THE LIVING EYE

Harvard Studies in Comparative Literature

Founded by William Henry Schofield

40

Jean Starobinski

THE LIVING EYE

Translated by
Arthur Goldhammer

Harvard University Press
Cambridge, Massachusetts
London, England   1989

Chapters 1–3 were originally published in *L'Oeil vivant* (1961);
Chapters 4–7 in *L'Oeil vivant II: La Relation critique* (1970).
Copyright © Editions Gallimard, Paris.

The translation of this volume has been aided by grants from
the Georges Lurcy Charitable and Educational Trust and
from the French Ministry of Culture.

This book is printed on acid-free paper, and its binding materials
have been chosen for strength and durability.

Library of Congress Cataloging-in-Publication Data

Starobinski, Jean.
   [Œil vivant. English. Selections]
   The living eye / Jean Starobinski; translated by Arthur
Goldhammer.
   (Harvard studies in comparative literature; 40)
   p.   cm.
   Translation of selections of L'Œil vivant.
   Bibliography: p.
   Includes index.
   Contents: Poppaea's veil—Jean-Jacques Rousseau and the peril of
reflection—Pseudonymous Stendhal—The critical relation—
Psychoanalysis and literary understanding—Hamlet and Oedipus—
The interpreter's progress.
   ISBN 0-674-53664-9
   1. Criticism. 2. Imagination. 3. Psychoanalysis and literature.
I. Title.
PN81.S6813 1989   88-29398
809'.93353—dc19   CIP

Preface

It may be that the works a writer undertakes over the course of his career develop out of dreams, questions, and problems that occupied his mind while working on his earliest projects. If I had to retrace the prehistory of *L'Oeil vivant* (1961) and of my work on Rousseau (1957), I would have to go back to the time of the war, to the anxiety aroused in me by fanaticism in uniform whose irrational imperatives had unleashed a worldwide conflict, and to the astonishment I felt at the seductive power exerted by leaders whose "charisma" stemmed essentially from their knowing how to make use of a certain kind of mask. My interest centered on modern ways of using masks and their powers of fascination. Meanwhile, in literary history, I was obliged to take note of a literary tradition of denouncing masks. The antithesis of appearance and reality is a commonplace that has been transmitted from age to age, expressing itself in every era in a variety of literary genres, tones and contexts. My first project, of whose difficulty I was well aware, was this: to write a history of the use of masks in terms of the most typical examples, coupled with a history of the kinds of accusations that had been leveled at masked behavior. I wanted to combine a history of mystifying alienation with a history of demystification. I dreamed of a great work that would be entitled *Interrogatoire du masque* or *Les Ennemis des masques*. Of these overly vast ambitions only what was viable remains.

L'Oeil vivant (1961) and *La Relation critique* (1970), the two collections of essays from which this English volume derives, are separated by an interval of ten years. The two works are complementary without being similar. Each has a character of its own. The first consists of a series of more or less developed monographs on authors who attached particular importance to the opposition between appearance and reality. The second is devoted to theoretical problems with a bearing on self-expression, the imagination, and interpretation. It includes essays on the history of ideas and considerations of different types of reading: stylistics, hermeneutics, and the language of psychoanalysis. Just as the first volume did not refrain from touching on philosophical questions, if only by allusion, so when it came to the second, primarily concerned with theory, I did not wish to deal with theoretical issues solely in the abstract, in isolation from illustrative examples and application to particular cases.

In *L'Oeil vivant* I made a case that was consistent with recent work by phenomenologists, preceded by a long line of other philosophers: that the dichotomy reality/appearance or being/appearing (*être/paraître*) was a rhetorical opposition. Appearance, inseparable from its verbal and gestural uses (lying, hypocrisy, dissimulation, mask), is also inseparable from any manifestation of being. Appearance is suppressed only when being withdraws into an ineffable self-sufficiency. In *La Relation critique* the very notion of relation indicates the sense in which the initial antinomy was transcended.

The opposition between appearance and reality and the metaphor of the mask belong to the visual register. Attention therefore had to be focused on the gaze or, more precisely, on what writers said about seeing, on the way in which each of them elaborated a dramaturgy of optical relations: to see and be seen are the main modalities of preverbal relation. In literary works, however, preverbal relations are interpreted, imagined, and shaped by means of language. They belong (or seem to belong) to a world prior to that of the written text that evokes them. With respect to them the text functions as a metalanguage. It causes them to live, it revives them, in a *different* system of relations. Do critical scrutiny and analysis apply a new metalanguage to the literary text? Of course, but they do not offer an interpretation of the same order as the text itself. It is not venturing too much to say that the critical text makes visible (and therefore restores to the order of the "seen") some of the relations that constitute the text under interpretation, and that in so doing it proposes a second-degree formalization of the text that is at once dependent and independent, audacious and tenuous. The critical text is to the primary text as the latter is to the preverbal (hence imaged, imagined) language of exchanged glances.

Can these essays be categorized as "new criticism," as it was defined in France? Was I a representative of "thematic criticism"? Some commentators evidently thought so. When I wrote the essays in

L'Oeil vivant I had a specific problem in mind, and I set about
working at the crossroads of philosophical inquiry, close reading of
literary texts, and intellectual history (though its place in that
particular work was not prominent). I had no intention of neglecting
social history. My purpose was not to focus on any special category
of objects in the works I studied (as Gaston Bachelard did when he
examined, in a series of admirable volumes, each of the four elements
of ancient cosmology). Nor was it to explore systematically certain
categories of subjective experience (as Georges Poulet did in studying
the consciousness of time). Yet some readers thought that I had
chosen the "theme of the gaze" as the guiding subject of my critical
research: they mistook the unifying motif of one particular book for
a methodological principle. I needed an emblematic instrument, a
focus that would help to bring related problems into clearer view. The
"theme" I chose was merely one angle from which I could approach
a multifaceted subject. It was, to use a slightly different image, one
possible "take" on the works under study. But the aim was always to
seek a more global meaning and perhaps a comprehensive truth. In
the book I wrote on Rousseau before writing *L'Oeil vivant*, the motifs
of "transparency" and "veil" (and related images) guided my analysis
throughout: Rousseau's frequent, almost obsessive use of these motifs
forced me to ask what such emphasis might have meant. Using the
themes in this way did not tie me to them, however, except in an
occasional and temporary manner.

I hope that *La Relation critique* and my other published essays on
the problems of criticism have shed sufficient light on my work as an
application of the "criticism of consciousness." It is in no sense a
prestructuralist or antistructuralist criticism. Saussurean linguistics
was part of my intellectual baggage as a student in Geneva. Much
later, in a conversation with Eric Weil (one of this century's great
philosophers), I recall our coming to the conclusion that the prettiest
girl in the world also has a skeleton. Structure is a necessary but not
sufficient condition for the production of a literary text. In "The
Dinner at Turin" I showed that there were singular homologies
between the syntactic organization of Rousseau's sentences and the
rhythm of the development of civilization as described in his philosophy of history. In fact, those remarks on structure led me to assume
intentions that manifested themselves simultaneously at the level of
both philosophy and literary form. I saw no need to decide whether
these intentions were conscious or unconscious. The fact that they

were evident was enough, and I saw little to be gained by searching for their psychological origins. Concerning subjectivity I had little taste for going beyond what the text warranted. Some critics took me to task for my "idealist" presuppositions. If it is idealist to think that there is no action without an acting subject (who acts under certain definite conditions) and no thought without a consciousness that uses the linguistic and interpretative tools provided by the age, then I am perfectly willing to be described as such. But this is no longer idealism. Literature holds proof that there exist regions in history not governed by the anonymous determinisms that shape a part of our destiny. The literary act, by modifying the language, ceases to be a conditioned phenomenon and becomes a conditioning intervention.

I therefore did not seek to treat texts as masks behind which lay a psychological truth open to self-empowered interpretation. I am aware, however, that some of what I have written has been vulnerable to the charge of "psychologism," and especially in the case of Rousseau that I may have given the impression of claiming to decipher him better than he was able to do himself, from a superior position and as if it were up to the critic to unearth secrets that no one else had ever discovered. The dominating vantage of the critic is merely the privilege he derives from being a spectator who arrives on the scene after the fact, in a new age of knowledge and in the name of greater enlightenment.

I am thinking in particular of remarks addressed to me by Paul de Man in *Blindness and Insight*. He cited a passage from *L'Oeil vivant* ["Jean-Jacques Rousseau et le péril de la réflexion," Gallimard edition, p. 182], to which he appended a commentary in which he attributed to me the intention of gaining access, by way of intuition, to a truth about Jean-Jacques that lay beyond the words the writer himself had set down:

> [Starobinski suggests] that the more paradoxical statements of Rousseau should not really be taken at face value: "it often happens that he overstates his aim and forces the meaning, in splendid sentences that can hardly stand the test of being confronted with each other. Hence the frequently repeated accusations of sophistry . . . Should we take those lapidary maxims, those large statements of principle at face value? Should we not rather be looking beyond Jean-Jacques's words toward certain demands made by his soul, toward the vibration of his feelings? We do him perhaps a disservice when we expect him to provide rigorous coherence and

systematic thought; his true presence is to be found, not in his discourse, but in the live and still undefined movements that precede his speech."

Benevolent as it sounds, such a statement reduces Rousseau from the status of philosopher to that of an interesting psychological case; we are invited to discard his language as "des phrases splendides" that function as a substitute for pre-verbal emotional states into which Rousseau has no insight. The critic can describe the mechanism of the emotions in great detail, drawing his evidence from these very "phrases splendides" that cover up a by no means splendid personal predicament. (Paul de Man, *Blindness and Insight*, 2nd ed. [Minneapolis, 1983], pp. 112–113)

In fact, if there is an error in the incriminated lines, it is that I failed to indicate clearly enough that I was employing the oblique device that stylisticians have dubbed the *style indirect libre*. The assertions that Paul de Man considered mine, and in which he believed he recognized a presumptuous claim of superior psychological knowledge, are actually assertions made by Rousseau himself. It is Rousseau who, when the need strikes him, asks that he not be read "at face value." I was merely summarizing (rather than citing verbatim) any number of statements by Rousseau—availing myself of the device of identification so often used by Poulet, which involves mingling (for a moment) the voice of the critic with the voice of the author. Thus in those lines it is not I who reproaches Rousseau for his "splendid phrases" and who asks the reader to join him at the level of feeling: I am simply taking note of what he repeats time and time again. Evidently I erred in allowing myself to paraphrase to such an extent, since a reader as astute as de Man was unable to recognize Rousseau's discourse as relayed by my simple description, with no indication of my differences with Rousseau or any statement of my doubts concerning Rousseau's expectations of his readers.

I should have included a more extensive analysis of the rhetoric of contradiction employed by Rousseau, of his manner of invalidating the vulnerable objective text, only too accessible to rational criticism. I should have pointed out in a more systematic way how Rousseau constantly resorts to notions of "emotional disposition" and "sentiment" in order to invalidate any negative judgments his reader might form by reading the texts strictly according to their obvious meaning. Careful as Rousseau was to lay the foundations of his argument, he also knew that facts cannot be demonstrated. He used facts of the heart to create an impregnable fortress against criticism that was aimed at the explicit content and intellectual organization of his discourse. It was Rousseau who wrote: "Forget about my fine style" (*Letters Written from the Mountain*, preface). And it was again Rousseau who, in the *Dialogues*, expressed the hope that he would find a reader who would "take the trouble to look for [his] true sentiments beyond [his] poor expression of them." Hence he is not always to be taken literally: "his heart, seething with emotion, is subject to straying from its course and going beyond the intended goal" (*Oeuvres complètes*, vol. 1, pp. 694–695). There is, in the Rousseau of the *Dialogues*, constant reference to a previous expression more truthful than the present one: "It is not in his present works that he ought to be judged . . . One must go back to the time when nothing prevented him from being himself" (p. 905). Similarly, and especially when he feels caught in some wrongdoing, he invokes an *intention* prior to the words that he may imprudently have set down. He writes, for example, to Madame d'Epinay:

> I cannot stand for you to mistake my expressions . . . Learn my dictionary better, my good friend, if you want us to understand each other. Know that my terms rarely have the ordinary meaning and that it is always my heart that converses with you, and perhaps you will some day know that it does not speak like any other. (*Correspondance complète*, ed. R. A. Leigh, vol. 3, letter 391, pp. 295–296)

Of course it is clear that in order to denounce those "expressions" that have been poorly understood, Rousseau uses other expressions; and in order to say that his sentiments are not perfectly captured by the words he has written, he is obliged to write other words. The self's denial of authority to its own language is reminiscent of negative theology's opposition to any attempt to express or qualify the nature of God.

What is the nature of the "critical relation" in all this? On the one hand, it is to take Rousseau literally and heed his account of an inner certainty that he invites us to share through sympathy, even though he has declared his inability to communicate it whole. On the other hand, criticism should seek to uncover the explicit contradiction into which a writer falls when, in a strategy of defense and seduction, he writes asking to be understood according to his own personal "dictionary." The task of criticism is to see and to make others see what the relation of author to recipient becomes when the person who writes, wishing to be loved but not bound, wishing to determine yet remain free, simultaneously affirms and denies his language. A whole school of modern literature is here coming into being. Even as the writer establishes meaning, he declares it to be revocable in the name of a higher meaning, or of a more adequate but yet-to-be-enunciated truth of which he is the sole possessor. Moreover, since the simplicity of the relation is thereby disrupted or, rather, since its complexity is thereby better revealed, the need arises for a reflection devoted to the accidents of the relation, to its diversions and perversions: the time has come for a criticism of relation and for books entitled *The Critical Relation* and *Transparency and Obstruction.*

Jean Starobinski
Geneva, September 1988

Contents

TRANSLATOR'S NOTE

I would like to thank Jean Starobinski for his invaluable comments on the translation. In the course of reviewing the manuscript, he made a number of changes and additions to the texts originally published in *L'Oeil vivant* and *La Relation critique*. The English version reflects these revisions by the author.

1 Poppaea's Veil

The hidden fascinates. "Why did Poppaea conceive the idea of masking the beauties of her face, except to make them dearer to her lovers?" (Montaigne). In dissimulation and absence there is a strange force that compels the spirit to turn toward the inaccessible and, for the sake of conquest, to sacrifice all it possesses. Fairy tales, works of realism as far as the mechanism of desire is concerned, know only hidden treasures, concealed in some dark depth. If these treasures must belong to someone, they will go to the one who has renounced everything, even the hope of becoming their master. The essence of mystery is to compel us to regard as worthless and tiresome anything that does not make it more easily accessible. Yes, the shadow has the power to make us release all our prey simply because it is shadow and provokes in us a nameless anticipation. Fascination persuades us, so that we may belong to it, to give up everything, even concern for our own lives. It takes all we have simply by promising everything we want. At first we were able to dream of laying hold of what lay hidden, but the roles were quickly reversed: all at once we found ourselves passive and paralyzed, having renounced our will and allowed ourselves to be inhabited by the imperious call of absence.

Moralists, of course, have deemed this sacrifice outrageous. What! Lose all that one has for an illusion! Allow oneself to be robbed of the present and to live forever after in destructive ecstasy? Scorn visible beauty for love of what does not exist? The passion for the hidden has not lacked critics, who reproved it sometimes for concealing the allure of the devil, sometimes that of God. But what we need is an explanation of the passion not unduly hasty to dismiss it as a mystification.

The hidden is the other side of a presence. The power of absence, if we attempt to describe it, leads us to the power possessed in varying degrees by certain real objects. These objects point beyond themselves toward a magical space. They are indices of something they are not. Obstacle and interposed sign, Poppaea's veil engenders a perfection that is immediately stolen away, and by its very flight demands to be recaptured by our desire. Thus the impediment created by the obstacle gives rise to a vast profundity, which is mistaken for essential. The fascination emanates from a real presence that obliges us to prefer what it hides, to prefer something remote, which it prevents us from attaining even as it offers itself. Our gaze is irresistibly drawn into the vertiginous void that forms in the object of fascination: an infinity opens up, devouring the real object by which it made itself sensible. In truth, if the object of fascination calls for the abdication of our will, it is because that object itself is annihilated by the absence it provokes. This strange power in a way stems from a lack, an insufficiency in the object. Rather than hold our fascination, it allows itself to be transcended in a perspective of the imagination, an obscure dimension. But objects can seem insufficient only in response to an exigency in our gaze, which, awakened to desire by an allusive presence and finding no employment for all its energies in the visible thing, transcends it and loses itself in an empty space, headed for a beyond from which there is no return. Poppaea runs the risks that her face, unveiled, will disappoint her lovers, or that her eyes, wide open and beckoning, will seem still covered by a dark veil: desire can no longer cease to search elsewhere.

To be fascinated is the height of distraction. It is to be prodigiously inattentive to the world as it is. But this inattention in a way rests upon the very objects it neglects. Having responded too impetuously to the veiled seductress, our gaze hurtles beyond the possessable body and is captured by the void and consumed in the night. Poppaea Sabina (in the "portrait" of her painted by an unknown master of the School of Fontainebleau) allows her body to be glimpsed beneath the gauze, and smiles: she is not culpable. Her lovers do not die for her; they die for the promises she does not keep.

If one looks at the etymology, one finds that to denote directed vision French resorts to the word *regard* [gaze], whose root originally referred not to the act of seeing but to expectation, concern, watchfulness, consideration, and safeguard, made emphatic by the addition of a prefix expressing a redoubling or return. *Regarder* [to look at, to gaze upon] is a movement that aims to recapture, *reprendre sous garde,* [to place in safekeeping once again]. The gaze does not exhaust itself immediately. It involves perseverance, doggedness, as if animated by the hope of adding to its discovery or reconquering what is about to escape. What interests me is the fate of the impatient energy that inhabits the gaze and desires something other than what it is given. It lies in wait, hoping that a moving form will come to a standstill or that a figure at rest will reveal a slight tremor, insistent on touching the face behind the mask, or seeking to shake off the bewildering fascination with depths in order to rediscover the shimmering reflections that play on the water's surface.

Some, invoking the example of Greece, have argued that the realm of the visible, the realm of light, was also the realm of measure and order: figures circumscribed by their forms, space made rhythmic by a harmonious module, by a law granting to each vantage an empire at once sovereign and precarious. But there is a hidden extravagance in the apparent triumph of measure. The will to delineate, geometrize, and fix stable relationships implies a violence beyond the natural experience of the gaze. The space of geometrical measurement is the product of a vigilant effort, which, compass in hand, *revises* the affective prejudices to which living space owes its "deformations." It is hard to deny that in this there is extravagance of the second degree, which consists in seeking equilibrium by rejecting the spontaneous extravagance of desire and anxiety.

It is difficult for the gaze to limit itself to ascertaining appearances. By its very nature it must ask for more. In fact this impatience inhabits all the senses. Beyond the usual synesthesias, each sense aspires to exchange its powers with the others. In a celebrated *Elegy* Goethe said: the hands want to see, the eyes want to caress. We may add: the gaze wants to speak. It is willing to give up the faculty of immediate perception in exchange for the gift of *fixing* more permanently whatever flees its grasp. By contrast, speech often seeks to efface itself in order to clear the way for pure vision, for intuition perfectly oblivious of the noise of words. In each realm the highest powers are apparently those that impose a sudden, overwhelming substitution. And do not forget that the night of the blind is replete with unfulfilled gazes or, rather, gazes diverted toward the hands, converted into gropings. In the absence of a visual function, the gaze, an intentional relation with others and with the horizon of experience, may assume compensatory forms, proceeding by way of an attentively cocked ear or through the fingertips. For by gaze in this context I mean not so much the faculty of collecting images as that of establishing a relation.

Of all the senses, sight is the one most obviously ruled by

impatience. A magical wish, never entirely fulfilled yet never discouraged, accompanies each of our glances: to seize, to undress, to petrify, to penetrate: to fascinate—that is, to illuminate the flame of the hidden in an immobile pupil. All are implicit actions, which do not always remain mere intentions. By revealing the intensity of desire, sometimes the gaze produces real effects. "How many children if looks could impregnate! How many dead if looks could kill! The streets would be filled with corpses and pregnant women." Can it be that Valéry did not notice all the corpses and pregnant women in our streets?

If not betrayed by an excess or want of light, the gaze is never satisfied. It opens the way to an unrelenting assault. Intelligence, cruelty, and tenderness only begin to tell the tale. They remain unappeased, unslaked. These passions awaken in the gaze and grow through the act of vision, in which, however, they find too little to satisfy them. Sight opens all space to desire, but desire is not satisfied with seeing. Visible space attests to both my power to discover and my powerlessness to attain. Everyone knows how sad the concupiscent gaze can be.

Seeing is a dangerous act. It is the passion of Lyncaeus, but Bluebeard's wives die of it. On this point there is striking unanimity in myth and legend. Orpheus, Narcissus, Oedipus, Psyche, and Medusa teach us that the soul that seeks to extend the scope of its vision is destined to blindness and night: "Truly, the dagger fell from her hands, but not the lamp. She had too much to do, and had not yet seen all there was to see" (La Fontaine). The burning of the oil (or of the gaze) awakens the sleeping god and brings about Psyche's dizzying fall into the desert.

The gaze, which enables consciousness to escape from the place occupied by the body, is an *excess* in the strict sense of the word. Whence the severity of the Church Fathers: of all the senses, sight is the most fallible, the most naturally culpable—"Do not fix your eyes on an object that pleases them, and remember that David perished by a glance" (Bossuet). The "concupiscence of the eyes" includes and epitomizes all others: it is the quintessential evil. "Under the eyes all the other senses are in some way included. And in common parlance to feel and to see are often the same thing." Here Bossuet is merely repeating Saint Augustine. Our hunger to see is perpetually subject to frivolous curiosity, idle distraction, and cruel spectacle. The least pretext is enough to capture our eyes, to lure our spirit from the path of salvation. Augustine found it most difficult to deny himself the pleasures of the circus. But the arena is not the only place where animals devour one another, and everything becomes theater for the ascetic unfaithful to his resolutions: "When I sit at home and watch a lizard catching flies or a spider wrapping insects that fall into its web, is not my attention conquered?"

Yet the very same people who castigate the indiscretion and dispersion of the worldly gaze invoke the same power to direct it toward "supernatural light" and intelligible forms. What they see as the natural extravagance of the gaze ceases to be culpable if directed beyond this world. Augustine, wresting himself free of the temptations of light, "that queen of colors," hopes that darkness will favor the advent of a new light, this time spiritual, invisible to the eye of the flesh. Access to the *idea*, whose very name refers to the act of seeing, is "like a vision emancipated from the limitations of sight" (Maurice Blanchot). In carnal curiosity as well as spiritual intuition, the will-to-see claims second sight as its right.

It is my hunger to see more, to repudiate and transcend my provisional limits, that impels me to question what I have already seen, to hold that it is a misleading decor. Thus begins the strange rebellion of those who, in order to grasp reality beyond appearances, make themselves enemies of what is immediately visible: they denounce the illusion of appearances without suspecting that by revoking the privileges of first sight they leave second sight little hope, in their impatience reducing the admirable theater of vision to ruins. Probably they have no choice. In the exigent gaze lies a whole critique of the primary data of vision. This critique cannot avoid *discourse* in one of its many forms: geometry, with its logical arguments, corrects the vague apprehensions of the eye with the purity of the abstract; poetic language seeks to transpose visible appearance into a new essence, because to speak, to name things, tends to prolong (if not complete) the work of safekeeping that in the gaze remains forever incomplete and precarious. The extremity of the gaze is already something more than gaze, and pursues its aim in the act whereby vision renounces and sacrifices itself. Yet criticism, having condemned deceptive appearances, is not incapable of turning on itself. If a little reflection takes us away from the sensible world, a more demanding philosophy brings us back—as if, having braved the limits of the horizon and traversed the void, the gaze had no alternative but to return to immediate evidence: everything recommences *here*. Montaigne, in this view, would have proposed the most aggressive critiques of appearance in the name of a truth to be unveiled, a fascination to be conjured away, attacking masks and shams only to arrive in the end at a wisdom that would allow itself to be "molded by appearances" and would accept the veil by means of which Poppaea is able to arouse in us such delicious discomfort and impatience. Skepticism first warns us against universal deception, then leads us very gently to the idea of recommencing knowledge with a wisdom that, under the protection of the *reflexive* gaze, trusts in the senses and in the world the senses reveal.

My studies here are all concerned in one way or another with literary works that deal with the pursuit of a hidden reality, a reality temporarily dissimulated yet within the grasp of anyone who knows how to force it out of hiding and compel its *presence*. What was needed, accordingly, was to retrace the history of a gaze lured by desire from discovery to discovery. It was also necessary to show, in a variety of circumstances, how the pursuit of what lies hidden, being an exorbitant ambition, poses the risk of failure and disappointment.

This book is much less and much more than a systematic exploration of a theme. Much less, because I felt no need to catalog all the expressive means (physiognomy, seduction, language of signs) and perceptual devices (world view, interplay of surfaces and depths) involved in the exercise of vision. Much more, because by consistently attending to the fate of the demand implicit in the gaze and unsatisfied by first appearances, I was obliged to trace an adventure that was almost always played out in the *interval* between the intended prey and the eye that wished to subdue it. The gaze was the living link between the person and the world, between self and others: the writer's every glance questions anew the status of reality (and of literary realism) as well as the status of communication (and of human community). Hence I am not dealing with an artificially isolated theme of literature. In this inquiry I try to understand what constitutes the *necessity* of the works studied.

For writers—and also, despite appearances, for painters—the adventure continues beyond the first view, even if unsatisfied desire must later, after losing contact with the sensible, return us there. In these essays my aim is to describe a language that begins with a glance, at times dazzled, at times lustful, at times defiant, and then proceeds along other, often deviant paths in pursuit of what it finds lacking in its original vision. To have declined to follow the same path (or absence of a path), to have shunned its risks, would have been to flout the underlying law of the gaze, which refuses to be satisfied with what it is offered initially. Full knowledge of vision's *excess* is required, full understanding of the extravagance that causes the gaze to overstep its bounds and risk blindness. By refocusing on distant objects (whose fate is often merely to be glimpsed) consciousness begins by transforming itself. Its own tension, its own desire, undergoes metamorphosis. Hence these essays seek not so much to describe the specific world of sight as to retrace the shifting fate of the *libido sentiendi* in its relation to the world and to other human consciousnesses.

In Corneille everything begins in dazzlement. But dazzlement is a precarious thing, which lasts only a fleeting instant. Drawn to brilliant objects, the Cornelian hero struggles against falling adoringly into their clutches. The bedazzled consciousness throws off passivity and seeks to effect a reversal of roles. It aspires to be dazzling itself, to achieve the power that comes with brilliance. It claims this privilege first of all through the language of generosity. But glorious speeches are not enough. It is necessary to proceed to action—to action promised, perhaps imprudently, in language. Boasts of valor bind the hero and make inevitable the decision that consecrates his greatness. Thus is man born to the admirable destiny that he has invented for himself: he offers himself triumphant to the world's gaze. His greatest happiness lies neither in the act of seeing (*voir*) nor in the energy of doing (*faire*) but in the complex act of demonstrating (*faire voir*). What exploit, what wish will reveal the hero's everlasting brilliance and spread his renown? The one effective course of action, the one certain to produce the desired "effect," is self-sacrifice, in which the individual turns all his energy against himself, denying himself so completely as to be reborn for all eternity in the eyes of generations called to witness. In this way the hero establishes an immortal *name*. For this, however, he requires the consent and vigilant complicity of crowds of onlookers: if doubt is cast on human memory and the endurance of renown, everything crumbles in obscurity and vanity, leaving nothing but a dusty stage set; the generous hero becomes nothing but a parody of himself, a ridiculous actor in a "comic illusion."

In Racine passion and desire control everything. A strange weakness, a fatal blindness, prevents Racine's heroes from fully dominating their actions. An obscure and wicked force dictates their crimes, subjects them to misfortune, and exposes them to our piteous regard. They are beset by bewildering uncertainties that reason is unable to surmount. Though not incapable of recognizing their downfall, critical awareness does not prevent them from hastening to their ruin. Full lucidity comes to them only when it is too late, and the clarity of tragic knowledge coincides with a feeling of total impotence in the face of irrevocable misfortune.

An attentive reading of Racine's plays, a methodical analysis of his expressive means, reveals that the gaze takes the place of theatrical gesticulation and becomes the act par excellence. It expresses the pained keenness of a desire that knows in advance that possession equals destruction but is unable to renounce either one. For Racine the tragic is not associated exclusively with either the structure of the plot or the fatality of its outcome. It is the very heart of the human condition that is condemned, since every desire is caught in the inevitable failure of the gaze. No one accepts this failure. Racine's characters struggle in vain, which only compounds their guilt. Voyeurism—the desire to possess solely through sight, to wound through the act of looking—is exacerbated by the feeling that it must remain forever unsatisfied. In the cruelest scenes, in which the power to torture is expressed exclusively in the gaze, the frustrated torturer suffers as much as his victims. In the very heart of desire, in the intense glow of visual lust, we can thus make out a desperate, self-consuming flame. Incapable of obtaining the desired object, desire can transcend its suffering only by choosing catastrophe, only by dying in darkness. The hero plunges into the abyss, while in a heaven filled with light the implacable gods bear sovereign witness to a disaster that exalts their omnipotence.

For Rousseau the happiness of childhood lay in living a carefree life under the gaze of a witness raised to the level of benevolent deity. But soon this benevolence gave way to a sense of all-enveloping hostility. From then on it became impossible to desire publicly even the most innocent of pleasures without incurring criticism or ironic comment. Shamefaced desire was forced to beat a retreat, give up the idea of possession, and resort to the clandestine glance. Now we can understand why Rousseau exhibits such clear signs of voyeurism and exhibitionism. Fearful of guilty contacts or initiatives, he contents himself, from a distance, with seeing and being seen. At first these predilections take perverse forms, but later they are disguised and transformed through sublimation: in *La Nouvelle Héloïse* Wolmar, the virtuous atheist, proclaims his desire to become pure vision, a "living eye." In *Emile* the preceptor finds moral pretexts for observing his pupils' most intimate caresses. The "ridiculous object" is exhibited once again, albeit in novel fashion, in the virtuous cynicism of total confession. But to see and be seen is still too much. The hostility is too great, and Rousseau, incapable of combatting it head on, generally prefers to concede defeat and to retreat into a more secret realm. Desire, once manifest, becomes a *latent* power. It renounces all external objects. Reveling in itself, it exposes itself to neither error nor punishment. But this inward retreat, with its concomitant dissimulation of desire, is compensated by a discovery that *reveals* what had remained hidden since the inception of civilization: neglected nature and natural man. This is a most important discovery, since it establishes a norm against which existing societies can be properly judged and a more equitable community can be imagined.

Both the man of sentiment and the child are gripped by a quite irrational conviction, that to avoid looking at external temptations and to abandon hope of external conquest is to avoid being looked at in return, hence a way of escaping hostile scrutiny and warding off persecution. At the center of a world of enchanted fictions, Rousseau reconciles the innocence of time's beginning with love's most searing pleasures. He invents a bewildering and loving spectacle in which nothing prevents him from participating in person. Nothing intervenes to compromise the transparency of happiness regained. As in his child's paradise, his ego binds itself to benevolent *counterparts* through trusting dialogue: avoiding the misunderstandings inherent in speech, they communicate through the language of signs and understand one another at a glance.

Yet beyond this spectacle of the imagination and by dint of the enthusiasm that overcomes him, Rousseau attains an extreme of ecstasy, a pure sentiment of existence, in which all images disappear. The dreamer's inward gaze having exhausted the pleasures of fictive celebration, desire wants to know a still higher degree of satisfaction, and it succeeds in doing so. At this moment all vision is abolished, replaced by a voluptuous stupefaction that is both total light and absolute darkness.

More than anyone else, Rousseau forces us to acknowledge that the gaze, from the moment of its first awakening, bears within it a strange power of separation. It discovers objective space, but only at the price of acquiescing in distance. It obliges us to see things as distinct—distinct from us and distinct from one another. Thus it disrupts a prior unity, a unity originally enjoyed by being (*l'être*) in its blind self-absorption. When gaze becomes reflection this loss of unity is further accentuated, for to reflect is to relinquish contact with the immediate and to sink ever more deeply into the misfortune of separate existence. Discursive reason, insofar as it is a product of reflexive thought, marks the utmost estrangement from primitive unity. But the trial of division ignites and fans the flames of a desire to regain the lost unity: enduring loss leads to discovery of the need for communication, which will repair the fragmentation of reality. Logical reflection must not be banished. To be rid of it one must follow it unflinchingly to its ultimate conclusion. When speech, having done its job, falls silent, consciousness enlightened by reason returns to the law of sentiment and to the undivided unity of the beginning. A cycle is completed: separate vision and the evil of reflection lead consciousness down a path that returns to the original happiness.

Rousseau is far from an irrationalist, but his rationalism goes along with the conviction (shared by the romantics) that "existential" truth belongs to the realm of time—or of the instant—and not to the realm of objective space subject to the quantitative operations of reason. Don't forget that this adventure of consciousness, whose goal is to transcend the servitude of conventional language, is presented to us entirely through the vehicle of language. If the reflexive gaze, rigorously pursued, can lead beyond the misfortune of reflection, then perfected language (that is, poetry or opera) seeks and finds an analogous power to transcend. It seems clear that Rousseau made a decisive contribution to the revelation of this power.

Stendhal, like Rousseau, began by experiencing a sudden shock of shame when confronted by the ironic gaze of others. But with Stendhal the feeling of guilt was less onerous. This accounts for the extraordinary vivacity of his riposte. How should one respond to a hostile gaze? By becoming someone else, transforming or masking oneself. Stendhal responds to an external affront by mounting a disciplined counteroffensive. His metamorphoses only appear to be escapes. One problem preoccupies him constantly: how to portray himself, how to influence the situation in such a way that his enemies, vanquished, cease to fight and unwittingly become allies in his own projects, auxiliaries in his pursuit of happiness. In extreme cases he would have to make himself fascinating by means of magic. Stendhal dreamed of this, not without self-indulgence. For a long time he believed that with logic, lessons from professional actors, and his knowledge of Destutt de Tracy he would be able to create a seductive and triumphant character for himself. The society in which he lived was so vile that anyone who hoped to succeed required a mask. Direct energy and strength of character were regarded as suspect. Stendhal played the game well enough, though he expressed nostalgia for those times and places when men won power and esteem through noble deeds. Why didn't he settle for what he had? What dissatisfaction drove him to ask for more? In the end he required nothing less than literature, which he saw as a game of chance. He created characters who lived lives different from his own but in whom he could feel himself living. He looked to the future to provide his audience. Above all, he transformed himself through the effect that the written work had upon his life.

And what about reading? What about the critical gaze? The exigencies that animate it are not unlike the ones we find in the creators. Sight is asked to lead the mind beyond the realm of vision into that of *meaning*. The critical gaze deciphers words in order to intuit their full meaning: this perception is a visual act only in the metaphorical sense. Thus the critical gaze *loses itself* in the meaning it awakens. It blazes a trail, but only to make pure pleasure possible without laborious access (Mallarmé's "pur plaisir sans chemin"). It transforms the written signs on the page into living speech and, beyond that, establishes a complex world of images, ideas, and feelings. This absent world was waiting for help, anxious for protection. Once awakened, however, this imaginary world requires the reader to make an absolute sacrifice: it no longer allows him to keep his distance. It demands contact and involvement; it imposes its own rhythm and its own destiny.

The critic is a person who, while consenting to the fascination of the text, nevertheless seeks to maintain his *right of scrutiny*. He desires greater penetration: beyond the manifest sense that is revealed, he perceives a latent significance. Beyond the initial "sight reading," further vigilance is necessary if he is to advance toward a *second meaning*. Do not overestimate that term, however: unlike medieval exegesis, modern criticism is interested not in deciphering an allegorical or symbolic equivalent of the original text but in revealing the vaster life or transfigured death inherent in it. Frequently the search for what is most remote leads to what is nearest at hand: to what was obvious at first glance, the forms and rhythms that seemed merely to hold the promise of a secret message. After a long detour we come back to the words themselves, where meaning chooses to reside, and that gleaming mysterious treasure we had felt compelled to seek in a "deeper dimension."

The truth is that the critical gaze is drawn toward two opposing possibilities, neither of which can be fully achieved. The first is to lose oneself in intimate intercourse with the fabulous consciousness glimpsed in the work: comprehension then becomes a matter of progressive pursuit of total complicity with the creative subjectivity, a passionate participation in the sensual and intellectual experience unfolded in the work. Yet no matter how far he goes in this direction, the critic can never stifle the conviction that he possesses a separate identity, the banal but insistent certainty that he is not one with the consciousness with which he desires union. Even assuming that it is possible for him to utterly confound himself with that consciousness, the result, paradoxically, would be loss of his own voice. He would inevitably fall silent. Through sympathy and mimickry the perfect critical discourse would give the impression of the most complete silence. Unless he manages in some way to break the pact of solidarity that ties him to the work, the critic is capable only of paraphrase or pastiche. One must *betray* the ideal of identification in order to acquire the power to speak of this experience and to describe, in a language other than that of the work, the life one has found there. Thus, in spite of our desire to drown in the vital depths of the work, we are obliged to stand at a distance if we are to speak of it at all. So why not deliberately establish a distance capable of revealing in a panoramic view the *surroundings* with which the work is organically associated? We might attempt to identify certain significant relations unnoticed by the writer; to interpret his unconscious motives; to understand the complex interactions between, on the one hand, a life and a work and, on the other hand, their social and historical circumstances.

This second possible mode of critical interpretation I shall call the *panoramic gaze*. The eye wishes to lose none of the patterns revealed by distance. In this expanded field of view, the work is of course the primary focus, but it is not the only object that commands attention.

It is defined by other, nearby objects and makes sense only in relation to its context. There's the rub: the context is so vast, the number of relations so large, that vision succumbs to a secret despair. The whole picture consists of so many elements that the single gaze can never gather them all in. What is more, the moment one decides to situate a work in terms of historical coordinates, the scope of the inquiry can be limited only by an arbitrary decision. It could in principle be expanded to the point where the literary work ceases to be the primary focus, now reduced to one of many manifestations of an era, a culture, or a "world view." As the gaze expands to embrace more and more correlative facts in the social world or the author's life, the work vanishes. Hence the triumph of the panoramic gaze is also a kind of failure. The panoramic gaze causes us to lose sight of the work and its meanings by trying to give us the world in which it is immersed.

Perhaps the most comprehensive criticism is that which aims at neither totality (the panoramic view) nor intimacy (intuitive identification). It is the product of a gaze that can be panoramic or intimate by turns, knowing that truth lies in neither one nor the other but in the ceaseless movement between the two. Neither the vertigo of distance nor that of proximity is to be rejected. One must aim for that double excess in which the gaze is always close to losing its power entirely.

Yet criticism is wrong, perhaps, to seek to discipline its gaze in this way. Often it is better to forget oneself and make room for surprise. We may then be rewarded by the feeling that the work is developing a gaze of its own, directed toward us, a gaze that is not only a reflection of our interrogation. An alien consciousness, radically other, seeks us out, fixes us, summons us to respond. We feel *exposed* by its probing. The work interrogates us. Before speaking for ourselves, we must lend our voice to the strange power that queries us. Yet docile as we may be, there is always the risk that we will prefer comforting tunes of our own invention. It is not easy to keep our eyes open, to welcome the gaze that seeks us out. But surely for criticism, as for the whole enterprise of understanding, we must say: "Look, so that you may be looked at in return."

2 Jean-Jacques Rousseau and the Peril of Reflection

for Marcel Raymond

I

Desire and Prohibitions

Jean-Jacques, miserable apprentice, coveted only in secret. Roasts, fruits, sweetmeats (not to mention girls, of whom he knew nothing) —all of these he ogled with sidelong glances, followed immediately by blushes. Even when he had cash in his pocket, he was ashamed to enter a pastry shop, for then he would be obliged to point out the object of his desire, thus betraying to others the appetite that held him in its grip. This caused him insurmountable embarrassment. "I catch sight of the women behind the counter and can already imagine them laughing amongst themselves and making fun of the greedy youngster . . . But two or three young people over there are looking at me."[1] He feels dangerously exposed. If he exhibits his desire, the gazes focused on him will immediately turn hostile. When he restrains his greediness and goes hungry, he convinces himself that others are "devouring him with their eyes." The would-be eater suddenly discovers the risk of being eaten.

A reinvigorated commandment weighs upon his conscience: "Thou shalt not covet" — not even what you can buy honestly. Rousseau will not permit himself to be caught redhanded in the act of desiring, for this would exhibit a culpable weakness, a shameful need. Before he can be slandered by a single gesture or word, his imagination leaps ahead: in the gaze of the onlooker it glimpses adumbrations of irony, anger, and mockery. Paralyzed, he is a timid Tantalus, repressing his desire while feeling it swell within him: "I am frightened by everything and discover obstacles everywhere. As my discomfort grows my desire increases. But in the end I go home like an idiot, consumed by longing and with money enough in my pocket to satisfy it, but not having dared to buy anything."[2] Desire, thus disappointed and heightened, must invent other gratifications. It will seek to satisfy itself in ways more oblique or more direct.

Who is spying on his actions? Rousseau has no idea. His "eyes lowered," he cannot recognize faces in the distance, which only increases his alarm. He is the victim of anonymous scrutiny by an unidentified spectator. Thus he is subjected to ubiquitous peril. The hostile witness, who is nobody in particular, in effect becomes everybody. Things quickly get out of hand. Under the scrutiny of the witness (that is, under the presumed scrutiny of a faceless witness) Jean-Jacques's relation to the object he covets is completely distorted. The distance and the lighting change, and a new obstacle crops up. Desire, knowing that it covets a forbidden object, can no longer reveal itself openly. It is obliged to dissimulate. From now on it will be the hidden desire of a forbidden object.

We should not be too hasty to find Rousseau in the wrong. The situation that makes him anxious is quite real: other people are out there, and they are looking at him. Jean-Jacques invents nothing; he is mistaken not about the facts but about their meaning. What idea lies behind the gaze directed toward him? Does the person wish him good or ill? Perhaps there is nothing there that should concern him, only indifference, distraction, and the like. The "normal" man accepts not knowing how others see him. He trusts in appearances and does not insist upon guesswork. So as not to cut off the possibility of dialogue, we generally leave open a range of possibilities. Among the attitudes we ascribe to others, favorable thoughts more or less compensate for hostile intentions. Thanks to our polite precautions and the conventions of language, all eventualities combine, in the absence of more ample information, to create a neutral uncertainty, a wavering ambiguity. This affective ambiguity, which is not without its dangers, results from mutual respect for an always elusive liberty.[3] In everyday intercourse we readily accept the uncertainty that prevents us from making assumptions about the true feelings of others, thereby protecting our independence. We do not think of complaining about the perpetual oscillation between a phantom of benevolence and a phantom of wickedness, knowing full well that for our interlocutors our own feelings are no less hypothetical than those we think we can read in their eyes.

Jean-Jacques, however, cannot bear uncertainty. With a rapidity characteristic of all his emotions, he rules out every possibility but one: hostility. Before any meeting can take place, before any precise idea has had time to form spontaneously in the depths of other people's eyes, Jean-Jacques has deciphered what they will think of him. In place of confusion, of shifting possibilities, a cruel clarity is established, a judgment from which there is no appeal. Assigned an irrevocable meaning, the situation is frozen. Hostility is no longer merely a risk to be run but a certainty that precedes and poisons all subsequent developments. Rousseau's gestures are henceforth not so much initiatives as ripostes, challenges flung at his accusers, subtle or vehement denials, replies and justifications offered up to the vigilant scrutiny he believes to be pursuing him. The game has not yet begun, but Jean-Jacques, convinced that he has lost, is already dreaming of possible revenge on other battlegrounds, already preparing the defense he will plead before better judges than those of the moment. Taking the dimmest possible view of things quickly eliminates all suspense and ambiguity: defeat settles one's ideas. No choice remains but to live on in spite of others rather than in the hope of winning their friendship or esteem. Imagination identifies the enemy and sets up its fortifications, creating for itself a clear field in utter solitude.

Faced with this conviction—precursor to the paranoia of Rousseau's final years—psychology is not at a loss for words. Is not the ironic and severe reproach that Jean-Jacques reads in other people's faces the projection of an anguish whose shadow falls across desire in the very moment of its enunciation? Is not Rousseau projecting into his interlocutor's gaze a condemnation he feels inwardly, responsibility for which he is somehow relieved to be able to shift to others? There is an economy of suffering: better to be the object of others' hostility than to suffer inner conflict and torment. The hurt persists, but for the harried conscience it is a lesser hurt. A defense mechanism reestablishes the unity of the ego by obliging it to confront an encircling enemy. Yet projection does not result in true deliverance. Its effect is not to abolish division but to shift the line of cleavage outside the self. External discord is the price to be paid for alleviation of inward suffering. If the situation thereby becomes more bearable, it also becomes more clear-cut. Projected outward by the imagination, the menace takes on the appearance of a nameless and implacable fate. It must be endured as one would endure an undeserved accident, an unjust harassment: an endless task, but a cause to which the individual can *rally*, in contrast to the kind of chaotic battle that would have to be waged against sedition that beset consciousness and its creations from within.

Projection explains many things, but not its own cause. If Rousseau suffered an inner anxiety from which he sought to escape by imputing it to alien malevolence, what was its source? Was it a primitive and mysterious malady, the fruit of original sin, or a spontaneous product of the extreme sensitivity that Rousseau himself often characterized as *bizarre*? Respectful as we may wish to be toward a singular nature that was not wrong in considering itself unique, the need to look for other explanations is inescapable. To begin with, we need to pursue the psychological explanation to the end, that is, to the point where it reveals the confrontation between consciousness and the external world. To go back to the origin, to the root, is to grasp the conscious being in its beginnings, that is, at a point in its evolution when it is far more dependent on the environment, far less autonomous, than it will be later in its development. Through a dialectic that also applies to other domains, plumbing the depths of being leads us to the place where being opens itself up to the *outside*, where it submits to the constraints of nature and receives the imprint of society. Admittedly, the primitive being at the height of its dependence does not know that it is dependent. But the critic, whatever his duties of sympathy may be, must comprehend this ignorance, not share it.

When the mechanisms of projection lead Rousseau to invent hostility in other people, he mistakes their attitude because he fails to recognize the wholly internal nature of his feelings of guilt. Yet if we ask where those feelings come from, we must number society and its values among their causes. Is projection therefore correct in its indictment of others? No. It is a misplaced response, a deviant reaction, that will not admit how early the pain began and that strikes out blindly at the enemy. There is error not only as to the person but also as to the time: present hostility is blamed for a conflict whose origins lie much deeper in the past. In reality, the psychology of guilt implies a system of collective values in terms of which Evil is defined and punished. Guilt anxieties never arise except in the presence of an authority and a law that anticipate and punish the infraction. In order to feel guilty, one must have encountered in the outside world an accusation or threat in which the commission of a crime was presumed. Even before I am accused of anything, I become obsessed with the possibility of guilt from the moment I glimpse on my horizon an accusatory power that compels me to see myself from its point of view and to declare myself *wicked*: "Knowledge of sin comes from the law." It is as if feelings of guilt were a means used by authority to anticipate or forestall possible recalcitrants by *preoccupying* them, by conquering them from within.

Taken separately, neither individual psychology nor sociology offers a satisfactory explanation. If nothing important is to be left out of account, one must resort to a unified method capable of analyzing affective behavior in its social context. Rousseau's guilt does not leap fully armed from his peculiar character, nor is it the inevitable product of the austere education that an orphan received in the Geneva of the 1720s, a puritanical city troubled by conflict between the patriciate (the "negatives") and the humble class of artisans. This *unique* individual must have attempted to assert his identity in conditions imposed on him through his family and social class. True, Jean-Jacques was not "made like anyone who ever was"[4] and nature broke the mold when she made him. Yet he was also, by his own admission, a "citizen of Geneva." In presenting himself to the world, he stressed at one point his absolute difference, at another his membership in a civic community: two sides of a single human reality.

There is every reason to believe that Rousseau's feelings of guilt were first formed in the early stages of his personal history, during his first confrontations with the order (and disorder) of Genevan society. On this subject the *Confessions* speak only implicitly, which should come as no surprise: although the book claims to trace a "concatenation of secret affections,"[5] it actually expresses the convictions of Rousseau's final years. It is the work of a man who has retreated to his final defensive positions: he took up his pen in order to insist upon his essential innocence. We must content ourselves with indirect proof of his guilt feelings, for he always repeats that he never did wrong intentionally. Far from explaining how his guilt feelings originated, Rousseau shows us a consciousness obsessed with self-perpetuated suspicions and seeking deliverance through magical denial. In the most humiliating stories he is able to find yet another pretext for tranquil satisfaction. The cynical courage of the confession compensates for the offense he admits having committed. He tells all, and by so doing claims to reestablish his righteousness in the eyes of any reader who may have presumed for a moment to doubt it.[6]

In fact there is no shortage of clues that reveal how the emotional child's anxiety about his misbehavior developed during his early years in Geneva. Although no one really cares about his mediocre existence, Rousseau imagines a reproachful gaze precisely because the *idea* of an omniscient and just God was an inextricable part of the Genevan heaven—*pace* Kierkegaard's remark that Rousseau was "totally ignorant of Christianity."[7] To breathe the air of Geneva was to breathe the conviction of man's original lapse and to bear all the weight of God's potential wrath. The vigilance of the Consistory meant that the atmosphere of the city was always heavy with suspicion of scandal. The Company of Pastors kept an eye on everyone and everything. It was quick to denounce and stigmatize libertines for the least offense to law and order. It observed, reprimanded, and condemned. Affidavits recorded every misdemeanor: "Was seen playing cards," or "Was seen disguised as a man or a peasant woman" (an accusation directed, as it happens, against Rousseau's mother).[8]

For an orphan *du bas* (of the lower orders and of the downhill section of the city), whose father was a "man of pleasure" forced to flee Geneva after gravely offending a citizen *du haut*, there was no doubt little indulgence in the Gaze. Were there not good reasons to fear that he would become, like his elder brother, a debauché and outright scoundrel who would eventually flee the city and never be heard of again? The authorities kept a weather eye for incipient evil, hence wrongdoing was, for its part, also wary. Chance always intervened, moreover, to make sure that Rousseau would not escape the inquisitorial gaze. The first book of the *Confessions* mentions hardly any instance of mischief or larceny that went undiscovered or unpunished. He is caught when he plants a walnut tree on the terrace at Bossey,[9] and again when he engraves medals in Ducommun's atelier.[10] He steals some asparagus only to sell it to "a woman who saw that he had just stolen it."[11] If he filches apples from his employer, luck would have it that he is caught in the act.[12] Does he hamstring himself with too many precautions? Or is he too incautious by half? No matter: he always manages to betray himself. When the little Goton girl plays schoolmistress and administers the spanking he desires, the news spreads quickly. The neighborhood urchins gather to jeer him: "Goton tic tac Rousseau."[13]

It no longer makes a difference if the gaze softens, recedes, or turns aside. Jean-Jacques continues to feel it, to carry it within himself, just as we continue to see light after its source is extinguished because of retinal persistence. Even if external surveillance disappears, the idea of its presence persists. Believing himself to be under scrutiny, Rousseau restrains his lusts and forbids himself to give in to desire.

His imagination takes over where persecuting authority leaves off. It fills the gaps, collaborates, gives authority the continuity that it lacks. Soon the face of indignation, with himself cast as its favorite victim, becomes an integral part of his self-consciousness. The reproachful gaze is internalized—it is no longer a separate power, no longer even perceived as a gaze. Where once it settled, there remains a permanent mark. By the time this *introjection* is complete, the suspect has been found guilty, convicted on the testimony of an accuser he carries within himself. Then and only then are all the necessary conditions satisfied, allowing an inverse *projection* to recreate the persecuting witness where none exists. In the depths of a childhood at once overly free and overly repressed, the groundwork for a Reign of Terror was being laid. Driven by an impetuous temperament to desire madly, Rousseau feels his desires only if he feels them immediately punished or punishable. A taboo stands between him and all carnal satisfaction.

After fleeing Geneva Jean-Jacques continually encounters the same point-blank accusatory gaze, all the more cruel for being more imaginary than before. The outcome is no better when he is faced with real hostility. He can never confront the enmity of others with a cool head. Unable to identify his enemies, he believes himself to be the victim of universal indignation and iniquity. His persecution anxieties are but an amplified version of his adolescent worries. And his innumerable flights (in real space, in felicitous dreaming, in musical pleasure, in ostentatious virtue, in memory) are only so many repetitions of his first departure from Geneva: half submission to fate, half deliberate attempt to run as far as possible from Sin.[14]

We are now in a better position to distinguish between society's role and Jean-Jacques's initiatives and reactions. The environment supplied the all-seeing religious police and austere morality, quick to suspect vice and condemn it, as well as the social inequality that left Rousseau's family in a position of resentful humiliation. Though a "citizen," he was only a "representative," stripped in fact of privileges accorded him in law. Confronted with these circumstances, Rousseau invented his response. Guilt feelings, protestations of innocence, and flight are not behaviors strictly determined by the environment. An element of personal interpretation is required, an extra option. Seldom is Rousseau the explicit focus of an accusatory gaze. Usually he is confronted with an imperative, a *general will* to morality, which involves no personal guilt. The law implies an anonymous, ambiguous culpability; it condemns such evil as *might* arise, without naming anyone. But Rousseau feels that he has been singled out. A diffuse accusation fills the air, and his anxiety forces it to solidify and precipitate out. Although indignation has not focused its gaze on him, he makes himself its object.[15] He might have identified instead with the awful eye. Indeed, that is precisely what he does do in certain circumstances. Why did he not choose the side of the righteous? His virtuous extremism (which can be interpreted as a defensive maneuver) proves that he was in fact free to choose between the role of accused and that of accuser. Nor is this choice *dictated* by the situation. It requires an overheated imagination and a peculiar need to take a stand, to objectify oneself as the guilty party or to project guilt onto others. Why, when all is said and done, did Rousseau express so well the historical situation in which he was placed? Because he confronted that situation not as it was in fact but in light of what impassioned interpretation made him think its ultimate consequences would be.

Desire Foils the Enemy

Escape the disapproving gaze and surreptitiously take hold of the coveted object: this was a temptation that Jean-Jacques knew and sometimes succumbed to. If occasionally he filched things (usually "snacks"), it was in order to avoid the shame of revealing his desire. In this way he believed he could achieve immediate ecstasy, without asking anyone's consent and without having to interpose any coin, an abstract sign that tarnished every pleasure bought with money.[16] Unseen and unidentified: paradoxically, in becoming a thief he abolished crime, simply because he put himself beyond the range of the accusatory gaze. Stealing became an innocent act, but only on condition that consciousness regress in imagination to a stage before it comes to be inhabited by an internalized witness. Jean-Jacques resorted to thievery not in response to a challenge or a penchant for crime but merely to simplify the situation, to get rid of an "inconvenient third party," and he protected himself by taking refuge in a primitive amorality, prior to knowledge of good and evil.

It is as if his world were too small to permit the simultaneous presence of desiring consciousness, coveted object, and censorious witness. The confrontation of these three elements resulted in an intolerable malaise. One of them had either to disguise itself, change its nature, or disappear. Thanks to the resourcefulness of imagination and the flexibility of desire, many solutions were possible, and Rousseau did not fail to try them all, without order or method, driven solely by the need to calm his anxiety and feel pleasure despite adversity. Avoiding the witness' gaze was only one possibility, the most impulsive but also the least certain of success: the witness never vanished from the horizon for long. Trying so hard to avoid scrutiny was likely to bring about its unexpected return. Jean-Jacques's clandestine activities were nearly always found out. Was this simply bad luck? Perhaps he provoked the catastrophes that brought shame down. Perhaps he desired them so that he might be forced to invent other solutions. When caught, he dropped his prey and opted for the perfection of a world of shadows. Unreal taboos called forth imaginary gratifications.

If the witness cannot be pushed aside, desire must seek through metamorphosis to render the situation compatible with its pursuit of happiness. Without sacrificing intensity desire will change its nature, modify its hopes, set itself new goals. Not only will its distance from the object vary, but the object itself may alter its shape and assume new identities. For to desire differently is already to desire something else. Here we touch upon a dominant characteristic of Rousseau's behavior, his frequent alternation between nonchalance and ardor. More than that, the focus of his passion shifts in singular ways. The pleasure he seeks sees no definite object as its sine qua non. Instead, it is associated with a state of exaltation, the pretext for which may vary indefinitely. Notwithstanding failures and obstacles, Rousseau finds or creates new objects, which enable him to remain in a state of desire. He is willing to consent to substitutions as long as nothing compels him to sacrifice the effervescence of his "expansive soul." He can fairly easily accept a new object in place of one he is not permitted to conquer. Every object is replaceable, first by its image and subsequently by a series of symbolic substitutes or analogies. Through a decree of the imagination, the innocent object of a permissible desire secretly represents the forbidden fruit that had to be given up.

Desire, if nothing interferes with it, is not a stable sentiment: it hastens after pleasure, drawn toward an object whose possession cannot be deferred. It persists until it has been satisfied (and thus annihilated) through attainment. The desirous gaze, focused on its prey and bewitched by it, cannot rest in the face of this existence different from its own. It is animated by a kind of impatience, tugged by a kind of tension. In fixing the object it covets, it already makes it a silent avowal, a kind of overture. If it conforms to its own law, it will transform itself into action, exposing itself to the perils of attack. From the outset it hastens toward its goal, toward the blessed mire of possession.

In the case of Rousseau, one effect of the presence of the reproachful witness is to repel or amputate the active component of desire. Rousseau desires but dares not act. Desire's energy persists in *marking time* rather than marching forth into the world with all its risks and perils. The crime that Jean-Jacques is afraid to be caught committing seems to reside not so much in desire itself as in its aggressive edge, in overt conquest, which disturbs the order of things and arouses the vigilance of the censors. How can crime be abolished without abolishing desire? One way is to stand still and leave it up to the object of desire to make the advances. The shameful part of desire can then no longer be imputed to Jean-Jacques; others will run the risks of desire in his stead. On this point the *Confessions* leave no room for doubt. Exhibitionism and masochism are attempts to reverse the normal movement from consciousness to object of desire.

The attack must then be mounted from outside. Willing and passive, Jean-Jacques will allow himself to be attacked and mistreated by his partners. He will do almost nothing beyond offering himself to the gaze of washerwomen and girls in the street. It is up to them to understand what is expected of them, indicated only by a sign, by the presence of the "ridiculous object."[17] In a paradox analogous to that noted earlier in connection with theft, Rousseau's immoral attitude, his masochistic or exhibitionistic perversion, actually diminishes his feelings of guilt. Compared with the taboo that prevents active satisfaction of desire, passivity is an alibi. Rousseau makes himself desirable; causes himself to be punished. But he ventures nothing. The pleasure he is able to feel in this way has to do with his imagination of the fascination that others feel in his presence. Not only is he desired, but he sees himself desired. Through the feelings he attributes to others, he turns his desire back upon himself and becomes its object. He wants to feel moved by their gaze or their blows. Thus the detour that makes it possible to achieve pleasure in spite of the reproachful witness (or even with his cooperation) has the effect of reducing desire to a more infantile level, to a form of autoeroticism. Since the *outside* is the dangerous domain of the hostile witness, the only "space" desire can occupy is the intimate space of the self. It must somehow find its satisfaction within itself.

Between the active initiatives of outward-directed desire and the passivity of desire that, taking itself for its object, settles within itself, we find a range of intermediate experiences, a spectrum of introversion. Desire often renounces the idea of being anything more than pure gaze, fixed upon the beloved: energy directed toward a distant goal is arrested en route, completely spent in the visual act. Vision that does not develop into purpose cannot achieve fulfillment; no real person is encountered or conquered. Jean-Jacques does not go beyond the stage of febrile contemplation, in which passion, forever unrequited, suffers but also takes a lasting pleasure, for it has already denied itself any access to what it covets. Instead of offering access to an object, desire remains a wish, sustained by its lack of gratification. It ascribes to itself a magical omnipotence and is enchanted by its innocence. To be sure, the gaze cannot escape the object of its fascination, but it remains without project or future. Fascination becomes an end unto itself, and the object acquires the status of image. For him whose only wish is to see, the goal is both infinitely close and infinitely far away.

Jean-Jacques creeps stealthily toward Mme. Basile's bedroom. He wants for once to see her in a place other than the shop, where anyone can see her. He enters the forbidden chamber where she sits by herself, alone with her beauty. He wishes to remain unnoticed, to worship her in secret and from a distance. His happiness lies in stealing images of intimacy and innocence from afar. And he achieves his aim, for he has time enough to gaze secretly upon the face of his beloved. "Her whole form displayed a charm which I had ample time to dwell on and which deprived me of my senses."[18] His is a solitary ecstasy, without reciprocity. As long as he reduces himself to pure gaze and remains invisible, Jean-Jacques is free to contemplate the young woman's every feature, gesture, and sigh. This is all he requires. Carnal possession does not occur to him; visual possession is enough. He has come in search of his own fascination, and he has found it. Jean-Jacques, "deprived of his senses," no longer occupies his own body, and Mme. Basile is therefore unaware of his presence. Both are absent. What remains? A vertiginous gaze: "I threw myself on my knees just inside the door and held out my arms to her in an access of passion, quite certain that she could not hear me, and imagining that she could not see me. But over the chimney-piece was a mirror, which betrayed me."[19]

And so he is caught: the stolen thief. The mirror captures his reflection and betrays his presence. In Geneva some time earlier, his employer had caught him in the same way as he stole apples from a cupboard. In the grip of desire, he had climbed up on a kneading trough in order "to peer into this garden of the Hesperides." Suddenly the tables are turned: an unexpected gaze catches sight of him. "The larder door suddenly opened. My master came out, folded his arms, looked at me, and said 'Bravo!' "[20] This adventure is repeated in Mme. Basile's bedroom. The spy is unmasked by the hidden mirror and he becomes prey. All at once he is precipitated into the most embarrassing situation. As spectator he had felt nothing but pleasure. But the moment he is seen he must justify his presence, and that presence is culpable: shame paralyzes him. What to do? What to say? How to explain himself? How to explain the innocence of his enterprise (which looks like guilt in the other person's eyes)? In the event Jean-Jacques is incapable of speaking, acting, or fleeing. He behaves like a fascinated animal, struck motionless by fright, cowering in absolute obedience. But his crime is a lucky one, for Mme. Basile is as immobilized by fright as Jean-Jacques. The mirror, which compromised the pleasure of solitary adoration, becomes the intercessor in a miraculous encounter. For once, no words or explanations are needed. The rush of emotion alone is enough. Without knowing whether his love is accepted or rejected, Jean-Jacques achieves amorous fulfillment in pure presence. Kneeling before Mme. Basile he abandons himself to feelings of guilty subservience and adoring repentance: his ideal of love. His joy stops at the "first fruits of possession," but precisely because possession is not complete it is not obliged to endure the death of desire, which is the law of all possession. This is a love that never gets past its beginnings and that, in its very incompleteness, without obligation to confront its end, finds itself inexhaustible and immortal. The following lines can be read again and again: "I do not know what effect this scene had upon her. She did not look at me or speak to me. But, half turning her head, she pointed with a simple movement of her finger to the mat at her feet."[21]

At this moment, then, the mirror is not the instrument of a gaze directed upon itself. It occupies a point on the path that connects Jean-Jacques to his beloved. Rousseau presents himself obliquely, through his reflection. He assures us that all this has come about unwittingly, and we must believe him. Yet it is easy to imagine that this indirect approach suited him better than any other and that he might have chosen it deliberately. It enables him to show himself "in effigy" without subjecting his real person to Mme. Basile's gaze. In a marvelously synthetic way, the mirror here serves both timidity and exhibitionism; it both betrays and protects. It shows, but what it reveals is only a reflection. It heralds a presence but reduces that presence to an image. Mme. Basile's reserve and timidity are tantamount to actual complicity. (The complicity is so perfect that one wonders if Rousseau didn't invent it when he came to write the account of his adventure.) Having noticed Jean-Jacques in the mirror, she knows that he is present but does not turn her eyes toward him, thus sparing him the shame of being stared in the face. She remains mute and unseeing, as if she knows and accepts the role assigned her by Jean-Jacques, that of an icon. She meets him halfway, but by way of a reciprocal estrangement that safeguards the precious distance between them. Two refugees in the pure world of images and reflections, neither is guilty. Their meeting takes place without them, each being nothing but a phantom for the other. This is a necessary condition if Jean-Jacques is to experience the highest happiness, namely that state in which exaltation, by its very intensity, culminates in depersonalization. Magic triumphs, establishing distance and contact simultaneously, accomplishing the miracle of union at a distance.

To show oneself; to see without being seen. Modern psychology has demonstrated that exhibitionism and voyeurism form a dual system of opposed yet complementary tendencies. Every exhibitionist is at times a voyeur. Rousseau is an excellent example of this, as the scene just described illustrates quite clearly. The pleasure of spying in secret is followed by the pleasure (not unalloyed with anxiety) of being furtively seen and, once seen, both punished and accepted. "She pointed to the mat at her feet." He is both welcomed and punished—as he likes.

Exhibitionism and voyeurism are two aspects of Rousseau's lonely quest for fascination, in which women are only a means to an end. When Rousseau in Turin shows his "ridiculous object" to serving-women, he is really trying to fascinate himself by eliciting an angry glare that causes him to anticipate, in his imagination, the imminence of the spanking he desires. The pleasure he creates for himself is that of seeing himself as prey, and he does so by provoking a public scandal and furtively participating in the supposed emotion of the aroused witnesses.

The same masochistic contrition can be achieved in other ways. In Lyons, Jean-Jacques secretly watches a girl bathing. After a short time he reveals his presence by singing some verses. The girl, upset, blushes, causing intense pleasure in the indiscreet onlooker, who thus measures from afar the power of his presence: "Would that I could give you back all that transpired in my soul at the sight of your confusion!"[22] A fine example of visual sadism, in which Rousseau for a moment plays the role of tormentor. But he cannot sustain it for long. Shame overcomes him, and the tables are turned. The moment he knows he has been seen, the cruel spectator becomes another man, a confused, humble fellow, who discovers the image of his guilt in his victim's eyes. Now it is his turn to endure her gaze, to kneel as a penitent prepared to accept punishment or pardon: "I lacked the courage to stare at you for long. It seemed to me that in your eyes you reproached me for having added wickedness to licentiousness. And these reproaches seemed to me inspired not by anger but by regret at finding me so guilty. Oh! How I detested my cruel joke! How happy I would have counted myself had I been able to hurl myself down at your knees to beg your pardon!"[23] He renounces his cruel pleasure, but only because he hopes to find a more exquisite pleasure in repentance.

At Meillerie, across the river from Clarens, Saint-Preux spends entire days at the telescope in hope of a purely optical penetration and possession: "From there through air and walls he dares in secret to penetrate your very chamber."[24] Does he manage to catch a glimpse of Julie? No, the distance is too great. He can barely make out "those fortunate walls that enclose the source of [her] life." This approximation is enough; imagination will supply the rest. No matter that the gaze cannot see the beloved but can only glimpse in the vaguest way the place where she lives and the surrounding landscape. That suffices to reconstitute her adored figure in memory. Saint-Preux sees Julie but in a sort of voluntary hallucination, in which he reconstructs her image from external signs.

Here we see in the making one of those conversions to the imaginary so frequent in Rousseau. Because the distance is too great, because the magnifying power of the telescope is too small, the indiscreet gaze is unable to make out the desired form. But never mind: the will-to-see, seconded by memory, becomes a creative power. The gaze transforms itself into vision and produces on its own the image of which it is deprived by hazy distance: "Quickly forced to turn inward, I contemplate you at least in the circumstances of your innocent life. I follow from afar the various occupations of your day, and I imagine them in times and places of which I have occasionally been the fortunate witness."[25]

Thus the telescope becomes the paradoxical instrument of retrospective evocation and private meditation. The gaze happily bridges distance in time rather than space. A diversion has taken place, substituting a *clear* vision of the past for the elusive phantoms of the real horizon: "I see an elegant but simple costume embellish charms that have no need of embellishment."[26] To see is to awaken in oneself the desired spectacle. If, originally, there is something of the voyeur in Saint-Preux (and in Rousseau), he quickly becomes the spectator of his own visions and thus ceases to offend propriety. The voyeur's assault is transformed into innocent reverie. This has two benefits. First, the desirous gaze, which can no longer be caught in the act of transgression, exempts itself from censure. Second, the inner spectacle has at its disposal a multitude of intimate details, remembered or invented. And Rousseau of course ascribed greater intensity to mental images than to actual sensations: "Objects make less of an impression on me than their souvenirs."[27]

The gaze fails to seize its prey, halting at objects made sacred by Julie's touch. In the end it invents the whole of the spectacle it coveted in reality. What a strange diversion, from the beloved to the things that surround her and finally to the fictive image of the desired being. This movement is characteristic of Jean-Jacques's affective behavior. Among other things, it reveals the possibility of slipping into fetishism. Unable to have the adored woman, incapable of thinking her accessible with impunity, desire shifts to the objects that are in contact with her, to her clothing. Rousseau kisses Mme. de Warens' bed and is filled with joy because "dear Mama" has slept there.[28] And when he swallows a morsel that has touched her lips, he is filled with ecstasy.[29]

In the bedroom where he waits for Julie, Saint-Preux is moved by the sight of her lingerie, which he touches and kisses:

The parts of your clothing that lie strewn about inspire in my ardent imagination images of the parts of yourself that they concealed: this slight hairpiece adorned by abundant blond hair that it feigned to cover; this happy scarf against which for once at least I shall not be obliged to murmur; this elegant and simple robe, so typical of the taste of the woman who wears it; these slippers so dainty that a lithe foot fills them easily; this body so slender, which touches and embraces . . . What an enchanting form! In front, two gentle curves . . . O spectacle of voluptuousness! The corset has ceded to the force of the impress . . . Delicious imprints, I shall kiss you a thousand times![30]

In Saint-Preux's imagination Julie's body rises up from these intimate objects, formed or deformed by contact with her flesh. The erotic value of these rags and relics comes from Julie's extraordinarily radiant power. Everything she touches, everything in her vicinity feels her influence, receives emanations of her presence, and thus takes on a sacred value. Intimate objects are visible messengers of the ideal woman. They involve her in the world of things. Yet while representing her indiscreetly they allow her to remain at a distance, intact. The true erotic "fetish" is the product of a fission, a splitting made necessary by the sentiment of guilt. On the one hand the proscribed beloved is not profaned in the flesh. On the other, desire can be satisfied by fastening on a symbolic substitute for the coveted person. Once again, an attempt to diminish the fault implicit in possession of the desired woman results in apparently perverse behavior. But Saint-Preux does not really behave like the fetishists described in psychiatric texts. His desire does not settle on things, and things do not help him to forget the primary object of desire. On the contrary these objects, which do not resist his eyes, his hands, or his caresses, help him to imagine Julie's presence. Through them the form of the desired body can be divined, while remaining the secret object of an "inward gaze." They suggest the brush of flesh, but despite its intoxicating proximity that flesh remains imaginary. Saint-Preux *burns* as he touches fabrics that have touched Julie's body. She is there, close by but beyond possession, perfectly absent, while Saint-Preux is overcome by an emotion that stems from an image docile to his thought. His happiness results from the singular conjunction of pure absence (which just barely misses being presence) with a paroxysm of emotion that certainly would have been less intense in the arms of a real woman. It is true that Saint-Preux possesses Julie. The ecstasy is fleeting, and in order to give full range to the fictional possibilities of separation, the moments of carnal happiness are quickly relegated to the past. The sacrilege must be committed in order to justify the virtuous effort of redemption. Saint-Preux must also take with him assurances that will serve as pretext for a repetition—imaginary, remembered, indestructible—according to the needs of reverie. But Saint-Preux is himself an imaginary double of Rousseau, and his triumph over Julie's virtue is merely a pleasant fantasy that Rousseau inscribes on the finest gilt-edged paper in a careful hand and with "blue and silver sand to dry the ink."[31] By degrees we have moved away from carnal possession only to return to a distant gaze upon the beloved, and from the gaze to the internalized image. Desire flows back upon itself, limits itself to *dreaming* of its power and satisfaction: under these conditions lust becomes tolerable and incurs no reproach. It has sacrificed its dearest intentions to the anticipated wrath of the hostile witness and at the same time has adopted a primitive and infantile attitude in which the witness does not yet exist. Thus it is not simply appeased but nullified.

The most effective alibis are not those that divert the gaze to other objects but those that make it possible to deny the very existence of desire. When the relation to objects ceases to be one of covetousness and becomes one of contemplation; when desire, confronted with the most attractive of women, appears to give way to childish confidence or virtuous emulation; then permissible intimacy begins its reign. Now the exchange of glances is no longer shameful, and the most affectionate gestures no longer have the erotic meaning that would have laid them open to reproach. At the cost of a total repudiation of lust, Jean-Jacques feels that he has acquired a total right to pure presence in the world inhabited by the woman he might have loved. This is Saint-Preux's situation when he returns from distant isles to the home of the married Julie. It is also the situation that Jean-Jacques accepts in the home of Mme. de Warens, accepts, that is, until she takes decisive steps to change it, thereby provoking in him a strange anxiety. And he would have liked to establish a similar relationship with Mme. d'Houdetot after the initial weeks of "folly." When glances are exchanged, Jean-Jacques cannot be happy and free of anxiety unless desire is concealed or deferred or transformed into something else: asexual sympathy, disinterested affection, filial love, musical or literary tokens. He is able to look Mme. de Warens in the eye because he persuades himself that he does not desire her: "I felt neither emotions nor desires in her presence; my state was one of blissful calm, in which I enjoyed I knew not what."[32] Thus he is both happy and reassured. His ecstasy is innocent because it knows no object, for he is living in the limpidity of a pure relationship into which lust has not introduced any *inclination*, any internal disequilibrium. After denying or repressing lustful thoughts, he can see nothing illicit in his need never to be far from "mama." "When I could see her I was merely happy. But my disquiet when she was away became almost painful."[33]

Lost Happiness, Imminent Happiness

The world becomes intolerable when desire, the object, and the witness meet. One of the three must disappear. Either desire is superfluous, or the object is, or the witness. We have just seen how Rousseau sought to resolve the difficulty by repressing, one by one, each of these incompatible terms.

Sometimes he eliminates the witness (as in clandestine theft). Sometimes he abolishes the external object (by shifting the scene to the imagination and making himself the object of a narcissistic love). And sometimes he eliminates his desire (through virtuous sublimation). Some of these invented solutions are perfectly "moral," others frankly perverse. Each one constitutes a possible (though never entirely calming) response to the same initial anxiety. Perverse tendencies are one kind of diversion among others, sought out by desire in order to escape the disapproval with which its audacity is likely to be met. Rousseau seems to feel more profoundly guilty about the dark crime of desire than about the manifestly deviant behavior in which he engages in order to obliterate the initial misdeed.

To speak of diversion is to suggest that desire is so malleable that it can be turned aside from a course it would otherwise have followed. It is to assume that desire is from the outset fairly clear about what it wants. But isn't this to ascribe to desire a clearer awareness and more precise choice than it is capable of? Does it know the forbidden fruit? Has it ever seen it? Can it recognize it? The proscription in fact attaches to no object in particular. It falls upon any desire that dares to reveal itself openly. Hence diversion usually occurs even before desire has settled upon a definite external object. Imaginary and symbolic compensations do not take the place of conscious passion. So great is the initial anxiety that every desire starts down a deviant path; its first object is already imaginary, already aberrant. It is a lesser evil that does not know what it is a substitute for, what untenable ecstasy it replaces.

Rousseau is incapable of sober desire. With him the adventure of desire does not begin with the selection of a real object. He is constantly searching for such an object without ever being able to define it. What is present initially is blind emotion: an avid power, as yet incapable of choosing among the many figures available to it in the outside world. From the first we find Rousseau governed by the confused vehemence of his feelings, largely uninterested in overcoming his difficulty or reluctance to leave the infantile world of egocentric and fantastic reverie. The avowal at the beginning of the *Confessions* is to be taken seriously: it was through the reading of novels that Jean-Jacques first became aware of his own existence.[34] From the first the ego discovers itself in the act that leaves it in thrall to fantasy, in the movement that propels it beyond the father's workbench and the humble reality of the home into a world of emotion and fictional adventure. The whole of Rousseau's work attests to the fact that desire bears within itself, for better or worse, an unlimited power to produce changing images capable of eliciting emotions.

A primary dictum of psychology holds that recourse to the imagination is a way of compensating for failures encountered in the quest for tangible possessions. Such a search for compensation is not lacking in Rousseau. On many pages of his autobiographical writings he mentions it explicitly.[35] That the appeal to the imagination is often the result of disappointment cannot be denied. In its final disillusionment Jean-Jacques's loving soul plunges itself into consoling fantasies. Unable to satisfy its appetite with the bread of reality, it feasts on the cake and wine of the imagination. Yet whatever validity there may be in this interpretation, it remains incomplete. If Jean-Jacques retreats into imaginary worlds in order to shield himself from hostile scrutiny, and if he derives from those worlds a hundred times the pleasures he was unable to achieve in the tumult of the real world, it is not simply because he finds the prey he failed to capture in reality reflected, indeed embellished, in his imagination. For the imagination is a native country, a homeland from which he is never entirely able to detach himself in order to enter the world of men.

There is a spontaneous movement in Rousseau's imagination, a confused hunger, a fanciful anticipation that, starting from a wholly illusory happiness, wants passionately to see that happiness come true.[36] This is the initial form of Rousseau's imaginary activity. It does not shun the world but prepares to penetrate it. It paints itself an enchanting portrait animated to its taste, anticipating, conjuring up figures that, if not yet real, are soon to become so. The carnal prey that will reveal desire, the living women who will receive its homage, arise in response to dreamy expectations, which have long heralded and prefigured their coming. A repertory of fantasy precedes and envelops them, as their images gradually take shape against a shadowy void. The beloved object is the visible figure in which an insistent reverie finds its culmination, supplanting an obsessive fantasy. Rousseau approaches reality only as he pursues his quarry in imagination. If the real object proves disappointing, it is because he looks to it for total confirmation of a felicity he has already experienced in a dream. The imagination offers archetypes, a priori models, not easily matched. The compensation he sometimes seeks after the fact is merely a return to the prior stage. It is a retreat, but one in which consciousness returns to the morning light in happy anticipation and with expansive emotions. Rousseau's fictional ecstasies involve an undeniable element of hindsight.[37] He evokes idealized images of missed opportunities and paints brilliant pictures of handsome objects that have resisted capture. But he relives this past as though he could transform it into a future, as though by invoking hope he could see again what is no more. The awakened dreamer nullifies time, experiencing unrequited desire as a quasi-future. What is most precious in the imaginary compensation is not the pleasure of possession but the initial euphoric hope of imminent gratification, the free acceptance of possibility untrammeled by the trivial laws of this world. The compensatory imagination derives its efficacy from the resources of anticipatory reverie.

Important as the role of magical memory is, Rousseau's reverie is a "prospective" movement that deploys its visions along an unobstructed horizon, safe from the dampening gaze of the witness. Janus-like, the imagination looks both front and rear. In order to liberate the future it plunges into the past. In an endless circuit dreams draw upon embellished souvenirs of actual encounters, but those encounters were consequences of still earlier dreams, previous pursuits of mysterious chimeras. More than the material reality of things and people, what attracts Jean-Jacques is the possibility of using them to play out a mental adventure; his is an imagination of the second degree, in which real people are desirable for their affinities with the figures of his personal mythology. He pursues real prey only in order to possess their beloved shades. In Sophie d'Houdetot, Rousseau believed he had found an incarnation of Julie d'Etanges,[38] whose image he had built up out of memories of Eléonore de Warens (and others). Yet he does not stop at a past actually experienced with "mama" but goes on to reinvent her youth, the mysterious time of her first loves: Julie is his dream version of Eléonore as adolescent. Conversely, Rousseau would not have been able to form so strong an attachment to Mme. de Warens had he not found in her the Lady of his first fictional imaginations, as well as the imagined features of a mother he never knew. If need be, he could drop the prey in favor of the shadow without any sense of loss. Pygmalion first falls in love with a fleshless image, but his desire fashions and brings to life a figure of flesh and blood; yet he continues to adore the first, incorporeal image, which he can scarcely distinguish from his own ego.

With what dreams did Rousseau ultimately compensate for his failure to obtain each of the real objects he desired? Equally pertinently, what dreams preceded each of those objects, and how was desire diverted to them? Psychoanalysis, not unreasonably but also without convincing proof, would suggest some sort of fantasy about the maternal breast. And before that? From conjecture to conjecture one could follow the trail a long way back, but without ever being sure of reaching the end. The capacity of substitution, the power of compensation, are here equal to the persistence of desire.

From Darkness to Darkness through the Imagination

Prior to discovery of the real object come the imaginary prefigurations that herald it. But imagination itself stands out against an imageless background. Several times in the *Confessions* Rousseau speaks of a primary state of desire, which is pure feeling that has not yet opened its eyes to the real world or to the spectacles of reverie. It is an obscure commotion, a burning sensation that is only vaguely aware of itself and still more ignorant of what might satisfy it. Where should he look? He does not know or wish to know. Jean-Jacques, if we take him at his word, for a long time remained the prisoner of a blind anxiety, exalted and disoriented without knowing why. In a boy who had devoured so many novels such innocence is astonishing. Puritanical terrorism no doubt played a part. This delay in the "choice of object" attests, I think, to the early influence of the taboo; it is the defensive response of a consciousness that wishes to protect itself against an accusation it knows to be imminent: desire denies having any object at all, or that it is interested in anything or anyone. It claims to be wholly absorbed in itself, enduring its effervescence as an overwhelming if delicious inevitability. It is thereby relieved of guilt, for it knows not even what it is desirous of. Rousseau lingers in innocence, as he will later linger in imagination: so many ways of not doing wrong, of avoiding sin. Isn't this, as he puts it, what saves him from himself?[39] A strange salvation: abandoning himself to the most dubious of bewilderments, Jean-Jacques thinks he is saved. The meaning of the confession is clear. He wants to be saved not from sensual turmoil but from the unpredictable new man he would become were he to come into contact with an *external* reality that would overpower his senses.

Feeling comes first. Then internal images are produced to bolster that feeling:

> My senses, which had been roused long ago, demanded delights of which I could not even guess the nature. I was as far from the reality as if I had been entirely lacking in sexuality. My senses were already mature, and I sometimes thought of my past eccentricities, but I could not see beyond them. In this strange situation my restless imagination took a hand which saved me from myself and calmed my growing sensuality. What it did was to nourish itself on situations that had interested me in my reading, recalling them, varying them, combining them, and giving me so great a part in them that I became one of the characters I imagined, and saw myself always in the pleasantest situations of my own choosing. So, in the end, the fictions I succeeded in building up made me forget my real condition, which so dissatisfied me.[40]

Image making, then, came only after a certain delay. Its effect was to reduce the tension of the situation, to lessen anxiety, to make the obscure fermentation of desire more tolerable. What is most authentic here is not the creation of images (all borrowed from books) but the silent intensity of the primitive emotion: feeling, looking for a way out, turns to images for both diversion and temporary satisfaction. The point bears emphasizing: Rousseau's imaginary life was above all a deployment of the powers of feeling, an expansiveness without definite object that reveled by turns in the keenest joys of pride and the pleasures of abject humility. Since Jean-Jacques is no longer satisfied to feel emotion for no reason, he invents detailed pretexts and demands a fictional stage setting. Feeling needs to wrap itself in a justifying story. But for Rousseau the images are mere auxiliaries of feeling; they have no originality of their own. Now we can understand why Rousseau's contemporaries were able to see him as the very type of the man dominated by his imagination, while modern exegetes of the imaginary (like Gaston Bachelard) find no evidence of truly creative reverie in his work. Everything is in the dynamic quality of the emotions, the pathos of the situation. Little room is left for the "material imagination," that is, for an oneiric exploration of nature. Rousseau is interested not so much in the world as in people, and not so much in people as in the emotions he feels in their presence. For him, reverie is above all the place where sociability is fully realized. While he requires a rustic setting if he is to dream, his favorite theme is "elite society." In his reveries he idealizes relations with other people. Rousseau is never isolated in his imaginary theater; he responds to his interlocutors. Alone in nature, he peoples his solitude with kindred spirits, and the wood is limited to the modest function of backdrop. The imagination adjusts the moral tensions as required and invents conflicts, disputes, repentances, pardons, sacrifices, and the like.

In this imagined world, glances meet affectionately, obstacles loom only to be quickly pushed aside, and misunderstandings are dissipated when the moment is ripe. The pleasure and the feeling of deliverance here have to do with the fact that the initiative of the gaze now comes from Jean-Jacques and Jean-Jacques alone. Friends, mistresses, confidants—all are products of his vision, and it is he who controls and commands at will the gazes that his fictitious partners direct toward him or return in response to his own. He knows implicitly what their eyes and faces are trying to express. Mysterious as they may be in his imagination, there is nothing in them that escapes him by its very essence. All their intentions are clear. He does not encounter in them those obscure, unfathomable, unknowable depths that inevitably arouse suspicion in real witnesses. Indeed, Jean-Jacques's gaze upon his visions and the witness' gaze upon Jean-Jacques are mutually exclusive. That is why he guards his solitude so jealously, even at the risk of being taken for a misanthrope. He can converse with his dear phantoms only if no one sees him. The "expansive" power of his affectionate soul cannot deploy itself unless he is surrounded by a sort of vacuum, devoid of human presence. This singular conquest of a fictional space presupposes a maximal shrinking of real life. Psychologists are not wrong to describe Rousseau's case as one of *introversion*. Reverie creates the illusion of access to the world, whereas in reality it draws exclusively upon a space it produces for itself.

Jean-Jacques's emotional lability creates space for itself not only by varying the episodes in his imagined stories but also by identifying one after another with the various actors. In the life of the imagination the great thing is not so much the spectacle that one sees but the admirable character that one is (or becomes). For Rousseau the charm of an epistolary novel like *La Nouvelle Héloïse* is that in writing he can pass from one subjectivity to another, identifying successively with Saint-Preux, Julie, Claire, Wolmar, and so on. His heroes are all generous, some passionate, others virtuous. There is no wicked character in this small, select circle. Thus Rousseau is permitted to ally himself fully with each one in turn. In identifying with his fictional characters he savors the pleasure of being someone else without thereby being false to himself. He never moves outside the enchanted atmosphere of affection, virtue, and redeemed guilt. His entire soul is divided among the several characters of the novel. What is more, the revels of the imagination and the most singular of metamorphoses remain compatible with the uniformity of a frugal life, in which day after day solitary walks regularly follow hours devoted to the copying of musical scores. Should we smile when he tells us that he was never more himself than on his days of reverie? Not at all. For Jean-Jacques, being himself means being free to *become someone else* in his imagination, contemptuous of straitened circumstances and hostile plots.

Born of blind desire, which has yet to catch sight of its object, the imaginary adventure ends in ecstasy, where all objects drop from view. The most precious moments of reverie are those in which consciousness, inundated by overpowering feelings, forgets all the images that have served it as pretext. Thus the domain of imagination proper is flanked on one side by initial obscurity, and on the other, by a final dazzlement that in a sense rejoins the obscurity of the outset. Everything begins in the silent churning of "burning blood." Visions, fantasies, "golden ages," "elite societies"[41] serve only to bring the spirit to the point where it is annihilated in a paroxysm and where the body, overwhelmed but triumphant, knows nothing but the mysterious pulses coursing through it. It is aware of no presence other than its own, on the brink of absence. This total presence, which has absorbed all differences and ceased to engage in dialogue with any alien figure (even imaginary ones), is often equivalent to a feeling of oneness with the universe. Identification with cosmic totality is the highest point that imagination can reach but, once reached, all images evaporate. The quiet reveries of the Lake of Bienne and the "stupe-fying ecstasy" of the third letter to Malesherbes (two states distin-guished by the intensity of the vibration, the one associated with extreme tenuousness, the other with a tumult that surpasses "the limits of beings"[42]) are both "reveries without object,"[43] exaltations whose ground has become so immense and limitless that the soul is enticed into a state of bewilderment in which all distinct representa-tions evaporate.

Images vanish, the gaze loses itself in the infinite. The expansive power of desire, having created the imaginary world in order to negate and transcend the imperfections of the real one, completes its trajectory with a final negation, which abolishes the imaginary spectacle itself.[44] As the successive stages are traversed, the progress of negation is apparent. The imagination opposes society's lies and vices by constructing a realm apart, inhabited by perfect types and superlative virtues: a rebellion that breaks no chains but supplants the unjust world with the idea of an "other sphere." Only this fanciful world, in which consciousness is free to savor the "pleasure of being cause," is affected by a weakness inseparable from its perfection. Its beauty is associated with nonbeing. "I always sought what did not exist."[45] "Is it my fault if I love that which is not?"[46] The perfection of the imaginary world is wholly sustained by the effort of the self, which cannot indefinitely hide from itself the fact that its creation proceeds ex nihilo. The images it evokes to satisfy its need of love are a trap, which fascinates and alienates the individual's freedom. The very ease with which the fancies of the imagination are dispatched reveals their nothingness, "suddenly saddening"[47] the soul. This void too must be filled, the nothingness negated in its turn. Just as the soul once wrested itself from the world in order to devote itself to the imagination, now it must wrest itself from the imagination in order to devote itself to the mysterious truth that appears to it across the nothingness of the imaginary. Cosmic ecstasy, or the sensation of raw existence, will have the value of a negation of the negation (endured in solitude): a return of primary plenitude following a detour by way of illusory appearances. This requires a kind of grace, by which I mean an excess of expansive energy or a power of total abandonment.

Even if ecstasy does not feel that it is subject to the law of time, it does not survive the moment that bears it. What remains? When excessive happiness evaporates, when imagination flags or becomes disenchanted, the gaze falls on the real world. In order to avoid the cruel hostility of the crowd, the eye must repose in the innocence of natural objects: trailside plants, familiar animals, a frugal table of modest dishes cooked by Thérèse. After ecstasy there always comes a moment when Rousseau surrenders "to the impression of objects but without thinking, *without imagining*, without doing anything other than feeling calm and happiness."[48] He experiences the happy exhaustion of the evening's walk home. And in the final years, when his imagination has dried up or "cooled," Rousseau finds in botany the same circumscribed pleasure, limited to the perception of agreeable objects. The obscurity that supplants the images of imagination is the empty heaven, the eye open to the world. Let a ray of light traverse it and this obscurity becomes pure transparency. "Fleeing from men, seeking solitude, no longer using my imagination and thinking even less, yet endowed with a lively nature that keeps me from languid and melancholy apathy, I began to take an interest in everything around me, and a quite natural instinct led me to prefer those objects which were most pleasing to me."[49] These rustic objects and consoling romances yield a lively pleasure made livelier still by Rousseau's certainty of his absolute innocence: all men are called to witness. Gaze upon him as long as you wish. Who would wish to take umbrage?

The Dreamer Banishes All Images

No escape into the imagination: that is how Rousseau describes the condition of the *man of nature*. He lives in harmony. He covets only those objects for which nature causes him to feel a need. His desire is always such that it can be immediately satisfied, never outstripping the resources offered by the physical environment. In the primitive forest, virgin and fertile, unthwarted desire is also desire with uncoerced limitations. No virtuous effort is required of the man of nature in order to maintain his equilibrium:

> His imagination paints no pictures; his heart yearns for nothing; his modest needs are readily supplied at hand; and he is so far from

having enough knowledge for him to desire to acquire more knowledge that he can have neither foresight nor curiosity . . . Imagination, which causes such ravages among us, does not speak to savage hearts.[50]

According to the hypothetical history set forth in the *Discourse on Inequality*, imagination develops only with foresight and reflection, that is, only when man through self-improvement abandons his natural condition. The imagination is one of those admirable but deadly powers that foment dissatisfaction, dividing the mind against itself and forcing it to quit its native ground of immediacy.

Hence it should come as no surprise that Rousseau, in the theory of education set forth in *Emile* and reflecting a need to prolong childhood and delay puberty, frequently suggests that the imagination be stifled as long as possible: "The waywardness of youth begins not with temperament or the senses but with opinion."[51] The imagination is supremely dangerous, for it opens the eyes of ignorant youth, pointing out desirable objects and inaugurating a period of guilty and wretched desire. Nothing is worse than premature discovery of sexual desire and its object. All powers of anticipation, whether intellectual or emotional, must therefore be quelled. Above all one must flee the cities, where men live exclusively through anticipation. Once the senses are awakened, however, once desire has recognized its object, imagination assumes a new aspect and becomes the auxiliary of virtue. Surrounded by temptations to which he is now sensitive, the young man is saved by the diversion available through "imaginary realization." Amorous reverie directed toward fictitious persons is thus to be encouraged, for it will provide the adolescent with good reasons to spurn easy pleasure. Sophie and Emile, fascinated by the image of the beloved ideal, keep their souls pure until they meet.[52]

Furthermore, while imagination is a power fatal to man's primitive state, in which he knows only familiar and innocent things, it nevertheless possesses privileges that give it an important function in the intellectual realm. Until the adolescent has fully mastered the use of his rational and discursive faculties, there is no point addressing him in the language of strict reason. Better to speak to him in ways that "strike the imagination," through concrete signs and examples. Therein lay the ancients' secret of eloquence: "What was said most forcefully was expressed not in words but in signs. One did not tell, but showed. The object exposed to the eyes shakes the imagination, arouses curiosity, and leaves the mind eager to hear what one is about to say. And often the object itself has said it all."[53] Rousseau exhorts us to "filter the language of the mind through the heart." No other method is as good for speaking to the young, "who do not think so much as imagine."[54] While striving to prevent those flights of imagination that might awaken sensuality too soon, one turns to the imagination to forestall premature recourse to reflection.

In the state of nature the imagination is corrupting. In the state of our imperfect societies, it is the sole resource of virtuous and loving souls. If it first separates us from harmonious reality, in return it protects us from a debasing contact with fallen reality. Although factitious society is itself a work of the imagination, maximal use of the imagination is enough to deliver man from its snares and restore the memory of primitive happiness. How, indeed, can Rousseau know what the state of nature was like? The answer is: through an effort of the imagination, "setting aside all facts."[55] For the man who must endure the iniquity of the corrupt world, the state of nature exists only as an *image*. Rousseau wanders alone in the forest of Saint-Germain in search of an "image of the first days."[56] The only way to recover the happiness of the golden age is to dream, without even trying to make Arcadia the specific theme of reverie. In the imaginary state, desire and its object are precisely correlative, perfectly in tune. In the object there is no opacity, flaw, or obstruction, none of those superfluous, unpredictable elements that divert and disconcert desire in reality.[57] The imagined figure conforms perfectly to the desire that conjured it up. Dream consciousness aspires to a condition in which it experiences happiness through the perfect match between the need it feels and the imaginary object that spontaneously arises to meet it. The result is an equilibrium analogous to what the state of nature possess in the plenitude of reality. The analogy is confirmed by Rousseau's use of the same term to describe happiness in the state of nature and happiness in the fancy of reverie: to be sufficient unto oneself (*se suffire à soi-même*).

The analogy is so striking that it is reasonable to ask whether the portrait of the state of nature is not entirely patterned after the *activity* of the imagination, of which it is a fabulous amplification projected into the past. Every desire finds immediate satisfaction, every impulse meets with nature's benevolent acquiescence, and no witness intrudes upon the solitary celebration. Happiness in the state of nature is as easily acquired as happiness in the imagination, except that in the state of nature the imagination is unknown. If it is true that the imagination fictively reestablishes the state of nature, it is also true that the state of nature is the myth reverie needs to justify itself. Jean-Jacques's dream is legitimate because, merely by being a dream, it shares man's primitive innocence. The man of nature is Jean-Jacques's warrant for not feeling guilty about fleeing the world and its duties.

What would happen if society were to perfect itself, if it were to adopt laws that would enable it to overcome its vices? Reverie, in Alain's words "always ambling and melancholy,"[58] would presumably lose its importance. The wonderful self-sufficiency of primitive and independent man would be recaptured in absolute dependency on the law, which guarantees man's liberty qua citizen. Desire, having sacrificed every particular will for the sake of the general will, takes on a new form and thereby acquires the right to reveal itself openly. It wants the good of all and may seek without shame to satisfy itself to the full. Not only does the law accept desire; desire itself has become the law. It no longer has anything to fear from the hostile witness. It assumes the role of witness: exposing itself to the scrutiny of all, it scrutinizes in turn the entire collectivity, where nothing is hidden from it. This exalting privilege is the very essence of the civic celebration. Why would consciousness take refuge in the imagination when it is free to exercise its sovereignty in public?

In the city of the *Social Contract*, whose virtuous institutions Rousseau imagined in 1752, citizens are not allowed to leave the State:

> If I were chief of one of the peoples of Nigritia, I declare that I would have a gallows set up on the country's border, where I would summarily hang . . . the first citizen who attempted to leave . . . He does harm by setting a bad example and harms himself by seeking vice. In every sense it is the law's job to prevent him from doing so. Better that he should be hanged than that he should be wicked.[59]

Such remarkable severity is immediately applicable to Jean-Jacques's own past. Did he not leave the State? Did he not roam far afield in pursuit of self-invented fantasies? "Finding nothing in his world that fulfilled his ideas, he left his homeland while a young adolescent and set out in the world with confidence, seeking the Aristides, Lycurguses, and Astraeas with whom he believed it to be filled."[60] His "undisciplined imagination"[61] drove him into the world in search of an unattainable happiness. But the just city as Jean-Jacques imagined it is a city in which Jean-Jacques would not have dreamed.

I I

The Self Subsumes Sacred History

In Rousseau the "passage to the imagination" concerns not only certain episodes of his life but his total image of it. Using the great religious themes he knew in his youth, he transposes his life onto the plane of myth.

The result is a strange hybrid of sacred history and personal myth. Important episodes in the Bible not only become contemporaneous with Jean-Jacques's life but merge with it. Sacred history and autobiography mingle. The same can be said of Augustine, who made a point of comparing sacred history and personal history. There are many good reasons to think that Rousseau secretly identified with some aspects of Augustine's early life. When Rousseau speaks of his destiny he easily incorporates Innocence, Paradise, the Fall, Exile, and Martyrdom. In all of these he is no mere spectator but the authentic actor. (His attitude is something like pietistic fervor.)

Here we encounter his extraordinary powers of identification. "I became the character whose life I was reading,"[62] he says of his reading of Plutarch and the novelists. Perhaps the same thing happened when he read the Bible. Why should he have found the religious pretext any less useful? Among his childhood enthusiasms (all of which prefigure some aspect of his later work) the pastoral vocation was not the least important: "For I found preaching quite a lovely thing."[63] After becoming a puppeteer for a time, he just as readily assumes the role of "minister."[64] These were the games of a child eager to draw the attention of adults. But Jean-Jacques remained a child all his life: the puppeteer became the writer of *Narcissus* and the *Village Soothsayer*; the preacher, the "man of God," would reappear beneath the cassock of the Savoyard vicar and would speak through the mouth of the dying Julie. Preaching is far more than a mere ministry. It is a heroic vocation that imposes suffering and sacrifice, transforming life into a sovereign passion. Through preaching, the "beautiful soul" calls forth the unparalleled destiny that confirms its estimate of its own unique worth. Did Rousseau imitate the Bible? It is possible that he never thought about it after embarking upon his life of sacred solitude, which according to him had no precursor despite the obvious prototype in the solitude of the prophets and Christ. And there were other models as well: the cynics and stoics. All these echoes of the past mingled and fused so thoroughly that we cannot expect Rousseau to discriminate among the sources of his inspiration.

The religion with which he was imbued became an integral part of his identity. But this involved him in a supreme heresy, for he so identified with religion that Christianity and narcissism (that is, the choice of himself as the object of his desire) were one and the same. What role did faith continue to play in a religion freed of all dogmatic constraint, mingled with the impulses of the man of desire, and placed on the same plane as humor and predilection, naturalized as it were by the self? Jean-Jacques did not subjugate his life to the Christian order. His actions and wanderings were confined by neither city nor established religion. Yet if for him the sacred ceases to be an external authority, it does not altogether disappear. Rather it has been swallowed up by personal experience. Its theory, whose power as law he has shaken off, continues invisibly to animate his passions, desires, and feelings of nostalgia. The impulse from *within* more or less consciously mimics the injunction from *on high*. Law and love are heralded not by transcendent logos but by the "voice of conscience." The whole external structure of Christianity is deformed or destroyed, enabling Rousseau to internalize his religion as a purely subjective power, at one with the liberty and exaltations of the individual consciousness. Compared with the encyclopedists, he was a Christian. In the eyes of the churches he was not. His sensibility, especially his anguish over the fall, reveals him as a product of Christianity. But he repudiated the world that had formed him when he ceased to believe in Original Sin.

With ingenuous pride Rousseau arrogated to himself the right to relive in his own way the prelapsarian life and the expulsion from paradise. This is what he says of his unjust punishment at Bossey: "We lived as we are told the first man lived in the earthly paradise, but we no longer enjoyed it."[65] Is this simply an innocent metaphor? A mere analogy? Analogy leads to identification. Jean-Jacques relives Adam's catastrophe. In imagination he is the first man, an absolute beginning. How could he, as Kierkegaard would, compare his suffering to that of the saints? He is the unique protagonist; history's axis passes through his life. Others are to look to him as a "term of comparison."[66]

In the *Profession of Faith*, in which Rousseau strives to make conviction into doctrine, there is a revealing hesitation. On the one hand he accepts the traditional theological view according to which the choir of creatures is subordinate to a central God. On the other hand he proposes the heterodox image of a universe in which each creature may regard himself as the center of all things.

One could hardly wish for a clearer affirmation of the principle of universal hierarchy:

> There is some kind of moral order wherever there is feeling and intelligence. The difference is that the good is ordered in relation to the whole, whereas the wicked orders the whole in relation to itself. The wicked makes itself the center of all things; the good measures its radius and remains within its circumference. Thus it is ordered in relation to the common center, which is God, and to all the concentric circles, which are God's creatures.[67]

By contrast, here is a world in which order no longer implies hierarchy or "concentric circles" and in which each creature may claim the privilege of centrality: "There is no being in the Universe that one cannot in some respect regard as the common center of all the others, upon which all are ordered, in such a way that all are reciprocally ends and means relative to one another."[68] If this is true, then individual consciousness can grant itself absolute importance. Since each person is then a center, no one has the right to grant oneself exclusive privileges. A requirement of reciprocity arises, so that this multicentric, nonhierarchical cosmos is an accurate reflection of the republic of the *Social Contract*. All creatures enjoy equal sovereignty, in return for which they are equally subject to the universal order. In the description of the rural festival at the end of book four of *Emile*, this idea is expressed in terms of the culinary imagination: "The dishes would be served in no particular order. Appetite would dispense with the need for ceremony. Since each one would openly prefer himself to all the others, he would find it right that all the others prefer themselves to him."

Depending on whether we look at the rational or the irrational side of Rousseau's egocentrism, we may see it as either a symptom of morbid hypertrophy of the ego or a mark of the "Copernican revolution" brought about by Enlightenment philosophy: at last coming of age (as Kant put it), human consciousness took possession of its creative autonomy and freed itself of all dependence on dogmatic absolutes and their earthly representatives, churches and priests.[69] In many respects Rousseau is already one of the new men. But his anxiety, his feelings of guilt, and his need for justification are shadows of old norms that he still carries within himself, ineradicable shadows that completely engulf him. Hence the personal myth can be stated only in the terms and language that once belonged to theology.

The Child and God

The reader of the *Confessions* discovers that the expulsion from paradise is repeated several times. It is as if Rousseau felt the need to relive it in a variety of circumstances, much as neurotics will repeat a traumatic event in their dreams and behavior. The *Confessions* contain a series of affirmations, each of which solemnly proclaims Rousseau's entry into the realm of woe. "My birth was the first of my misfortunes."[70] But other solemn beginnings will resound throughout the work, as if the narrator were hesitant to indicate precisely when his destiny took its dark and fatal turn. Even in the most disastrous situations, unexpectedly positive things happen. Rousseau miraculously retains the power to recreate and reenter paradise. Yet in reconquering Eden his secret intention is apparently to lose it yet again, to confront one more time the misfortune of exile, as if to assure himself in a tangible way of the implacability of fate. As far back as we trace his childhood, he has *already* lost an earlier happiness, but every calamity, even those he deems definitive and irretrievable, leaves him a surprising measure of tranquillity and peace. This aptitude for regaining Eden is characteristic of Rousseau, as is his suffering at having been unjustly driven out after too brief a stay.

Rousseau knows both the divine life and the fallen life. Above all he knows the abrupt passage from one to the other. The felt contrast between the two states establishes the fundamental division in his emotional life, the bass clef of his affective existence. The theology of the fall secretly dramatizes his psychological reversals. It animates his antithetical style, his manichaean protest, his merciless critique of monarchical society. Obeying the same law of absolute contrast, his life is divided into zones of darkness and light. Rousseau's psychological experience, from the moment he acquires it and even more when he relives it in memory, tends to take on the dignity of myth, with all its characteristic prophetic and exemplary qualities. Incidental fortune and misfortune almost immediately lose their fortuitous quality and become sacred "archetypes."

Paradise is the bedroom of Aunt Suzon, archangelic musician, and later the countryside at Bossey. It is the orchard at Charmettes and the Hermitage before the quarrel. It is Montmorency before the *Emile* affair and the Ile Saint-Pierre before the expulsion order. In each asylum Rousseau knows "brief and delicious intervals" before once again encountering misfortune and persecution. Some of these intervals are very brief indeed, no more than an instant of awakening, as in the theater of Saint Chrysostom in Venice: "My first thought was that I was in Paradise."[71]

What is the nature of the dream of paradise? What is its peculiar tonality? Rousseau's work is filled with descriptions of sweet harmonious scenes. There is much greenery, and there are panoramic views encompassing tranquil expanses of scenery. There is blue water, scarcely rippled. The music is expressive and simple. If possible all these pleasures are mingled and confounded, for Rousseau's sensuality, not content with superficial sensation, needs to develop into a synesthetic tremulousness. And pleasure wants for its accomplice some grand moral idea that will well up from the heart and disguise the invasive emotion as a virtuous affection. Sometimes paradise discloses itself to Jean-Jacques in a stationary ecstasy. More often, however, it takes the form of a pleasure derived from the free expenditure of energy in some gratuitous activity, without specific goal or utility. It is the inaction "of a child who is constantly in motion for no particular purpose, or that of a dotard who roams the countryside." He has the right to "muse all day long" and "to obey nothing but the whim of the moment."[72] But happiness requires that other conditions be met: the young Jean-Jacques is not content simply to indulge in a thousand carefree games. He also needs the love and approval of grownups: Aunt Suzon, Mlle. Lambercier (before the unjust punishment), Mme. de Warens (before offering herself), and, ultimately, God. "Happiness, the golden age, means just this: to come and go beneath the gaze of a protective god or divinized individual; to be recognized and acknowledged by him as a child, and to offer to this transcendent being, this 'spectator' who does not encumber the child but leaves him all the freedom he might wish, a pure heart."[73]

Rousseau constructed his myth of paradise out of his need to reverse a situation in which he was subjected to the scrutiny of a disapproving witness. In Eden the spectator has not yet turned hostile; his gaze proclaims not reproach but benevolence. Before the age of culpable desire comes the fabulous age of innocent desire and free gratification in the presence of an approving witness. In the depths of the past, Rousseau imagines having known a state in which evil and prohibition had yet to arise. Not only have his desires not yet been contradicted by any obstacle, but he offers his inviolate heart in all its transparency to the divine persons who are the object of those desires. A transcendent guarantee heightens his happiness, and sovereign comprehension and approval preserve his security.

In paradisaical life, the encounter with divinity is wonderfully easy. A perfect, limpid relationship, a gratuitous and effortless miracle, the divine presence is in the very light that laps at the "lovely shore" of the golden age. Presence reigns in tranquillity and simplicity.

What boon permits spontaneous harmony to exist between the carefree child and the omniscient god? The child surrenders to the sensuous enthusiasms of the moment, whereas God knows all things through a unique, intuitive gaze. Both are liberated from the sequentiality of time because they exist in the present instant: that is their point of contact. The instant of youthful consciousness is infinitely limited, whereas the divine instant is infinitely extended. Despite the extraordinary distance between them, they share the same privilege. Limited to immediate sensations, the child passively endures the external world and need not struggle against any external obstacle. He is not opposed to anything, since he has yet to recognize himself as distinct from the world around him. At the opposite extreme, God is limitless energy, which, being omnipotent, encounters no obstacle: "The supreme intelligence has no need to reason. For it there exist neither premises nor consequences nor even propositions. It is purely intuitive. It sees both what is and what can be. All truths are for it but a single idea, all places but a single point, and all times but a single moment."[74]

The consciousness of the child (or savage) is but a pale reflection of this instantaneity of the divine:

His soul, which nothing disturbs, dwells only in the sensation of its present existence, without any idea of the future, however close that might be, and his projects, as limited as his horizons, hardly extend to the end of the day. Such is, even today, the extent of the foresight

of a Caribbean Indian: he sells his cotton bed in the morning, and in
the evening comes weeping to buy it back, having failed to foresee
that he would need it for the next night.[75]

By his own account Jean-Jacques is strangely similar to the Caribbean
Indian, with whom he shares the traits of forgetfulness and impru-
dence:

> He goes from one extreme to the other with unbelievable speed and
> without even noticing the change or remembering what he was a
> moment before . . . For J.-J., incapable of even the most elementary
> prudence and entirely in the grip of whatever sentiment moves him,
> is unaware as long as it lasts that he will ever cease to be affected by
> it.[76]

A fine example of a "coincidence of opposites": instantaneity
establishes a marvelous conjunction between a consciousness that
never escapes from the present moment defined in the strictest
possible sense and a power that draws upon all time. Neither will
abandon the immediate to immerse itself in duration and change.
Hence the constricted innocence of the child (ignorant of good and
evil) joins the infinite goodness of God. Though polar opposites,
divine life and youthful life are alike in the absence of all need. God
is sufficient unto himself because he can lack for nothing. The child
and the savage are nearly as autarchic because nature maternally
ministers to their every need, and because their imaginations never
inspire desire for what is superfluous. The resemblance is so profound
and the communication so easy that Rousseau in his moments of
happiness shifts effortlessly from extreme contraction to extreme
expansion, that is, from the condition of child to that of god. One
moment he is confined within the constricted paradise of sensation,
the next he is striving through his "universal system" to apprehend
the infinity of the "great being."[77] The childish states and the divine
states are both manifestations of a single theme: immediate existence,
which ranges from nullity to infinity, from a minimum to a maximum.
Depending on the extent of the "field" that dominates his consciousness, Rousseau will call himself as "carefree as a child" or as
"impassive as God himself."[78] The uttermost humility and pride
derive from a single source. Rousseau can be a child before a god, and
he can also become a god himself. Here the hierarchy and the relation
of transcendence are not established in any absolute way. It is not a

question of superior and inferior. The extremes are simply symmetrical, and neither prevails over the other. What counts is not divinity or childhood as such but the quality of happiness that they may share and that Jean-Jacques insists upon knowing. By working hard enough to simplify things or surrender to them, the ego can with total but fleeting clarity achieve its goal.

Many of Rousseau's assertions derive from firmly established tradition. That God knows all things intuitively and not through discursive reasoning is a commonplace of theology. Intuitive knowledge is infinitely superior to knowledge of any other kind, but it is not the province of fallen, incarnate spirits. Did Adam possess it? The question is controversial. In order to regain such power the human soul must at the least strive to return to "Saturn's heaven" and to approach the angels. In this life man achieves intuitive vision only on rare occasions and with the aid of a special grace at the culmination of a lengthy spiritual ascent. He comes into permanent possession of it only after the soul is separated from the body: "The joy of the blessed is to see God *sine medio*."[79] In ordinary circumstances, in his "worldly condition," man must follow the path of discursive reason. Though inferior to intuition, reason is a divine gift that bestows upon man an eminent dignity and raises him above all other creatures. He must content himself with this and not anticipate to the felicity of the angels.

Nothing could be more traditional, moreover, than God's benevolence toward children and the humble of spirit. The word of the gospel says as much. In strict orthodoxy, however, the child is blessed by virtue of his innocence, his obedient docility, incapable of rebellion or pride, and not at all by virtue of a supposed affinity or privilege shared with God, or a participation, however minimal, in the prerogatives of intuitive vision.

In the secularizing trend that, since the Renaissance, transferred so many once-divine privileges to nature and her creatures, intuitive vision was among those things that passed from the supernatural to the natural order. At first this took the form of angelism, or a desire to escape from the conditions of bodily existence: mystics and neo-Platonists attempted to arrogate to themselves the powers of pure spirit and developed techniques of intuitive vision, at times with the help of magic and other proscribed arts. The Renaissance interest in hiero-

glyphs stemmed from the same ambition: these were signs that made
it possible to take in entire propositions at a glance, by intuition, thus
permitting human knowledge to aspire to identity with divine knowledge and enabling man to encounter God through a shared language.[80]
More prudent theologians succumbed to the same temptations. In
1713 Father André, a Jesuit and disciple of Malebranche, was censured
for teaching that "in the state of pure nature, God would be the
objective beatitude of man, not only God as seen and savored in his
creatures, which cannot fully satisfy the human heart, but God seen and
savored in himself, through immediate possession."[81] Intuitive power,
thus ascribed to natural man, nevertheless continued to be directed
toward God. Its object was still absolute. And since sin had wrenched
all mankind out of the state of pure nature, Father André's proposition
remained purely hypothetical.

It was nevertheless indicative of a particular strain of thought.
Among philosophers the evolution was more clearly marked. Not
only was natural consciousness granted the gift of intuition, but this
faculty (which in the transition from Descartes to eighteenth-century
philosophy was transformed from a faculty of mind to a faculty of the
senses) took natural existence itself as its object. Access to transcendence was foreclosed. Intuitive knowledge no longer apprehended the
supreme presence of the divinity but instead the primary datum of
thought (in the *cogito*) or of sensibility. For Locke it consisted in
nothing other than "the knowledge we have of our existence." The
existence of God could now be known only indirectly, through the
indispensable exercise of discursive reason. Locke, followed by all
French philosophers other than Rousseau, attached no value whatsoever to religious enthusiasm. No longer was the function of
immediate knowledge to direct our gaze toward transcendence. It was
now simply the means of making a fundamental determination:

> As for our own existence, we perceive it so plainly and so certainly,
> that it neither needs nor is capable of any proof. For nothing can be
> more evident to us than our own existence. I think, I reason, I feel
> pleasure and pain: can any of these be more evident to me than my
> own existence? . . . In every act of sensation, reasoning, or thinking,
> we are conscious to ourselves of our own being; and in this matter,
> come not short of the highest degree of certainty.[82]

Intuition, "summit of the soul," was given only in rare moments of
illumination. Now it has become a sort of invisible background or

substrate to all our states of consciousness. It is the faculty whereby my existence remains a primary, absolute certainty, whatever I may do and whatever may befall me. Over the course of the eighteenth century the notion of intuition was in fact degraded to something resembling animal instinct. If man is the product of a lengthy evolution, if the origins of the human race can be traced back to the obscurity of animal life, then man's oldest faculty is not reasoning but intuition. Not only does intuition underlie every human thought and sensation; it is also the physical cause of the development of human mind. La Mettrie puts the point quite clearly:

> What was man prior to the invention of words and knowledge of languages? An animal of his species . . . with much less natural instinct than other animals . . . Reduced to nothing but the *intuitive knowledge* of the Leibnizians, he saw only shapes and colors without being able to distinguish among them.[83]

Deprived of the power of reflection, was primitive man happy or miserable? In this confused state prior to the acquisition of reason, did he possess privileges that we might legitimately regret? Yes. Even though "inferior" prelogical immediacy was nothing more than a substitute for the direct knowledge attributed to the blessed by theologians, or a reflection of the beatitude implicit in the exercise of "superior" supralogical intuition, the consciousness of the savage was nonetheless illuminated by it. Dragged down into the density of nature, this privilege was transformed into an entirely instinctive faculty. On the chain of being it was shifted from the divine to the animal end of the spectrum. Yet secularization was not total; the Genesis story and the myth of the golden age were not entirely forgotten. Even among materialists the vision of man's origins was still contaminated by poetic and religious elements. The "primitivism" of Alexander Pope, who revived very ancient themes, is still widely acknowledged:

> Nor think, in nature's state they blindly trod; The state of nature was the reign of God; Self-love and social at her birth began, Union the bond of all things, and of man. Pride then was not; nor arts, that pride to aid; Man walked with beast, joint tenant of the shade.[84]

For a while longer it would still be possible to confound the biblical Adam with the naked savage roaming the prehistoric forest. Different as they might be—the one illuminated by God and close to the angels, the other animated by dark forces and close to the beasts—they presented an image of primitive unity. Consciousness did not yet separate either one from the world or from other creatures. Both relished the happiness of undivided existence. A profound similarity therefore persisted in the functions assumed by the intuitive act. Once it linked the blessed to the Creator. Now it linked the living organism to Nature, which produced it. It still constituted an intimate connection, an essential contact, and in certain respects a filial relation.

Rousseau, like Locke, trusted in intuition in all that concerned the sensation of existence. But like the pietists and heterodox mystics, he also wished to obey the "divine instinct." He accepted the thinking of his age, according to which immediate knowledge was a primitive experience, but he did not wish to give up religious ecstasy. He needed intuition in all its forms, indeed in all its forms at the same time. For him, happiness was simultaneously idle passivity and expansive activism. It was to be found at both the bottom and the top of the hierarchy of spiritual activity, in childish abandon as well as in identification with God. Sometimes the object of intuition was the pure ego, reduced to its unique presence. Sometimes it merged with maternal Nature. And sometimes it reached out toward a transcendent "Great Being." Many commentators have called attention to the vagueness of Rousseau's vocabulary in this regard. The reason for the ambiguity (though never explicitly stated by Rousseau) is that for him superior and inferior were reversible terms, or terms susceptible of identification, as in the thought of certain mystics or in oriental philosophy. Wherever existence revealed itself to be most tenuous and diaphanous—whether through privation, inattention, or abandon— God was also to be found.

Such a philosophy, in which "primitive" immediacy can spontaneously turn into "superior" immediacy and vice versa, would seem unlikely to confront the problem of history: *beginning* and *end* would be the same. Historical duration would be bypassed or dismissed as illusory (as it is in oriental philosophy). And it may well be that Rousseau was tempted at times by such a repudiation of history. Would he otherwise have ascribed such value to paradisaical existence? In the child's life the instant is an atom of time prior to all historical becoming, and inchoate consciousness lacks the power to organize the multitude of sensuous experiences into a continuous duration. The divine instant for its part dominates all time and subsumes all history. Yet one whole side of Rousseau's work confronts the problem of historical destiny. For man cannot sustain himself in one instant of time. "Fatal hazards" and his own perfectibility dislodge him from the moment. Willingly or not he must become the creator of his own duration. He must become a historical being. At that moment primitive immediacy and superior immediacy are driven infinitely far apart; space distends between them. Between the elementary self and the divinized self there now must intervene not only a whole education but all the heroic effort of individual history. Similarly, for the human race, if the state of childhood and the divine state are destined to be reunited, it can only be by and through universal history. When a systematic view of social evolution based on Rousseau's thought was finally elaborated, it was expressed in terms of a cyclical movement, a great circle that opened and closed upon itself; the final achievement of unity was given the value of a return to the primordial unity. The beginning was recaptured, but enhanced and deepened by a previously missing dimension of consciousness. This unfolding, however, was identical with that of religious eschatology, from original innocence to final redemption by way of sin and the fallen life.

Accursed Time

In this fallen life man must extend his effort over time. This world is the world of mediated action, which obliges us to employ means to gain our ends, to use instruments, money, and conventional signs. It is a world of reflection, source of amour-propre and discursive thought. By these shackles every act is bound to a series of consequences. Instinctively Rousseau is hostile to all of this. Yet in repudiating the ways of this world he describes them, and in describing them he takes them upon himself. It is hardly novel to say that in combating the fallen life he becomes its captive. He tolerates this world impatiently as a fate he does not deserve; yet he knows that there is no other way, that he must follow the worldly path before he can abandon it. One whole aspect of human reality is condemned in the name of principle but at the same time presented as an indispensable condition of progress toward salvation. Most of the contradictions in Rousseau's thought result from the gap between this refusal and this acceptance.

It will suffice to direct our attention to two themes associated with the fallen life: succession and reflection. Consider first a well-known passage from the "Fifth Walk" in Rousseau's *Reveries of the Solitary*

Walker. Jean-Jacques first says that he wants no part of fleeting happiness embodied in "brief moments of madness and passion." He longs instead for a "single and lasting state." Yet in shunning discontinuity he must avoid swinging to the opposite extreme and subjecting himself to the ordeal of duration. His ideal is a state in which "time is nothing to [the soul], where the present runs on indefinitely but this duration goes unnoticed, with no sign of the passing of time" (*sans aucune trace de succession*).[85]

Another example can be found in the *Dialogues*, where the "sensuous souls," initiates in the Enchanted Kingdom, understand one another by instantaneous signs, because the "ponderous plodding (*pesante succession*) of discourse is unbearable to them."[86]

A third example: Rousseau has misgivings about his own desire to do good. Why? Because experience has shown that his good deeds have given rise "to chains of continuing obligation (*engagements successifs*) which I had not foreseen and which it was now impossible to shake off."[87]

And a fourth: the history of the human race has been a *succession* of states each farther removed from original goodness than the preceding one. The force that engenders this movement is perfectibility, "a faculty which, with the help of circumstance, progressively (*successivement*) develops all our other faculties."[88] It is of the essence of human perfectibility that it unfolds over time and results in a progressive transformation of man:

> In thus discovering and tracing the lost and forgotten paths which must have led men from the natural state to the civil state, in reconstructing together with the intermediate situations which I have just noted, those which lack of time has made me omit or which imagination has not suggested to me, no attentive reader can fail to be impressed by the immense space which separates these two states. It is in this slow succession (*lente succession*) of things that he will see the solution to an infinity of moral and political problems which philosophers cannot solve. He will understand that the human race of one age is not the human race of another age, the reason why Diogenes could not find a man is that he searched among his contemporaries for a man of a time that no longer existed.[89]

In order to understand the meaning of history, one must understand the law that governs the "slow succession of things," which is moral decline coupled with intellectual progress.

Perfectibility not only triggers the unfolding of history but gives us the power to reason, that is, to link our thoughts together in a methodical chain. Does human reason wish to prove the existence of God? If it does not rely on the evidence of feeling, it is condemned to failure precisely because it must then take the course of proof by logical succession: "If I come to discover *successively* those attributes of which I have no absolute idea, it is through obligatory conclusions, through proper use of my reason. But I affirm them without understanding them, and fundamentally that is to *assert nothing*."[90] Even Jean-Jacques's prayers reveal his impatience with temporal succession and his misgivings concerning reflection:

> I can think of no more fitting homage to the divinity than the silent wonder aroused by the contemplation of his works, which is not to be expressed by any external acts ... In my case, it is especially on rising, exhausted by insomnia, that a long-standing habit induces those upliftings of the heart which require none of the weary effort of thought ... I have read of a wise bishop who, on touring his diocese, met an old woman, whose sole prayer consisted of the exclamation, "O!" "Good mother," said he, "go on praying like that always. Your prayer is better than ours." That better prayer is also mine.[91]

No external acts? Whether Rousseau knew it or not, his attitude continued a long mystical tradition. Perhaps he recalled an article on the "Explanation of the Maxims of the Saints" in which Fénelon distinguished between "simple and direct acts" and "deliberated acts."[92] The former, performed without reflection of any kind, "are what Saint Francis of Sales called the summit of the soul or the peak of the spirit."[93] By contrast, deliberated acts are the work of souls that "still have interests of their own." They are also usually less certain. It is impossible for the soul to recall by a willful act of memory its direct actions, for "God in his jealousy deprives us of the capacity to discover through reflection after the fact such certitude and righteousness." Memory is powerless to recover the felicity that rewarded moments of perfect self-oblivion. The deliberate effort is destined to fail. For Fénelon, reflection is of course not a capital sin in itself, but it is associated with disappointed hope, with awareness of our loss of ecstasy. It is a vain attempt to recover lost certainty, accompanied by anxiety and regret. Rousseau, moreover, gave a considerably sharper edge to Fénelon's idea that reflection is associated with the soul's self-interest. For him reflection became the source of amour-propre, that "hateful passion," hence the cause of universal Evil.

In the psychological theory of reflection as Rousseau developed it, there remain innumerable echoes of the previous century's theologies and religious philosophies. Passages in Rousseau are astonishingly reminiscent of Malebranche. In the *Dialogues*, for example, we read:

> All nature's first movements are good and straight. As directly as possible they promote our preservation and our happiness. But soon, lacking the strength to continue along their initial course in the face of so much resistance, they allow themselves to be deflected by a thousand obstacles, which, turning them off their true goal, force them to follow oblique routes, in which man forgets his original destination.[94]

The same metaphors can be found in Malebranche's *Search for Truth*:

> Just as the author of nature is the universal cause of all the motions that are found in matter, so, too, is he the general cause of all the natural inclinations that are found in minds. And just as all motions are in straight lines if there be no foreign and particular causes that determine and change them into curved lines through their opposition, so, too, are all the inclinations that we have from God straight, and they could have no end other than possession of the good and of truth if there were no foreign cause to compel nature's impress toward wicked ends. Hence it is this foreign cause that is the cause of all our woes and that corrupts all our inclinations.[95]

To be sure, the "foreign cause" indicted by Malebranche is not an external obstacle but man's free will. Both texts nevertheless postulate, in identical terms, an analogy between physical motion and the inclinations of the soul (by abuse of language, Condillac would later say in discussing this passage from Malebranche[96]). Both texts affirm the existence of an initial rectitude that is subsequently deflected or deformed. Yet these remarkable similarities should not blind us to a significant modification: Malebranche ascribes the origin of motion to God, "author of nature," whereas Rousseau in this passage mentions only nature. In the one text nature is still entirely dependent on God. In the other, it is portrayed as the primary source. (In the "Profession of Faith" Rousseau locates the motor impulse in God, in conformity with Cartesian tradition. Despite this, however, it is evident that nature is no longer strictly dependent on divinity. The most one can say is that nature is the perceptible image of divinity, but one in which the creatures, having deprived their Creator of his spontaneity, tend to substitute themselves for him.)

Evolutionist anthropology and the theology of the fall meet and mingle in what Rousseau says about reflection. Yet the fusion of the two views is never complete. In the second *Discourse* the theological point of view and the "naturalist" point of view seem to coexist. Man, being perfectible, has raised himself above the animal condition. At the same time he becomes corrupt and falls, thereby losing the innocent unity of primeval times. He increases his powers but becomes a divided, "alienated" being, a stranger unto himself and his fellow man and a prisoner of appearances. If there is progress of any kind, it is of inequality. Thus the image of progressive development and that of moral alteration are scandalously mixed. The scandal, moreover, was no less serious a matter for Christians than for philosophers. Consider the following well-known passage, in which Rousseau plays both registers at once without attempting to harmonize them—whence its shock value, which has earned it innumerable commentaries:

> If [nature] destined us to be healthy, I would almost venture to assert that the state of reflection is a state contrary to nature, and that the man who meditates is a depraved animal.[97]

Is this written from the standpoint of natural science? Is Rousseau talking about an evolution that begins with animal life? In that case the norm is indeed health, but infidelity to that norm would be not depravity but disease. That is precisely what Hegel would say later: "Man is a sick animal." In Rousseau's sentence, however, the word *depraved (dépravé)* abruptly introduces a reference to a moral, indeed a religious, value.[98] It is an antonym not of *healthy* but of *righteous* or *just*. Rousseau's assertion, shifting insidiously from one plane to the other, substitutes a norm of morality for a norm of health. This sentence, with its inner pathos and tension, reveals in a kind of shorthand the presence of two superimposed ideologies. The ideal synthesis, which would reconcile the terms in conflict and make it possible to look upon human history as a *natural* process yet without denying primacy to *religious* values, would be *natural religion*. Did Rousseau achieve this? The idea certainly was not alien to him,[99] but instead of a synthesis he offers us the spectacle of unending vacillation. If, as Engels maintains, there is a dialectic in Rousseau, it depends in large part on the fact that the materialist interpretation and the theological interpretation coexist in his thought in opposition to one another. Rousseau fleshes out the meager skeleton of sensualist anthropology with what remains vital in Judeo-Christian thought. The result is not a system but a tumult of ideas, which contributed a great deal to the extraordinary political and philosophical ferment of the late eighteenth century.

The Bewilderment of Splitting and the Need for Unity

In fact Rousseau's theory of reflection is a focus of conflict. He gives us abundant proof of this, even when he limits himself to implicit avowals. The appearance of reflection among men is not only subject to a dual interpretation (progress and fall); it is the product of dual sets of causes, for it results from the combination of an *internal* disposition with an *external* obstacle. Man would not perfect himself if difficult "circumstances" did not lay down a challenge and compel his perfectibility to come into play. In other words, human inwardness takes shape and becomes aware of itself only in contact with the resistance of the external world.

That is not all. Reflection is double in its effects as well as its causes. An "active principle," it unifies the external world by introducing into it a network of ratios and relations. It takes scattered, isolated sensations and creates unified objects. But it also makes us aware of difference. It destroys the alliance of sympathy that previously united man with nature, animals, and his fellow man. The price to be paid for the unity it brings to the objective world is the condemnation of consciousness to the misery of separation.

In the realm of thought, reflection is what gives us access to being (it confers "a meaning on the word *is*"[100]). By contrast, in the moral order it raises anxiety about appearances and causes us to forget our true being. Reflection is no less ambiguous when it comes to liberty. To reflect is to compare, to judge, to exhibit spontaneity and freedom. But our judgments may be false. Our liberty subjects us to the risk of error. Worse still, in comparing ourselves to others, we fall prey to amour-propre: "Social man lives always outside himself. He knows how to live only in the opinion of others, and it is, so to speak, from their judgment alone that he derives the sense of his own existence."[101] His situation therefore becomes one of dependence and servitude; he is subjugated. Thus reflection makes us free, but it also makes us slaves.

The final ambiguity lies in Rousseau's attitude toward reflection. In moments of anxiety, when he tries in every way he can to prove himself innocent, he denounces reflection as the cause of all the "hateful passions" and of universal perversion. Reflection, he says, destroyed man's original goodness. Through his hostility to reflection he affirms his own unity, innocence, and purity. Although to us it seems that Rousseau at such times is continuing to reflect and to act deliberately, perhaps more than ever, he utters a magical denial, and in order to reassure himself (especially in the *Dialogues*) recites a litany of exorcism: his true nature is one of unreflective spontaneity; reflection is absolutely foreign to him; if he ventured to try it, it was by accident, against his will, under the influence of malevolent friends. Sometimes he almost seems to guess that he is pursued not by Jesuits, the government, "those gentlemen," or the mob, but by his own reflections. (Did he not have real enemies? Was he not in fact under surveillance?[102] Of course. And for him that is reason enough to blame everything on external hostility.) The conspiracy that envelops him is the pretext he needs to project outside himself a part of himself that he disavows. For to admit reflective activity in oneself is to accept the threat of truncation and fragmentation. This risk seems to make Rousseau extremely anxious. He therefore rids himself of his anxiety by blaming it on an illegitimate faculty—reflection—which he attempts to extirpate from his image of himself. Thanks to this defense mechanism he temporarily regains his tranquillity and security. In doing so, he seems not to notice that he himself has carried out the mutilation he feared. By pruning reflection (that active, aggressive, "male" force) from the self, he eliminates the distressing tension caused by internal splitting, and he regains the precious conviction of personal unity (a passive, innocent, "female" attitude). But he thereby invests the external world with all the aggressiveness he has refused to assume inwardly. The quantity of anxiety is not diminished. It has simply become more tolerable, because its supposed source is now external.

By contrast, when Rousseau's besetting anxiety subsides, when his mind is less captive, he maintains that the only hope of overcoming the ambiguities of reflection lies in reflection itself. He asserts not only that "regression" is impossible but that additional intellectual effort is required. Man must look to "perfected art for the remedy to those ills that rudimentary art inflicts on nature."[103] A philosophy of history is thus outlined in which there are three ages: mankind, having lost through reflection the plenitude enjoyed in a state of nature, attains a higher unity as legislation and education gradually resolve human conflicts. The vices of reason can be cured only by employing all the resources of reason. Man can overcome inner division, social inequality, and subservience to opinion not by regressing to the unreflective life but by drawing upon all the consequences of his perfectible nature.

Rousseau's divided feelings about reflection call for a more general remark. If he exhibits a "bipolarity," it lies not simply in his tendency to shift back and forth between *for* and *against*, alternately embracing antithetical terms, but primarily in his tendency, in dealing with any particular problem, to alternate between a rhetoric of antithesis and a dialectic of transcendence. Sometimes things solidify into a Manichaean system of opposites from which there is no escape. Other times conflicts are resolved by moving to a higher plane. At times all effort is directed toward the struggle against absolute Evil. At other times a flexible program for progress is invented, and reconciliation seems possible. The role of Jean-Jacques's emotions is not difficult to make out. The antithetical approach corresponds to his penchant for opposition and aggression. The logic of transcendence corresponds to the outpourings of his affectionate imagination, avid to explore every open path and to embrace the entire world. The psychological explanation by itself is inadequate, however. One must never lose sight of the social content of Rousseau's work. In his hesitation between antithetical conflict and a synthetic approach, how can one fail to see an expression of the situation of French society before the Revolution? Revolutionary negation and Jacobin passion would draw upon Rousseau's rhetoric of antithesis as their prime ideological arsenal. But the critique of the social order as absolutely wicked is combined with a utopian eschatology, which justifies hope and gives meaning to innovative actions, to temporizing, to provisional measures, and perhaps even to certain compromises (after the new bourgeois order has achieved stability).

Even in the realm of self-knowledge, where the legitimate rights of reflection have to be acknowledged, reflection remains suspect. When he attempts to persuade us of his perfect sincerity in writing the *Confessions*, Rousseau seems particularly intent on convincing us that he was able to grasp the truth without exposing himself to the perils of reflection. We watch as he seeks refuge prior to or beyond the domain of reflective thought. At times he pretends to divorce himself entirely from his own life, carrying reflective splitting to such a degree that the reflected image becomes an object for the reflecting consciousness, a remote object that can be observed from outside. At other times he assures us that he is incapable of forsaking the undivided unity of unreflective feeling.

"This is my portrait, not a book. I shall be working as it were in a camera obscura. No art is needed beyond that of tracing exactly the features that I observe there."[104] In Rousseau's time the camera obscura, which placed the art of portraiture within the reach of everyone, was a highly complex apparatus. Curio shops housed bulky advanced models, actually *rooms* that the painter entered in order to trace the image of the model, which was projected onto ground glass plates by a series of lenses and mirrors. The obedient hand almost passively traced the profile and shadows of the image. Then came Daguerre, who sensitized the plates with silver salts, completing the transformation of the camera into an automaton, in which images recorded themselves. That is the truth Rousseau believed he had achieved in speaking of himself. Before his own image he wished to be as neutral, as mechanically faithful, as a camera.

Almost immediately after conceiving the project of a detailed and facile *copy*, Rousseau veered toward the opposite extreme. Instead of aiming for perfect objectivity, he would now trust in a no less perfect subjectivity, letting emotion invade him in an unpredictable, undisciplined manner. This uncontrolled spontaneity would be truth itself, revealed in its nascent state: "By surrendering to both the memory of the impression received and the present feeling, I shall paint the state of my soul twice over, in the moment when the event occurred and in the moment in which I described it."[105] As docile to subjective evidence as he was to the authority of his objectified image, Rousseau limits his role to one of welcoming an overwhelming emotion. The truth will cost him no effort. He will allow himself to be seized by it, he will surrender without resistance, as if sincerity found its guarantee in utter passivity and abandonment. Fear not the distortion of language and style. As written by Jean-Jacques the story of his life will be one of ideal, involuntary presence, in which each word, pervaded by the spontaneous welling up of emotion, will allow absolute certainty to emerge: "My uneven and natural style, sometimes rapid and sometimes diffuse, sometimes measured and sometimes mad, sometimes grave and sometimes gay, will itself be part of my story."[106] Yet another automatic mechanism: not that of the camera obscura but that which records the subtle variations of the soul as they occur. "I shall apply a barometer to my soul."[107] A very sensitive instrument will authentically transcribe the slightest fluctuations. Since every fluctuation of the soul is communicated, expression is but the passive trace of Jean-Jacques's inner state recorded on the page, immune to possible alteration.

Rousseau was not the first to use the camera obscura metaphor. Descartes compared the "internal concavities" of the smooth, shiny brain to a mirror upon which the images of external objects are projected via the optic nerves. The reflected rays converge upon the pineal gland to form a simple figure.[108] Locke argued that "the understanding is not much unlike a closet wholly shut from light, with only some little openings left, to let in external visible resemblances, or ideas of things without."[109] For both Descartes and Locke the camera-obscura metaphor applied exclusively to perception of the sensible world. Rousseau, introducing a singular change, made it the allegorical image for the self-portrait he would attempt to paint in the *Confessions*. Between the self-as-model and the self-as-painter there would be as definite a distance as that which separates consciousness from external objects. And this was precisely the ontological gap that Rousseau would attempt to bridge when he set himself up as "judge of Jean-Jacques." In the *Dialogues* he would claim to have perfected the split between the self and its image, which confront each other as two strangers: "I was necessarily obliged to say how, if I were someone else, I would see a man like me."[110] By means of this radical separation Rousseau hopes to liberate his gaze, thereby enabling it to render impartial judgment and to provide a disinterested description.

For Rousseau, then, self-knowledge stems from two different, indeed diametrically opposed, attitudes. On the one hand, ego becomes a stranger to itself in order to perceive itself as spectator, as an external object. On the other hand, it seeks to know itself through feeling, without abandoning its presence, by way of an immediate intuition that prevents any division of consciousness from occurring. No middle ground is possible, apparently, between complete unity and total fission. This is the duty Rousseau sets for himself, as he proudly informs us, and from then on we are not permitted to withhold our confidence. How can we presume to challenge the sincerity of one who places himself in the position of enduring the truth?

But he promises more than he can deliver. Perfect splitting and total self-absorption are extreme states toward which consciousness may doggedly strive but which it can never attain. Philosophers, most notably Jean-Paul Sartre, concede that this quest is doomed to failure.[111] They even go so far as to suggest that it is never undertaken except in the obscure hope that it will eventually fail. Such quietude, fulfillment, and security seem desirable to us because the natural condition of self-consciousness is precisely the opposite, compounded of insecurity, restlessness, and uncomfortable presence or distance. On the one hand, reflection rescues us from the blind spontaneity of instinct. On the other hand, however, it remains eternally unfulfilled, so that we never achieve the clarity of vision necessary to see ourselves with the same precision with which we can perceive objects.

In reflection the primitive unity of consciousness cracks. A person who adopts a reflective attitude toward himself loses the full self-possession that is the privilege of obscure acts of feeling. To see oneself in reflection is to encounter a ghost, nearby yet unattainable. Hence it is to dispel a precious presence: we retreat into nothingness in order to represent our own existence. We thus become slaves of appearances, which we have caused to step onto an imaginary stage so that we may scrutinize them with our own eyes. Henceforth all the moral dangers of falsehood lie in wait: vanity, amour-propre, and so on. That is the *theory*. It is therefore understandable that Rousseau was sometimes tempted to be done with reflection and to deny the very possibility of inner vision. For instance, he declares: "We do not see the souls of others, for they are hidden, nor do we see our own, because we have no intellectual mirror. We are in every respect blind, but blind from birth."[112] We possess neither vision nor a mirror in which to see our own image reflected. We are condemned to darkness.

Does this mean that we must do without any knowledge of ourselves? Not at all. Although we cannot see in the dark, we still have the evidence of inner experience. For Rousseau it is easy to say, "I feel my heart."[113] We do not see our souls, but the shadows in us are endowed with feeling and speak more plainly than our vision.

We can learn still more about the status of reflection by pursuing the mirror theme in Rousseau's work. It is important to consider not only those circumstances in which mirrors appear but also those in which, though evidently needed, they are peculiarly enough nowhere to be found. We shall see Rousseau suffer the discomforts of reflection as he attempts to avoid his own image in mirrors and reflecting surfaces.

The meeting with Mme. Basile is the only episode in which the mirror's appearance is manifest. Earlier I remarked that in this episode Jean-Jacques was in no way seeking to discover his own image. But because through a fatal and fortunate chance the mirror happened to be there, Jean Jacques was able to show himself while remaining hidden. This accident can be read as a very curious symbol.

The manner in which Jean-Jacques approached Mme. Basile—hiding himself while betraying his presence through an oblique reflection—is duplicated in many other circumstances and lies at the root of Rousseau's aesthetic vocation. He is a timid person. In proximity to others, surrounded by the stupefying chatter of the salons, he feels foolish, embarrassed, and ashamed. Yet he is aware of his true worth. How can he make others recognize it? "The decision that I made to write and to keep myself hidden is precisely the one that suits me."[114] It is tantamount to showing himself to the public in a reflection, an oblique image like the one in Mme. Basile's mirror; only now it is Rousseau who, after consulting his heart, creates his own image. He will be known and admired without having to expose himself in person. His work will hide him while impressing his name upon the public mind. All of Rousseau's writings, from the first *Discourse* on, are the manifestation of a soul that wishes to be loved for its personal merits. They are a *double* of individual existence. They oblige the reader to imagine a Jean-Jacques Rousseau who is tempted by vice but virtuous, childish but heroic and devoted to the noblest principles, a great soul who suffers at the sight of corruption and iniquity. That is indeed what he wants to be. He creates himself through the image that he exhorts the whole world to have of him. The hidden man will be able to arrogate to himself the glory and applause that are in fact addressed to his public reflection. In order to exist, this reflection needs a fascinated readership for its accomplice. Again the imagination is pressed into service: it is the same as in the episode with Mme. Basile, except that the role of the mirror is now filled by Jean-Jacques's written works, by his literary activity. And the laws of optics are henceforth less simple. No longer is it enough for a ray of light to bounce off a reflecting surface. Now, behind the surface of the work, Jean-Jacques's imaginary projections must meet those of his readers to constitute a unique image. What if those projections fail to coincide? Then there will be two images of Jean-Jacques: the reflection will be doubled. He will have to eliminate the false image (the one formed by others, misled by the wicked), and that will not be easy. The correction of this false image—a combat of the innocent imagination against the malevolent one—is the endless task of Rousseau's late works: the *Confessions*, the *Dialogues*, the *Reveries*, and the *Circular Letters* will prove inadequate to the task.

Mirrors are dangerous. In old legends the myth of Narcissus is sometimes combined with that of the Siren. Reflection ceases to be docile and passively obedient. It frees itself, begins to move of its own free will, and becomes a supernatural creature, whose fascination is fatal to those captivated by it. The "monstrous" Jean-Jacques (whose nonexistence Rousseau attempts to prove in the *Dialogues* by comparing him with the "real" Jean-Jacques) is a figure of this kind, a reflection of a reflection. Rousseau in his imagination blames the imaginations of his contemporaries for this distorted projection. The image of the monster—which is traced in Jean-Jacques while its origins are transferred to the gaze of others—is an obsessive idea, endowed with an inexhaustible desire for evil. The monster gathers poisonous herbs and extracts their poisons. He rapes young girls. He is rotten with venereal disease. Jean-Jacques's heroic image also takes on an autonomous existence, and it is perhaps no less persecutional. Once invented and made public, the *admirable self* invests itself with unlimited authority. It imposes behavior in keeping with its standards and insists upon extreme, ultimately untenable values. The woeful fate that Jean-Jacques considers to be so undeserved is actually a response to the idealized reflection that seizes control of his life. Eventually there comes a time when Rousseau, no longer able to see himself in this image, tries to escape from it and return to his "true nature," which is weaker, more sensual, more contradictory. The *Confessions* and *Dialogues* have a purpose other than that of dispelling the monstrous image of Rousseau, which is to withdraw the image of a Jean-Jacques more virtuous than nature—a tyrannical model that compels existence to strive for a height of moral perfection where the air is no longer breathable. (Hence the cynicism of the *Confessions* has two purposes: by unveiling all his weaknesses, Rousseau proves that his faults have rarely harmed anyone but himself; at the same time, however, he intends to free himself of any obligations incurred as a result of having tried for a time to fill the role of a heroic and virtuous figure.) But neither the image of the monster nor that of the hero can be repudiated entirely. They have come to life in the imagination, and they cannot be deprived of that life by fiat. In combating the obsession with false images that have acquired an unacceptable freedom, Rousseau feels a constant need to reconquer his inner unity. Each new autobiographical work marks a new beginning in this indefatigable quest. He insists that it is possible for him to erase his image in that distorting mirror, the eyes of others. "Is my essence in their stares?"[115] Others have robbed him of his image in order to distort it; he has the right to take it back, to refashion it in conformity with the truth.

Narcissus without a Mirror

Can we catch Rousseau in front of the mirror, though? Can we surprise the author of *Narcissus* studying his own image like the Narcissus of legend? Rousseau tells us that he always had a passion for water. But what did he look for? He prefers mildly agitated streams, the "silvery simmering" water of rapids and falls to either calm lakes or tumultuous oceans. Above all he likes gentle waves, whose rhythm induces a mild torpor in the mind as the canoe in which he floats alone drifts slowly at the whim of the current. Such water is not still enough or calm enough to reflect his own image. It is shimmeringly quiet but not a mirror. It is fascinating in itself, because of its own ceaseless movement and not because it allows Jean-Jacques to see himself. And even when he looks into the waters of Lake Leman, as he does during a hike described in book four of the *Confessions*, it is not to see himself but for the sake of a curious sentimental communion: "How many times, stopping to cry at my leisure and seated upon a large rock was I amused to see my tears fall into the water."[116] Thus the lake becomes the repository of his groundless sorrow, in a game in which Jean-Jacques takes pity on himself without expecting to see his own features. More revealingly, we find him in another episode stretched out in his canoe, "his eyes turned heavenward." He looks at open space, not at the reflecting surface. On the Ile Saint-Pierre he likes to let "his eyes hover over the horizon of this beautiful lake"[117] in a dream of flight. Under these conditions there are no limits to the expansion of sentiment. Reverie can invent whatever it will, or it can remain "stupid" and "without object." Transparent space welcomes all the fancied images. They can be made to appear or disappear as the dreamer desires, and some seem to take on a life of their own. Rousseau will thus take possession of himself simply by allowing himself to feel his existence, without having to look at himself. In ecstatic nakedness or imaginary expansion he is immediately present to himself. Why would he look for his reflection? To do so would be to destroy the precious unity he has regained.

What about Rousseau's narcissism? Let us go to the source, namely, to *Narcissus*, which he claims to have written at Annecy and which Marivaux retouched in 1742 or 1743. Valère spends his time staring at himself in a looking glass. His father scolds him for "preening in front of the mirror." As the action begins, we see Valère in the act of grooming himself. But he does not approve of the image reflected in the mirror. He is disappointed by his appearance. Some absent quality prevents him from really loving himself—he is dissatisfied: "How do I look to you this morning? I have no fire in my eyes. My complexion is dull. It seems that I am not up to my usual self."[118]

The mirror, unfriendly and cruel, is not responsible for turning Valère into Narcissus. His narcissistic vocation is not settled until he falls into a different kind of trap: his feminized portrait, his face embellished with a woman's allures. For his latent narcissism to manifest itself fully, he needs to be provided with an excuse not to recognize his own image, a "heterosexual" camouflage that will allow his self-indulgence to blossom into real passion. Here error is indispensable. Seductive power lies not in a pure reflection but in a slightly altered one, disguised just enough to acquire the appearance of an external *object*. Therein lies a paradox: this Narcissus is in love with himself only because he is unaware of his resemblance to the image (though he ought to know it well enough after so many hours in front of the mirror). His passion, one might say, respects the proprieties. It wants to be directed toward *another*. But the ego tricks itself and becomes rapt in an image of itself disguised behind the features of someone else. Valère is of course the victim of a deliberate trick. But he is in every way a willing accomplice. He wills his error and persists in it until the final moment. Once again we are witnessing a "passage to the imagination." Objectively it is the same face that is reflected in the mirror and recorded in the portrait. But the effects of the portrait are far more telling. It stimulates a never-ending reverie.

The unknown woman becomes the pretext for a passionate pursuit, in which desire invents its object and invests it with every charm. Incognito, the portrait opens the way to every possible mental representation, and Valère euphorically throws himself into the quest.

Note that the *distorted portrait*, which is a love trap in *Narcissus*, will later become a theme of madness and persecution (especially in the *Dialogues*). Corresponding to the fraudulent portrait that seduces Valère is the alleged misrepresentation of Rousseau by his enemies, who paint him as a monster in order to bring universal opprobrium upon his head. The procedure is the same, but the emotional sign is reversed. None of this is surprising from a psychoanalytic point of view, since certain persecution manias are classed as narcissistic disorders. The persecuted ego makes itself the center of the world. It thinks it is the object of universal attention. In this way it asserts its own importance. The enormity of the persecution can then be cited as an excuse: I am not the one who thinks I am exceptional, for they are subjecting me to unprecedented torments. By the detour of a league and a plot, Rousseau's ego sees itself as playing a role of unlimited importance. Government, police, dignitaries, men in the street—all are concerned, he tells us, only with him. The persecuted ego finds in its persecution an odd proof of its power. It is alone, but all the powers leagued together are unable to subdue it.

More generally, we may say that Rousseau's narcissism occurs in two rather different forms, both *mirrorless*. The first narcissism possesses all the prerogatives of *self-love*, which Rousseau discusses several times, always to exonerate it as opposed to guilty amour-propre. Hardly different from the instinct of self-preservation, self-love appeared to him to be the most archaic of human passions: through it each individual strives to preserve his or her own vital energy. In the second *Discourse* it is a special form of self-love that accounts for the primal attraction between the sexes. At this stage, love is anonymous, indiscriminate, and impersonal. It is directed in a confused way toward all females. Before a more specific choice can emerge, along with more marked preferences and a more exclusive attachment, vanity and amour-propre—products of artifice—must enter the human soul and displace the *natural* imperative of self-love. Even before the formation of the couple, however, self-love is contented self-presence, confident attachment to one's own body and to the surrounding world. It is a power of sympathy and identification. There is no division between inside and outside. Natural desire is so instantly gratified in the natural world that man literally has no time to feel different from his surroundings. Such is man's harmony with nature, so immediate is his pleasure, that appetite, untroubled by excess, never becomes unhappy lust: the necessary fruit falls into the outstretched hand. In the world of self-love, desire is always legitimate and never suffers privation or opposition. (This world is also one in which each person, regarding only the self, is in turn regarded by no one or everyone. Taboos have yet to be instituted, and persecutors have yet to arise.) Here the unity of man and nature is neither obscure nor unwitting. It is innervated, as it were, by a rudimentary sensibility, which enables consciousness to perceive itself dimly, with a calm feeling of well-being. The ego envelops itself in affection, making no attempt to determine whether the source of that affection is internal or external. It is not a matter of indifference that the first example of the effects of self-love in *Emile* concerns the child's attachment to its wet nurse: the euphoria of vegetative satisfaction. In this narcissism of self-involvement, Narcissus has not yet opened his eyes, so to speak. He has not yet discovered the fountain or leaned out over the water. Nor is he aware of the "twin sister" bestowed upon him by Pausanias. His contacts with his image is internal; there is no distance between him and it. Perception is introceptive; the subject does not distinguish between itself and the perceived object. There is still no sign of the subsequent discovery of amour-propre and its woes. "The child's first sentiment is to love himself."[119] This act, still utterly unreflective, introduces no division of the self, no possibility of judging oneself or others.

This is also the inexhaustible theme of the *Dialogues*. Jean-Jacques wants to be sensitive—a sensitive soul—but above all he wants to be sensitive to himself, to feel "internal delights" inwardly, with no gap between himself and his object into which a mirror might be inserted or the consciousness might be split. Note, incidentally, that this image of Jean-Jacques is presented in the *Dialogues* by a Rousseau who is himself divided, who looks at himself and paints his own portrait, who compares and judges—an extraordinary dissonance.

The undivided narcissism of self-involvement is followed by an-other, antithetical form of narcissism: self-projection. It would be better perhaps to call this attitude not narcissism but pygmalionism, for Pygmalion is its mythical exemplar. Instead of falling back immediately upon itself, love alienates itself in the form of a *work*. Through the work, however, it still seeks union of self with self. Love abandons the ego only to pave the way for a happy return. "I adore myself in what I have made."[120] This is hyperbolic narcissism, more demanding and creative than the first form of narcissism and devoted to the imagination and to the perpetual dissatisfaction that will keep it indefinitely but deliciously in a state of breathless anticipation.

Here again the mirror is unnecessary because it is in a sense traversed and transcended. The object of desire is not the similarity of the reflection but the illusion of difference, a difference that Pygmalion imposes upon the stone statue yet hopes to abolish in a warm embrace: "May my Galataea live, and may she and I not be one. O! may I always be another so that I may want always to be her, to see her, to love her, to be loved by her."[121] The creature of the imagination is a projection of desire. In order for the magic to work, the mirror must be enchanted, must feminize the received image so as to permit a quest for an androgynous union. Pygmalionism requires powers not possessed by ordinary mirrors. What triumphs is not so much the faculty of seeing oneself as the talent for making oneself into someone else. (Transported to Yonville, pygmalionism becomes bovaryism. But we should not forget that Mme. Bovary is Flaubert.) Solitude is thus populated, filled with "elite societies," and Rousseau is able to converse with "people of his heart's desire." Far less inventive is the unimpeachable testimony of the mirror, which can only repeat the face presented to it. The mirror exacerbates solitude by showing it a mirror image of itself. It creates no ideal companions, "virtuous friends," or "faithful mistresses." Jean-Jacques's fascination with himself, his narcissistic enchantment, must be mediated by Julie's gaze.

Necessary Reason

Even if Jean-Jacques does not renounce his preference or nostalgia for the sensuous life, for the intuitive vision that turns Eden green once more, he is nevertheless compelled to be valiant in his approach to the fallen life, to life in this sad world of sequence and consequence, reason and discursive thought. But now he knows that the act of thinking is fraught with danger, that nothing sustains it other than the memory or desire of certain thoughtless states of repose or fulfillment. One thing he knows for certain: to speak, to reason, to write is to be in the wrong place, estranged from oneself, vagabond, a prisoner of appearances, and subject to the judgment of others and to misunderstandings of every sort. "Thinking for me is a very difficult labor, which tires, torments, and displeases me."[122] Words in themselves possess no guarantee of stability. They are threatened by excess, solitude, mistakes of all kinds. Their only firm mooring is the previous overwhelming intuition, which they seek to recreate.

The act of writing, which unfolds in time and makes use of conventional signs, is profoundly a part of the fallen life. Recall that in the *Confessions* Diderot's advice urging his friend to respond to the question put forth by the Dijon Academy is portrayed as a diabolical suggestion. "From that moment I was lost."[123] The fatal event is not the revelation on the road to Vincennes (an intuitive, momentary illumination) but the decision to transform that revelation into discourse, the shift from pure spontaneity to eloquent demonstration. Appreciate the full measure of the distressing distance between Jean-Jacques's sobbing ecstasy under the oak at Vincennes and the sleepless nights during which, "with incredible difficulty,"[124] he turns his sentences over and over in his head. In maintaining that he deserves to live in paradise, which accords with his true nature, Rousseau repeatedly proclaims that his original vocation was neither to write nor to think. An accident, an external influence, turned him from his true goal, which was repose and tranquillity. This at any rate is the vision of himself that he sets forth in his last works, where he attempts to exorcise the curse occasioned by his career as writer. Thinking and writing lured him from his appointed course, fatally interrupting his journey. Now he must work to persuade posterity that nearly all his books began with a moment of pure intuition, tender and passionate, and that it was only as a result of some incomprehensible weakness that he allowed himself to become involved in developing a discursive argument. Initially there was only a simple reverie, the vision of an inner landscape, in which he felt at home "from the first inspiration"[125] (*du premier bond*: literally, from the first leap, as Rousseau describes his initial, purely imaginary conception of the novel that would become *La Nouvelle Héloïse*). Next come sentences "unrelated to one another and in no sequence," upon which by subsequent effort he attempts to impose some systematic order. On one occasion he is quite clear about this: "Nothing comes to me whole."[126] His discourses are not true discourses. They are scattered ideas, momentary humors, linked together by "a charlatanry of transition."

This results, in the style of Rousseau's ideas, in an elusive quality of tremulousness and enthusiasm, an alternate tightening and relaxation as he seeks the final formulation and attempts to create (or recreate) the illumination of absolute conviction. Often he will force the meaning or say more than he meant to say, producing splendid but ill-matched sentences—whence the oft-repeated accusation of sophistry. His fidelity is above all to his initial passion, his virtuous indignation, his shudder of emotion. Must we take literally his lapidary maxims and declarations of principle? Should we not set greater store by a certain soulful imperative in what he says, in the vibrancy of his emotion? We do him an injustice, perhaps, in requiring him to be consistent and systematic in his thought, when his real presence, as he himself avows and repeatedly insists to the reader, is not in his discourse but in the warm if confused animation that precedes language and resorts to words and ideas only to make its presence felt, much as it might have resorted to music. Jean-Jacques's "consolations" are by turns romances and pages of prose: the medium is of little importance as long as it reveals a quality of soul and helps to reestablish an absent *calm*.

Yet we must be careful not to overlook the efforts of a mind eager to take hold of a logical order not among its natural gifts. Rousseau plays the game of reflection by the rules. He seems to have accepted the fact that, to save himself from reflection, he cannot shun it but must practice it with rigor, attempt to tell all, and gather together in logical order a totality of disparate states that sentiment would rather subsume in an immediate unity: "There is a certain sequence of impressions and ideas which modify those that follow them, and it is necessary to know the original set before passing any judgments. I endeavor in all cases to explain the prime causes, in order to convey the interrelation of results."[127]

The task that Jean-Jacques sets himself includes all the operations he finds so difficult: sequence, interrelation, causality, logical development. He believes not only that these are linked in a fundamental way with man's unhappiness but also that they are unsuited to his nature. He believes, further, that he has been summoned to provide proof of his innocence, and since he cannot give that proof in the form of an immediately intelligible sign, an instantaneous expression, he must resort to all the devices of discourse and pass through all the stages of reflection. Like the fool who dives into the water to avoid the rain, he hurls himself bodily into reflection in order to be done with it as quickly as possible.

At this point Rousseau's *rationalism* comes into play.[128] If one is driven out of the child's paradise and instinctual repose, one has no choice but to follow the path of reflection in the hope of recovering lost happiness at the end of the journey. Since discursive reasoning cannot be avoided, we may as well get through it as quickly as possible by facing up to all its requirements and reasoning in accordance with the strictest logic. We must plumb the depths of this intellectual purgatory before we can achieve tranquil certitude. Once the truth has been demonstrated, it becomes a possession of feeling. Once irrefutable conclusions have been formulated, philosophy stands aside and leaves us in the presence of its results. After the most exacting labor, reason reasonably condemns itself and submits the thinker once more to intuition (now founded on reason): "Thus my rule of submitting myself to sentiment more than to reason is confirmed by reason itself."[129] Here the most important reference is the third *Reverie*, where Rousseau tells us he constructed his system in order to live out his days in certainty and repose. He has consulted reason once and for all, subjecting himself in his reflections to the most rigorous of methods, and he has made the most strenuous efforts. This anxious labor is the price he has paid for his ultimate tranquillity.

> I felt keenly that the tranquillity of the rest of my life and indeed my whole destiny depended on it . . . I made up my mind once and for all on the questions that concerned me . . . Since then, remaining steadfast in the principles which I adopted after such long and careful meditation, I have made them the constant rule of my belief and conduct without wasting any further thought on the objections which I was unable to answer or on those which I had not foreseen.[130]

So well does Jean-Jacques endure and transcend the ordeal of reflection that he is no longer aware of the arguments on which he based his conviction. In any case, if reflection is banished, security must remain:

> Sunk in mental lethargy, I have forgotten the very arguments on which I based my belief and my principles, but I shall never forget the conclusions I drew from them with the approval of my conscience and my reason, and henceforth I shall never let them go.[131]

The time of thought is now over. No longer will Jean-Jacques subject any question to deliberation, for reason has done its job and must disappear in the resulting state of repose. Vanishing along with reflection is the pain that is its constant accompaniment.[132] Once again the world is harmonious and amicable, as in childhood. By world, however, he means *nature*. For other men have not been delivered from reflection and continue to do evil.

"A Feather That Falls in the River"

Such is the journey that Jean-Jacques's consciousness feels compelled to make. Driven out of the paradise of the unreflective life (divine or natural), his only hope of returning or of finding repose in silent certitude is to follow the detour that leads from one end to the other of reflective existence. There can be no return to harmony unless we learn how to think about and live with our temporal condition with reason as our only aid. In solitude, therefore, Jean-Jacques sets out upon a journey that his work at one point appeared to ascribe to universal history.

The spiritual journey described by Rousseau also inspired Kant's philosophy of history, and still later it was summed up by Kleist: "The gates of Paradise are locked and the Angel is behind us. We must skirt the world and see if Paradise does not perhaps have a rear entrance . . . In order to return to the state of innocence, we must once again taste of the tree of knowledge."[133]

Kleist's *Theater of Marionettes*, in which poetic allusions to sacred history reemerge into the open, is concerned with an aesthetic problem: grace. Reflection destroys grace. The mirror that shows us our image for the first time is an instrument of evil. Consider, for example, the adolescent who, upon noticing in a mirror his resemblance to an ancient statue, immediately loses the power to repeat the naive gesture he has just made. Grace vanishes, replaced by stiffness, artifice, and mannerism. Kleist, also tempted by analogy, condenses the notion of intellectual reflection with the image in the reflective surface of a mirror. Reflection is Narcissus' gaze upon himself. Grace can exist only beneath or beyond reflection, in the marionette (or animal) and in God. Because it is unselfconscious, "the soul (*vis motrix*) of the marionette . . . coincides at every moment with the center of gravity of its motion." Because God is infinite consciousness, he coincides with his center of gravity, which is the world.

We see that, as reflection dims or weakens in the organic world, grace becomes more radiant and imperious. Nevertheless, just as two straight lines that meet on one side of a point suddenly, having traversed infinity, meet again on the other side of that point; or as an image in a concave mirror, having traveled all the way to infinity, suddenly reforms in proximity to us; so too is grace revealed once more, after knowledge has also passed through a kind of infinity.

Reading these lines of Kleist's, how can we help thinking of the extreme states toward which Rousseau constantly inclines? To be sufficient unto himself, like God: divinization is for him a frequent temptation. But more frequently still he experiences the temptation of the mechanical life. Here he defines himself as an automaton, almost a marionette:

Prudence, reason, precaution, foresight: for him all these words are without effect. When he is tempted, he succumbs. When he is not, he remains in his torpor. Thus you see that his conduct can only be uneven and fitful, at moments impetuous, and almost always weak or ineffectual. He does not walk. He leaps and falls back on the same spot. His very activity tends to limit itself to what circumstances oblige, and if he were not driven by his most constant desire, he would remain forever immobile.[134]

His habitual state, he assures us, "was and always will be intellectual inertia and mechanical activity."[135] To become God or to become an automaton: for him these are two opposite ways of avoiding the dangers of reflection (not, of course, in order to attain the gracious beauty that interests Kleist but to recover innocence). Yet if reflection really were transcended once and for all, Rousseau would not experience the twofold temptation that he does, toward both divine life and mechanical life, forward as well as backward. If there were no other proof, this alone would suffice to show that Rousseau was not yet entirely delivered, that he remained in the middle of the journey. Try as he will to convince himself that he has come to the end of the road, can he be sure? Is the time of division, of obligatory reflection, really over? Has reflection arrived at its goal? Rousseau would like to think so, but even he is not sure. That is why he succumbs to anxiety even as he expresses the certainty he desires: "Then I would say to myself, my heart nearly bursting with agony: 'Oh, who can protect me from despair.' "[136]

The most profound tranquillity remains subject to "flickers of anxiety" that "have no more effect on my soul than a feather falling into the water can have on the course of a river."[137] In the end, Rousseau would like his soul to be no more than a stream that follows its natural course. Leaving behind all the other metaphors of innocence and quietude, his last image is one of elementary motion, a flowing stream. But if the feather cannot alter the course of the river, still the water is a reflective surface, and a threat subsists in its very limpidity. For it is still a mirror, which divides the fullness of the world and which robs the landscape of its reflection, the sky of its clouds. Through reflection, moreover, fugitive and dangerous shadows are always reborn.

3   Pseudonymous Stendhal

When a man puts on a mask or takes on a pseudonym, we feel challenged. He denies us his person. We, in turn, want to *know*, and we set out to unmask him. From whom is he trying to hide? What Power is he afraid of? What Gaze makes him ashamed? What was his face like, that he felt the need to hide it? And still other questions follow from these: What is the meaning of his new front? What significance does he give to his hidden activities? What character does he now wish to simulate, having dissimulated the one that wished to disappear?

Political caution no doubt played a part in Stendhal's use of pseudonyms. Fouché and the White Terror partly explain and justify César Bombet. Customs agents and concierges (and jealous husbands) very likely had good reason for wanting to open Stendhal's mail or to decipher the secret writing of his diary. He had reason to worry. For this somewhat too garrulous champion of liberty the danger was real, as the archives of the Austrian police and the papal chancery prove. But the danger was only a pretext, almost an excuse. Stendhal devoted far more attention to the matter than the real threat required. Even when he was not threatened, he enjoyed wearing masks—and not only those that enabled him to disappear or to travel incognito. For Stendhal, to use a pseudonym was not to escape into anonymity. It was a way of shaping appearances, of deliberately altering human relations. He sought to escape from the nominal value system only to master it and outwit its rules.

To take a pseudonym is to engage in an act of protest. Whatever else it may be, it is first of all a repudiation, out of shame or resentment, of the name transmitted by one's father. A name, like a doll whose heart (or symbolic place of the heart) one pierces, contains in substance the life one wishes to destroy. If the name is truly an identity, if through the name it is possible to attack and injure a person's essence, then repudiation of the patronymic is a substitute for patricide. It is the least cruel form of murder in effigy. Humiliated by his father, Stendhal avenged himself by calling him (most notably in letters to his sister Pauline) "the bastard." The insult is aimed directly at the legitimacy of the name. In his filial hatred Stendhal concocts the most extraordinary reasons for denying any connection with the Beyle family. He adumbrates nothing less than a system of filial interpretation: he feels too different from Chérubin Beyle to be his legitimate son; hence he is probably the secret heir of a more illustrious line. The "myth of birth" (which would later have its role in *The Charterhouse of Parma*) was among the deepest reveries of young Henri Beyle. It was Stendhal himself who wished to be a bastard, but the derogatory accusation was projected onto his father.

A name awaits us before we are born. It was there before we ever knew it, like our bodies. A common illusion is to believe that our destinies and truths are inscribed in our names. In this way we invest our names with the dignity of an essence. To some extent Stendhal succumbed to this illusion. If he refused the name Beyle, it was because it signified a predestined fate of which he wanted no part. His name bound him to France, to Grenoble, to the bourgeois class, and to his father's world of hoarding and sordid calculation. (And phonetically Beyle could be confused with *bêle*, bleats, and take on animal connotations.) Sensing a danger that his name would hold him fast, he attempted to improve his chances by giving himself a new one. A pseudonym would not have been necessary had he felt free in spite of his name, had he been able to accept his identity as a bourgeois of Grenoble as a matter of pure convention, an accident of social classification that in no way closed off any road he wished to travel.

By choosing a new name he gave himself not only a new face but a new fate, a new rank in society with the noble particule *de*, new nationalities. He was the last of the eighteenth-century cosmopolites but also the first of the nineteenth century's "good Europeans." Some of his pseudonyms were German: Stendhal, for instance, was the name of a Prussian city. Only in Italy, moreover, was happiness free to flourish, and in his imagination young Henri Beyle established a whole Italian genealogy for himself on his mother's side. His mother, with whom he was in love, does not belong in Grenoble. He therefore settles his memory of her in the warm and sensuous Lombard countryside. Whenever he traveled outside France, Stendhal felt that he was returning to his true world, and he liked living outside his country just as he liked living outside his name. His enthusiasm for travel and pleasure in flight were interchangeable with his penchant for pseudonyms.

There is no point listing all of Stendhal's pseudonyms, which number more than a hundred. Alongside this list we should set the list of pseudonyms he assigned to his friends, some of whom, caught up in the enthusiasm of the game, adopted those names for themselves. Their pseudonyms were tangible signs of the intelligence that set them apart from the world, evidence of their election. The "happy few" formed a select society who cultivated rational knowledge of the human heart. But these rationalists loved to surround themselves with the prestige of the invisible and went so far as to amuse themselves by affecting certain esoteric manners. Secrecy, or the feigning of secrecy, was part of their system, and their pseudonyms marked them as conspirators. In all clandestine societies initiates receive new names, and Stendhal and his friends were not far from using a language of initiation.

Stendhal's pseudonyms are astonishingly diverse. Some were used no more than once, while others persisted throughout his life. Stable pseudonyms coexist with unstable ones. Some of his pseudonyms are meant to please: Dominique and Salviati are love names, use of which makes him a more elegant and attentive lover. The whole effect of these seductive identities depends on the tenderness inherent in the names, which magically create an atmosphere of trusting intimacy. Sometimes, in order to make himself more illustrious, he borrows the name of a great prince. But we also find humorous pseudonyms, names that make him even more bourgeois than he really is: Cotonnet, Bombet, Chamier. Others cast him in a ridiculous light: Baron de Cutendre, William Crocodile. Some pseudonyms are for show, whether humorous, grandiloquent, or affectionate. Others are for flight, intended to make him invisible or to protect him from bores and nuisances.

Such a profusion of pseudonyms leads to the question, What's in a name? By forcing us to ask this question, the masked egotist has already won a first victory: he has manipulated us and left us in doubt. We discover that a man is never entirely either in his name or behind it, just as he is never entirely in his face or in back of it. We cannot persist for long in either the realist or the nominalist illusion. To us the name appears alternately as repletion and emptiness, now laden with an immense density of existence, now reduced to a superficial and pointless verbal convention. In the name a whole life is concentrated, reduced to a sign, but this sign is only an empty signifier. It has nothing to teach us. We no longer know with whom we are dealing. This is what the egotist wants: "I am not where you thought you could find me."

The use of a pseudonym is therefore a way of declaring independence not simply from one's social and family background but from other people generally. Our identities, which bind us to our names, also deliver us as hostages to alien consciousness. They leave us defenseless in the face of public judgment. The egotist seeks to regain possession of himself. He destroys the name that leaves him feeling vulnerable in the part of himself that reflects the onlooker's gaze. By breaking the bonds that made him vulnerable to others, he hopes to spare his pride from injury.

If it is true that our names contain what is unique about our lives even as they symbolize that uniqueness for other consciousnesses, then the egotist strives on the one hand to preserve that uniqueness while, on the other, preventing or distorting reciprocity between his own consciousness and that of others. He cannot prevent others from using his name, but he can see to it that his name no longer designates himself. Rather ingenuously he dreams of placing himself in the position of one who sees without being seen (a desire that we find quite clearly expressed at places in Stendhal's most personal writings).

The name is situated, symbolically, at the confluence, as Sartre puts it, of existence "for oneself" and existence "for others." It is both intimate truth and public object. In accepting my name, I accept the existence of a common denominator between my inner being and my social being. The purpose of a pseudonym is to introduce a radical disjunction at this level. It is intended to divide two worlds at the very point where they might have been joined through the agency of language. By this act the egotist rebels against his membership in society. He refuses to be delivered unto others when he is given unto himself. Freedom of action is inconceivable without insubordination. Hence he resorts to the pseudonym, which unties his hands. The first requirement of egotistic individualism is to sever the bond between personal existence and the warrant for that existence that we give to the world. He is a god, reborn from his own ashes, like the phoenix. *Noli me tangere* might be its motto. Therein lies its weakness. What is the egotist afraid of? That if he reveals his identity too clearly, he will bare himself completely, that his secrets will be "brought to light," which for him means almost the same thing as to be nullified, reduced to nought in the eyes of others. If the egotist had sufficient confidence in himself, he would not try to make such a mystery of his attractive qualities. If he often suffers from being misunderstood, he suffers far more from being understood too well. Afraid of being attacked personally, he works diligently to distinguish his person from his role.

In the equation $I = I$, the name replaces the equals sign in the eyes of others. Invested in our names, our identities become alienated; they come to us from and through others. But the egotist rises in revolt against the imposition of identity from without. What is to prevent him from achieving sole mastery over the equation that makes him identical to himself? By giving himself a pseudonym, he claims his radical autonomy. But does he really gain greater possession of himself? He gives himself a verbal identity as external and contingent as the one was imposed upon him by others, the only difference being that he gives it to himself rather than receiving it from others. The pseudonym makes the false swearing impossible because there is no one to be bound by any oath: the multiplicity of "selves" is an admirable alibi.

Noblesse oblige, as the saying goes: and what obliges in nobility is the name, the title. But the egotist is especially irritated by the sense that his name, by establishing an obligation toward himself, also establishes a necessary relation to others. No one is responsible who cannot be called by name and compelled to respond. If my name no longer refers to *me*, then I no longer have anything to answer for except to the person who still possesses the right and power to give me a name: "I answer to myself alone," says the rebel. Nothing prevents him from taking this principle one step further and renouncing his responsibility even to himself. At that point he ceases to bear his own name and is instead borne away by an imaginary one. He may then surrender to a dizzying sense of being propelled by an energy that seems to come entirely from the mask he wears rather than from the "real" person who hides behind the mask. The mask and the pseudonym generate a dynamic of pure irresponsibility.

Stendhal's use of pseudonyms has this quality of movement and, among other ends, aims at changing his position on the social scale, raising him from the status of Henri Beyle to that of Baron Frédéric de Stendhal. For Stendhal, however, the essential pleasure is not in the false nobility he grants himself but in the movement itself. For movement is the law governing the pseudonym's existence, the sine qua non of its success. Indeed, Stendhal is perfectly willing to assign himself ridiculous pseudonyms that bring him no advantage whatsoever. The important thing is never to linger over invention; the surprise that disconcerts others must be continually reproduced. The mask must become a procession of masks, and "pseudonomia" must give way to a systematic "polynomia." Otherwise the egotist will again fall into the clutches of others. The misunderstanding he sought to escape will only grow worse, to his own disadvantage. He must always run several lengths ahead of the pack. And he must conceal the systematic nature of his secret conduct. For to show any sign of system is to make oneself perfectly explicable, hence to relinquish all the benefits of secrecy. What pleasure would be left if Stendhal's system of escape were exposed? He who seeks mystery in too obvious a way risks having the opposite effect: rather than make himself an enigma for spectators, his dissembling defines him once and for all. Sometimes, as Stendhal is well aware, it is more effective to live with an open heart, always ready to confess and avow, than it is to wear a mask. His confidences, with their endless qualifications and contradictions, make him more mysterious than his elaborate strategies of impersonation.

Stendhal's tireless and elusive use of pseudonyms contrasts sharply with the simpler behavior of those who, in the hope of consecrating their glory, choose once in a lifetime a name that brings some advantage and, having chosen, never change it again. Writers and artists who choose pseudonyms are usually out not to deceive the public but, on the contrary, to enhance their public prestige. Seeking celebrity, they choose a name that seems to enhance their lives, characters, or destinies (as did Gérard de Nerval or Joseph Conrad, for example). They aim simply to amass a phonetic capital, which they believe indispensable to success. Stendhal did not escape this temptation entirely, but with him it was relatively unimportant. He is admittedly avid for glory and wants to make a name for himself, but he also wants that name to remain external to his identity, leaving him free to take up any of a thousand other names.

The theme of confinement in Stendhal bears emphasizing. A name, a body, a social condition—all of these are prisons. But their gates are not so tightly locked that escape is unthinkable. Of course it is easier to abandon one's name than to abandon one's body, and the use of pseudonyms is a substitute for the metamorphosis of dreams. (Impatience with the need to endure a body is found in nearly all writers who employ pseudonyms. Voltaire and Kierkegaard, different as they are, share an anxious concern for their bodies and ailments. In this sense pseudonomia is a form of hypochondria.)

The dungeon, with its chains, thick walls, and tall guard towers, is a natural metaphor for confinement. These images occur repeatedly in Stendhal's work. Heroes are imprisoned and escape—Julien at the seminary, Fabrice in the Farnese Tower, Hélène Campireale in the cloister, Lamiel at the Hautemares—each time reproducing an archetypal situation, into which the theme of passionate love strangely insinuates itself: confinement coincides with the inception of the highest form of love, which derives its strength solely from its impossibility. Desire implies distance and insurmountable separation. Octave, confined within the fatality of his impotence, loves Armance all the more ardently because he cannot abolish the impediment that separates them. But Octave is loved in return, as are all the other imprisoned heroes, despite the locks on their cells, or perhaps because of them. Extreme unhappiness turns into extreme happiness. The power of compensation that animates Stendhal's fiction is clearly evident. If society avenges itself on the exceptional individual by imprisoning him, the individual from his high cell can avenge himself on society by turning his solitude into a disdainful happiness unrelieved by hope. The motif of elevated places, which Proust noted as a fundamental theme in Stendhal, here merges with the theme of confinement. These glorious prisoners need but one long look to dominate the world. In these heroes visited in prison by love, we find among other things a figurative transposition of Stendhal's secret desire: to be loved in spite of his ugliness, in spite of the prison that his body and his age represented for him—to love and be loved from afar, through the power of the gaze. No destruction can threaten such love, whether because in the absence of fulfillment in possession and marriage there is nothing to destroy, or because in its very realization it remains furtive and clandestine, admirably curtailing the role of physical presence.

We are therefore dealing with a man unhappy to be what he is, disappointed in his body ("Why am I what I am?"), and caught between two contradictory temptations: to assert himself forcefully, thereby imposing his absolute uniqueness on others, or to undergo constant metamorphosis, to become someone else, to divide himself in order to become at once the perfect actor and the invisible spectator through an impenetrable disguise. These two tendencies, which Stendhal manages in such a way that they are not entirely contradictory, are expressed in two statements that should be taken together. "The only thing worth any trouble in this world *is oneself.*" But in the *Souvenirs d'égotisme* he says: "Will anyone believe me? I would wear a mask with pleasure, I would change my name with delight. The thousand and one nights that I adore occupy more than a quarter of my mind. Often I think of Angélique's ring. My sovereign pleasure would be to turn myself into a tall, blond German and stroll through Paris."[1] On the one hand he wants to be himself; on the other he savors the pleasure of working impossible tricks of magic in order to stop being himself. This is the contradiction that we must try to comprehend more fully.

Scattered through Stendhal's *Journal* and autobiographical writings are a thousand remarks on the use of the mask and the pleasure of "feeling alive in many versions." "Look upon life as a masked ball,"[2] is the advice that Stendhal gives himself in his diary for 1814. What is essential in this profession of faith is not the indictment of the social comedy or the excuse offered for the recourse to disguise, but the evidence it provides of a close connection between pleasure and travesty. What is signficant in Stendhal's hypocrisy, even more than the practical success of his stratagems, is the elegance of means, the aesthetic success of "playing well." In the masked ball hypocrisy becomes the rule of the game. The struggle for power or money is thus transformed into a kind of celebration, and in a final return to gratuitousness the hypocrite ceases to have any ambition other than the perfection of his game. He need only savor the inward enjoyment of being so perfectly outside himself.

Acknowledgment of the profound connection between the "pleasure principle" and the desire for metamorphosis can be found in an almost pure state in a curious text written by Stendhal near the end of his life: "The Privileges of 10 April 1840." Here Stendhal, at an age when most people are more concerned with their wills, formulated his enduring reveries as a contract between himself and God. The text begins with the notation: "*God* [English in the original] grants me the following privileges." Later we read:

Article 3: The *mentula* [penis], like the index finger for rigidity and movement, the latter at will. Size, two inches longer than the original, same thickness. But pleasure through the mentula, only twice a week. Twenty times a year, the grantee may become whomever he wishes to be, provided that individual exists. One hundred times a year he shall know for twenty-four hours the language of his choice.[3]

Desire for erotic potency, desire for metamorphosis, and desire for command of a new language are oddly juxtaposed. By normal standards of logic such different wishes should not be mentioned side by side. But here logic is wrong and the imagination is right. Improvising freely, it has translated a single emotional inspiration in a variety of ways. The wish for erotic power and the dream of metamorphosis, mentioned in the same breath, express two aspects of a single will to power. In both cases what is desired is the ability to manipulate by power of the conscious will either the sex life or the physical appearance. For Stendhal, the body is a contingent fact that he dreams of wresting from contingency in order to bestow upon himself, by an entirely voluntary act of will, a body of his own choosing. As for the mechanism of sex, so fundamentally governed by vegetative responses, so independent of the conscious motor powers, Stendhal wants it to respond as well to conscious command. Imperialism of the will here takes as its object not external nature or the cosmos but the body itself, which is to become an obedient tool. In the text cited above we can make out two aspects of the desire to wield conscious power over one's own body in order to possess the body of *another* person. For, broadly interpreted, erotic possession and metamorphosis are both ways of "entering the body of another." Desire here gives itself a choice between two types of fulfillment, imagining in turn the infallible triumph of an extroverted sexuality and the narcissistic satisfaction of inhabiting a body that will remain one's own even as it becomes the body of another.

In this refusal to accept the body as a given or a limitation, there is nothing in the nature of a disembodiment. Stendhal exalts corporeal existence by imagining it free of all servitude. It is a fine thing to have a body as long as one bestows it upon oneself. This fantasy is very similar to the mythical dream of gaining immortality by drinking a magical potion. As long as we inhabit an opaque body of which we are not the masters, we live in dubious cohabitation with death, for death attacks us by way of that in our bodies which is not subject to our will. To become lord and master of one's own body is to evade the threat of death, whereupon all servitude in the human condition disappears: man rises to the rank of the gods.

"Privileges" is a text from the pen of the aged Stendhal that reveals a "Faustian" desire for rejuvenation in a quite pagan context of death-defying recommencements. For Stendhal, metamorphosis is an opening to the future, an acceleration of life that nevertheless turns its back on death. (Note that according to Kafka metamorphosis is the exact opposite: it is an aggravation of the corporeal condition, a slowing of existence in which energy is frozen and paralyzed and access to the future is shut off as existence shrinks back by degrees toward its center until, finally, it is absorbed in the unique conspicuousness of destruction.)

In ancient myth we find two opposite types of metamorphosis: that of Zeus, for whom it is an instrument of aggression and amorous conquest, and that of Proteus, who derives from it the ability to flee would-be captors and make himself uncatchable. In Stendhal, conquest and flight are connected and figure as complementary attitudes. The desire to appear and the desire to disappear are part of a single "complex." Both are ways of establishing one's value in the eyes of others, ways of defending oneself from annihilation by an alien gaze. Stendhal, ashamed of his ugliness, knows that no one can love or desire him as he is. He hopes to be discovered behind an image other than the one that is really his. By wrapping himself in mystery, by refusing to be deciphered, he invents out of whole cloth a realm beyond appearances into which the external gaze is obliged to venture. Others must seek him out beyond his body in a trompe-l'oeil perspective. The perfect mask invites the onlooker to imagine a world behind the mask, a pure mirage toward which the victim nevertheless rushes headlong in order to offer himself or herself to the seducer.

Stendhal had still other ways of diverting attention from his ugliness. One was to compel others to look at themselves. In company he posed as a "connoisseur of the human heart," disturbing his interlocutors who found the scrutiny of his glance hard to bear. By turning the tables and making others aware of being stared at, he ceased to be the object of their stares. And it was easier to fascinate others who had been made anxious about their own mystery. He struck at them through their narcissism.

According to contemporaries, Stendhal was past master of the grimace. Recall the entry into the Ancelot salon of M. César Bombet, seller of cotton bonnets. The hours spent in front of the mirror—

grooming himself, adjusting his "borrowed toupee," dying his hair, doing his nails—were really makeup sessions, in which he prepared himself to confront society as an actor might prepare to confront his audience. If Stendhal took great pains to cut an elegant figure, it was because he guessed that the only way to nullify the effects of his ugliness was through an artifice of behavior by means of which his body would cease to be a thing and would become a sign. And when instead of aiming for elegance he lent himself to some farce, it was again to conceal his ugliness behind comedy and grotesque caricature. Whatever provokes laughter automatically elicits approval. People looked not at his dreadful nose but at the humorous point he used his nose to make. Thus by playing with his *physiognomy* (as his uncle Gagnon had recommended) he drew attention to himself but not to his ugliness. Concealed by the mobility of his features, his ugliness became almost unreal, leaving him free to savor the pleasure of giving pleasure.

Let us continue reading the astonishing "Privileges of 10 April 1840." We find several examples of metamorphoses imagined by Stendhal, and, much to our surprise, we discover that after priding himself on his worldly elegance, he expresses the wish to be transformed into an animal so as to experience the pleasure of an elemental vitality:

> Article 5. Handsome hair, fine skin, excellent fingers without scrapes, a light, sweet scent. On the first of February and the first of June each year the grantee's clothing shall become as they were the third time he wore them.
>
> Article 6. Miracles in the eyes of all who do not know him: the grantee shall have the figure of General Debelle, dead at Santo Domingo, but without imperfection. He shall play a perfect game of whisk, écarté, billiards, and chess but never win more than one hundred francs. He shall be flawless in pistol shooting, horseback riding, and fencing.
>
> Article 7. Four times a year, he shall be allowed to change himself into whatever animal he may like and subsequently to change himself back into a man. Four times a year he shall be allowed to change himself into whatever man he may wish; and, what is more, concentrate his life in that of an animal, which, in case of death or incapacitation of the number-one man into whom he changed himself, shall be allowed to return him to the natural form of the grantee. Thus, four times a year, and each time for an unlimited period, the grantee shall be allowed to occupy two bodies at once.

This double transformation, toward perfection and toward animality, corresponds quite well to tendencies in Stendhal's love life. He never loved a woman who was not either far above or far below his own station. Among his mistresses there are virtually no women of the bourgeois class, only duchesses and slatterns. Passion holds no attraction for him unless he feels compelled to transform himself. His first loves are for actresses, of whom he becomes enamored while reciting scenes from Molière and Racine. He loves them because they draw him into the world of metamorphosis and because more than other women they give him the pleasure he has anticipated, a pleasure that can flourish only in an atmosphere of theatricality. He assumes that after conquering his actresses he will love them more and longer than he would love other women, for with them he expects to be able to continue his metamorphoses indefinitely, even in the most trivial details of daily life. Such an inventive life is the only life not threatened by boredom, which looms on the horizon whenever the power of metamorphosis flags. In effect, Stendhal finds bourgeois women boring because he does not need to transform himself in order to conquer them. As for the woman of high society, the idealized figure "à la Corregio," she must remain forever inaccessible. Success with such a woman would mean never again needing to outdo himself. Metamorphosis having been rendered futile, love would find itself paralyzed at the same moment, as immobilized by boredom as a ship caught in ice. Stendhal's lovers therefore need distance and obstacles not only to make conquest worthwhile but even more to render necessary a transformation of self that in itself is already a form of ecstasy. Love for a woman already won can survive only by becoming either clandestine or illicit: Fabrice and Julien are obliged continually to repeat their masked exploits.

The text just cited calls for another remark. Stendhal dreams of occupying several bodies at once. The metamorphosis he desires is not a depersonalization but a multiplication of the self, indeed a "super-personalization." He wants to become not just *an* other but *several* others.

Stendhal adopts pseudonyms as both ends and means. He loves the pseudonymous life for itself, but he also loves it for the effects it produces and for the pride he derives from it. This means that in his metamorphoses he needs to stay vigilant so as to reap for consciousness the secret booty of his masked conquests. Even as he changes form he strives to maintain his clear vision. Like the general staff gathered on a ridge overlooking the field of combat, he keeps constant watch on the vagaries of a battle to which he has committed only the shadow of his thought. Unflagging attention is necessary if the desired outcome is not to elude him. Thus he constructs for himself an inner life, immediately certain that it is invulnerable because it is nothing but a pure gaze directed upon himself and others, safe from counterattack by the gaze of others. Having turned his face and body into instruments under his full control, he is no longer their captive; no longer must he endure them as a fate. The mask (and the pseudonym) thus appears to expand his freedom. Free will makes use of a body from which it has detached itself and which it may use as it pleases. In this way Stendhal succeeds in lightening his body, a great boon to a man who was always ashamed of his weight. But then the mask has always been used as an adjunct to dancing, whether in primitive celebration or in the modern ballroom: the mask makes bodies seem lighter. Irony, of which Stendhal was so fond, yields the same discontinuity, the same effect of levitation, for irony is nothing other than the spiritual quintessence of the mask.

Behind the playfulness that clouds appearances, Stendhal intends to preserve his lucidity intact as refuge for his enduring self, his unalterable identity. He preserves those functions he needs in order to see himself and feel himself act. A highly alert ego must be present to savor the sensation of successful activity, which is a form of pleasure. For Stendhal's love of metamorphosis is directly related to his love of action and energy. Doubtless there is first of all a failure of spontaneous action (as we shall see), and doubtless the recourse to metamorphosis reflects a need to follow a devious course in order to make contact with the world. Nevertheless, metamorphosis in Stendhal is essentially voluntary and dynamic, as the text of the "Privileges" shows so well. Hence Stendhal cannot be numbered among the proponents of passive metamorphosis. I doubt that he would have cared for drugs that transform existence in fantastic ways but at the price of consenting to passivity. The mid-nineteenth-century vogue for hashish and opium suited a type of sensibility very different from Stendhal's voluntarism. Metamorphosis can be experienced as an active or a passive phenomenon: one can metamorphosize oneself or one can undergo metamorphosis. Stendhal chose the former. He had such great need of other people that he could not surrender to a reverie in which he would not have to confront rivals and adversaries.

Stendhal's social ambitions were of course rather meagerly re-warded. The fall of the Empire marked the end of his social success. In the reactionary society of the Restoration he had little hope of advancement. Despite the most subtle of tactics, he ran up against insuperable limits and obstacles. Can one really abandon one's body? Mephistopheles is not always around to strike a bargain. If reality resists too stubbornly, dream is still free to claim every victory for itself. But to accept such victories would be to give up the game, to relinquish all hope of conquering the salons. Stendhal was unwilling to do this. A way of conquering the world remained open to him, even as he dreamed of metamorphosis: literature, which Stendhal first viewed as an indirect avenue to social success. Mark well the fact that he entered the social fray before trying the literary one. Even when he began to write, his goal was primarily to win prestige, not to produce a body of work. In seeking literary celebrity, he was striving for "spin-off success" in high society. The young Stendhal's dabbling in the theater was quite specifically aimed at achieving the kind of "Parisian" success that can launch a man's career in society. His plagiarisms were calculated to make money but also offered the pleasures of a low-cost metamorphosis. After stealing another man's book, Stendhal was ipso facto obliged to hide himself, to deny his theft: an excellent occasion for dissimulation. This situation, which he deliberately provoked, allowed him to satisfy his penchant for wearing masks; henceforth wearing a disguise was indispensable. But success is not to be had so cheaply. For want of other means Stendhal finally determined to yield up the substance of his private dreams to the public. This was his last trump card, and he was loath to play it too quickly. Had he been slightly more shrewd, slightly more competent in affairs, he might not have resisted the temptation to become a "celebrity author," a talented mountebank at once disdain-ful and flattering toward his public. But through clumsiness, which is to say, because of a bizarre inability really to break faith with himself—whence the embarrassment that paralyzed him in the pres-ence of others and ruined his political hopes—he remained attached to his dreams of happiness, his audacious desires, his private prefer-ences.

Stendhal's good fortune as a writer was that he was unable to abandon himself. In reverie he metamorphosized into Julien, Fabrice, Lucien, and Lamiel, changing his face, his body, his social rank, and even his sex, but always in order to tell the story of his life, altered to give himself either better opportunities than he actually had or more impressive misfortunes than he actually suffered. Unlike Balzac he never sought to find out the secrets of other people's lives. He recommenced his own life with another body as one might recommence a card game with a fresh deck. Stendhal's metamorphosis was never intended to achieve the radical alienation expressed in Rimbaud's "je est un autre." It sought to change not being but only contingency. Hence Stendhal was able to remain himself while assuming the fate of a Fabrice or a Julien in compensation for his failures. He consoled himself for his failure to be named prefect; the boredom of living under the "most knavish of kings" (Louis-Phillippe) found its compensation.

Compensation, for Stendhal, meant not simply imagining his characters happy in love but just simply imagining them in life. They lived before his eyes, other yet also himself. They lived as his proxies but without compromising him. He stood aloof from his invented brothers, guiding them from afar. And before long he was looking on as they emancipated themselves by making surprising decisions, almost independent of their author's will. Because they acted freely, they were truly alive. Yet they did not cease to act on Stendhal's behalf. Thus he obtained the pleasure he desired. He enjoyed a sense of living outside himself, of truly occupying "two bodies at once," for the figures of his imagination were possessed of healthy bodies and autonomous destinies. Note too that the characters themselves do not neglect the value of disguises. The desire for metamorphosis that conjured them up perpetuated itself in them. Consider the various disguises of Fabrice del Dongo: barometer salesman, hussar, peasant, worker, priest, English eccentric, valet. Delivered from his body and his boredom, Stendhal belonged to his characters, who led him where they pleased. His blood flowed in the veins of these "others," who developed as he did and thus remained a part of himself. Thus he created for himself the illusion of confronting his destiny in the external world, seeing all without being seen, as if looking down from a dark loge on a spectacle of happiness and power, finally achieved.

Commentators have been quick to portray Stendhal as an actor or a supremely lucid illusionist, in control of all his gestures, skilled at every kind of deception, and unerring in his calculations. But such complete mastery, cunning use of the self's native resources, and capacity for simulation—all qualities that Valéry rather too generously attributes to Stendhal—were not so much possessed as desired, not so much developed as longed for. The young Beyle's primary experience is that of awkwardness and shame. In society he feels superfluous, clumsy, embarrassed, incapable of saying anything witty, hence unlikely to attract. Others more gifted than himself scored successes before his very eyes. How should he take his revenge: in glory or in love? Though he felt that the world was not made for him, it was nevertheless his chosen field of battle. His social maladjustment was immediately translated into a need for conquest and projects of defense. His central problem was how to act on himself in order to act infallibly on others. He thus discovered the need for knowledge of himself and others: "self-interested" knowledge still subservient to his plans for winning prestige. "In order to speak well one must be self-possessed."[4] Self-knowledge was sought not for itself but for its tactical benefits. Self-knowledge led to self-possession, and self-possession made it possible to shine in company, to dazzle other people. Anyone without such ability could get nowhere. Like all timid men, Stendhal believed that women yield only to a display of extraordinary qualities. Love, he thought, had to be merited in open competition.

In Maine de Biran's first journal, a similar desire for self-knowledge is again associated with discomfort in society and dissatisfaction with self. Biran also speaks of "self-possession," but self-knowledge ultimately becomes a pretext for fleeing the world, since, as he puts it, "I can contribute nothing there that would allow me to make my mark, and I tarnish those qualities by which I amount to something in my own eyes."[5] He prefers, that is, to withdraw from society without having proven his worth, which he chooses instead to husband in solitude or with a few cultivated friends. Stendhal, however, aims to remain within the society he contests. He needs its antagonism and, ultimately, its recognition. "To have character is to have felt the effect of others on oneself, hence one needs others."[6] Stendhal therefore turns to Helvetius, the sensualists, the ideologues, and the physiologists for the weapons he needs to confront the world. The would-be student of France's foremost school of engineering requires a frankly mechanistic philosophy, in which man is seen as a clavier that one must learn to play. He trusts in his training, which he believes has given him the skill he needs to elicit whatever emotional response he desires. Provided he knows what keys to touch, all inward unpredictability is eliminated. A sovereign, hegemonic, imperial will can command the docile faculties. (At this point in history there was erected around the triumphant Bonaparte a myth of consummate self-control, of perfect subjugation of body to will.) Thus Stendhal dreamed of dominating himself, of using himself as one might use a scientific instrument, guided by a psychology whose results were summarized in easy-to-use theorems and tables. It was enough to observe, deduce, and make proper use of logic. If Stendhal initially felt a sense of inferiority in the presence of others, those feelings were converted to a sense of challenge. Stendhal immediately rationalized his aggressiveness and sought with the aid of mathematics to proportion the means of his counterattack to the ends.

But his project went awry as he was forced to admit that one cannot regain possession of oneself methodically, using a system based on primitive sensations; or after creating a tabula rasa in oneself, construct the self through logical associations; or establish between self and self a transparent relation of utility and prediction analogous to the relation that obtains between man and things. In every difficult pass, with every assault he wished to make, Stendhal proved unable to maintain the order of battle he had prescribed or to follow the strategic routes he had mapped out in advance, for in the event the order proved too mechanical, the routes too unswerving; when he attempted to follow them, they lost whatever plausibility they seemed to have in premeditation. Life cannot be poured into a ready-made mold. Experience demonstrated that freedom was constantly catching itself unawares and was never able to predict its own decisions. More than other men Stendhal was prepared to submit to the unforeseen, to acquiesce in the suddenness of an emotional upheaval that altered all previous prospects in a single blow. All Stendhal's calculations and preparations were intended to impose continuity in such a way as to repress the vehement discontinuity of feeling, which could make a rout of even the battles best begun. True, the same discontinuity was responsible for the "states of inverted sensibility" in which Stendhal enjoyed his finest moments. Though he looked for success in action, he also looked for a happiness that revealed itself in the sudden, unforeseen flash of a moment. In his "system," however, he subordinated happiness to action. In opposition to himself, he attempted to close his mind to all counsel but that of calculating reason and to establish a seamless style of life. But the vigilance needed for such a system to succeed was itself at the mercy of sudden and fortuitous disruptions, which made it necessary to start all over again. Such was the rhythm to which Stendhal had to accustom himself, to suffer and to enjoy. Nothing is more certain than that he began by wanting to suppress or overcome irrational discontinuity. Stendhal's rationalism was above all the system of a man endeavoring to rid himself of a very powerful "irrational" interior. But Stendhal was unable to conform to his system: he turned it into a mask.

Unity, coherence, maneuverability, mastery—all the qualities, all the power dreamt of by an adolescent eager to make the most impressive possible mark upon the world—can be found in Stendhal's fictional characters, yet none of these qualities enables them to achieve immediate success. Stendhal himself was destined to lead a life of instability, awkwardness, and error, but he refused to accept his instability and sought to compensate for it in every possible way. Later he would admit: "We know ourselves and we do not change; yet we must know ourselves." This is an admission of defeat on the part of a man who initially sought self-knowledge solely in order to transform himself. As he grew older, Stendhal began to love knowledge for its own sake, without hope of using it as an instrument to achieve some other end. This belated search for himself was intended not to prepare for the future (like the "Intimate Diaries" of 1806–1818) but to restore the past. The point was no longer to perfect his masks but to rediscover his true visage. It was at this stage of his life that he wrote the *Life of Henry Brulard*.

What does "know thyself" mean in the Stendhalian context? Is it a question of discovering or rediscovering one's "true" and enduring nature? Or is it simply a matter of enumerating certain elementary psychological mechanisms (impersonal mechanisms shared by all men) of which free use can then be made in contriving a character for oneself? Stendhal never gave an unequivocal and definitive answer. His work shows that both approaches were possible, and Stendhal never attempted to strike a balance between them. His life and his genius needed this degree of uncertainty and disequilibrium. At times he sought to discover the immutable truth about himself; at other times he felt free to make himself up in any way he fancied. Thus to know himself meant sometimes to determine what he was and accept it, sometimes to create himself out of whole cloth. In the first instance he was obliged to conduct an investigation, an "inquest," to unearth his real nature from beneath an accumulated weight of sediment and distortion. Here such notions as sincerity and naturalness found full employment. In the second instance, however, self-knowledge yielded not the secret of what he was but the raw materials with which to construct himself as he wished to be. By means of lucid and careful planning and judicious selection and scrutiny of his methods, he would be able to "define" and "conquer" himself through action. Where is the dividing line between hypocrisy and sincerity? If hypocrisy becomes a means of action, and especially if it augments one's power to act, it need not occasion any self-betrayal, for there is no preestablished truth. To the extent that hypocrisy increases a man's strength, it enables him to know what he can do, hence also what he is. From this point of view, being and value are synonymous. Hypocrisy, if it leads to power, oddly enough becomes a means of access to the self, a way of becoming oneself. In Stendhal's novels, especially *Lucien Leuwen*, it is quite clear that as long as the hero has no history he is suspicious of himself and unable to render judgment. In his own eyes he is nothing, he has no shape or character. It is by confronting the world, testing his mettle in contact with others, that he becomes himself. He knows himself only from the moment he has proved his worth (measured in terms not of morality but of energy and efficacy).

In the diaries for 1804 and 1805 the demand for perfect naturalness is strikingly coupled with tactical calculation. For Stendhal the contradiction entails no conflict. At times the terms can even be inverted: naturalness can be pressed into service for its tactical value. To make himself more attractive, Stendhal tailors his naturalness to order and calculates his spontaneity. Or else he will employ a premeditated dodge to bring about a "lovely moment of naturalness." Initially, however, Stendhal is always at a distance from himself. Lacking self-possession, he must make an effort either to be natural or to choose a proper strategy. He must find himself or construct himself before doing anything else. Unable to strike the right tone immediately, he is neither sincere nor seductive. Knowing that he sounds false, he tries to to recover his "natural self" through transformation. Different secret maneuvers are needed to recover his naturalness, which must be unearthed and liberated as a mineral is liberated from its ore. (Rousseau undoubtedly influenced this idea of a first nature enveloped but not destroyed by a sheath of custom, which must be unearthed and then honored.) An awkward adolescent, Stendhal feels that his movements never reflect his true first impulses, from which he is separated by a thick layer of learned behavior. That learned behavior must therefore be either eliminated or developed to such a pitch of perfection that a second level of naturalness can be pieced together. In his assiduous attentions to the little actress Melanie, Stendhal alternates between two attitudes: repudiation of all convention and perfection of conventional manners.

There are moments, however, when playacting and spontaneity appear to dissolve and merge, when the antinomy between facticity and authenticity seems to be resolved. On such exalted days surrender to the inspiration of the moment coincides with self-mastery and lucidity; self-possession coincides with spontaneity of impulse. Life is then rather like a commedia dell'arte, in which one makes up one's role as the play goes along, with each reply arising in its unsurpassable perfection from the depths of an unpredictable future. Fiction is experienced as truth, and truth deploys itself in fiction. The energy of feeling is liberated from all hindering hesitation. Freedom goes hand in hand with invention, and we seem to discover even as we invent our selves. Existence appears to be raised to a higher plane of efficacy, rapidity, and intensity. Natural self-containment gives way to a more tenuous, freer, less material relation of self-connivance. We dominate our lives rather than being mired in them. We become sure of ourselves as we are liberated from ourselves and find reason for fascination in our power to fascinate others. Thus Stendhal becomes himself by dint not of perseverance but of the inimitable way in which he continually breaks away from himself even as he sets forth the representation of his life. To be seen, but in perfection, to please ourselves by being seen through the eyes of others: in this way we construct, as a work of art, a consistent personality of the second degree upon the ruins of an unsatisfactory primary personality. An agile, perceptive self rises from the ruins of a ponderous existence. For Stendhal there is no contradiction in showing himself and masking himself simultaneously. Masked exhibition represents a superior state of power: the power to act on the spectator, to seduce the audience, without thereby making oneself vulnerable to the public gaze.

Stendhal thus redeems his ugliness. A life that is invented from moment to moment, haphazardly and without plan, constructs a perfection analogous to that of a work elaborated and planned in advance. As the unforeseen is realized, it solidifies into the foreseen. Having improvised as if at random, the result is a text in which nothing need be revised. Liberty at its most unbridled and adventuresome retraces its path, only to discover that not a single gesture or riposte failed to conform to the requirements of aesthetics. (Dandyism, without favoring the unforeseen to the same degree, obeyed the same rule: to make life into a work of art.) The disappearance of all boundaries between the factitious and the natural, the spontaneity of improvisation and the calculation of the masterpiece, is an occasion for great joy.

In such a special moment, every gesture and every word incorporates the ingenuousness of the absolutely natural and the magic of achieved perfection:

> This was probably the best day of my life. I may achieve greater success, but never will I exhibit greater talent. Perception was precisely what was needed to guide sensation; a little more and I would have allowed myself to be carried along by my senses. Perception made me shrewd enough to see that what was needed was to recite a *couplet*, and once the first word was out of my mouth I felt what I was saying. It is impossible to simulate passion any better, because I actually felt it . . . To convey the perfection of the genre in which I excelled, I should say that I played, as Molé, a role that Molière could have written, being at once author and actor.[7]

When Stendhal writes that "it is impossible to simulate passion any better, because I actually felt it," he is describing one of those dazzling moments in which the natural and the feigned are reconciled. At such times, contrary to what Diderot says in his *Paradoxe sur le comédien*, the play is all the more perfect for expressing a genuine sentiment, and the sentiment is all the more deeply felt because it is well acted. Stendhal feels himself fusing with his play. His joy is essentially that of having overcome the division between "inner" life and "outer" behavior, which he has turned into a highly organized system. At the culmination of a series of stratagems based on the distinction between appearance and reality, Stendhal feels triumphant only if he witnesses the disappearance of a duality he has imposed upon himself. Having mastered himself to the fullest possible extent, he willingly identifies with the arbitrary image he has adopted simply for the pleasure of the sport. He is finally what he wanted to be. His way of abolishing falsehood is not to return to the inner life (which does not exist) but to throw himself into his fiction to the point of merging with it.

The movement by which Stendhal grows aware of becoming

himself is a centrifugal one. Rather than match his action to his passion, rather than attempt to express faithfully what already exists within himself, he becomes what initially he played. His passion comes to him through his actions. As the pace of the play accelerates, authenticity is born. At that point Stendhal can no longer hold out against the fascination to which he has subjected others. He allows himself to be caught up in the play, creating from nothing an unanticipated "naturalness." In the end he finds satisfaction in the pleasure that enticed him beyond all foreseeable success. In Stendhal there is as close a connection between pleasure and self-awareness as there is between pleasure and metamorphosis. Surrender to natural- ness always brings happiness, but sometimes it is pure artifice that brings a gratuitous euphoria, which precedes and magically produces the advent of a naturalness beyond anything he had even dared to hope for.

What is the meaning of Stendhal's distinction (in the passage just cited) between sensation and perception? These terms of psychology, though borrowed from philosophers and despite their technical and impersonal character, reflect a striking aspect of Stendhal's behavior. They delineate two distinct levels of consciousness, an inner division of which Stendhal was profoundly aware. When sensation and perception are in proper equilibrium, he experiences a state of heightened pleasure. Such moments are brief, however, and he is more commonly aware of a discord between the two. Sensation, which is an aspect of the life of the body or at any rate confined to a fairly obscure realm of consciousness, is immediately available. By contrast, perception organizes sensation into clear consciousness and bestows upon it the dignity of the reflected phenomenon. Here we touch on a favorite theme of empiricist philosophy, which sought to distinguish between what belonged to judgment and what was subject to the body. Stendhal, however, is not interested in questions of metaphysics. For him, the conflict is between immediate existence (sensation) and reflected consciousness (perception). In his diaries we find him alternately blaming one or the other for his errors, failures, and timidity. Frequently sensation catches him unawares and throws him for a loop: a flood of sense data suddenly inundates and obscures a situation in which everything had been clearly prepared and premeditated. The more thoroughly Stendhal prepares himself, the more readily he falls victim to the unwanted resurgence of sensation: "In things where I am weak, I am never sufficiently resolved beforehand. As when I go to see a woman I love. The result of it all is that during the first quarter of an hour with her I have only convulsive movements or a sudden and general weakness, a *liquefaction* of solids."[8]

When excess is not on the side of sensation, however, it is on the side of perception (for there is always some unfortunate excess to ruin Stendhal's pleasure). Perception then robs him of sensation, stands between himself and the world, and prevents him from being present. To know what one feels is already no longer to be entirely there; it is to stand aside. Unlike sensation, which is pure participation, pure adhesion to the world, perception is discontinuity. Worse still, it can at times stifle sensation, nip it in the bud. When Stendhal is in a perceptive state, his sensation dries up. The gaze he directs at himself prevents him from spontaneously experiencing the situation in which he is engaged. He then loses his poise, does not know how to respond, and despite his perfect lucidity misspeaks himself, well aware that any effort to dissimulate his awkwardness will only compound the difficulties. On the other hand, in the triumphal note cited earlier from his diary for 1801, he applauds himself for having reduced perception to a minimum, to just the degree necessary to experience pleasure. Disencumbered of the excess of consciousness that threatens to stifle the spontaneous invention of sentiment, he can finally commit himself fully to action and thus succeed; his strength is restored.

In extreme moments of perfect happiness, perception will have totally disappeared. Happiness as Stendhal describes it implies an intense suspension of the reflective consciousness, a veritable loss of self. Whereas the rare equilibrium between sensation and perception is accompanied by pleasure, happiness is by contrast a state that belongs to pure sensation. Insofar as everything is subordinated to the quest for perfect happiness, it must be admitted that all the hyper-conscious maneuvers and hypocritical doublings paradoxically lead to moments in which consciousness vanishes in incandescence. While listening to the bells of the tiny church above Rolle, Stendhal experiences "perfect happiness"[9]—perfect because the ravishment of his senses is unnameable and leaves no residue in consciousness but a dazzling void. There can be no souvenir without perception, and when consciousness vanishes memory becomes impossible. "Moments of happiness so unhinge the soul that they elude its grasp."[10] In such happiness, which in order to exist must not be possessed, there is admittedly a rather romantic way of getting rid of the "for itself" (*le pour-soi*, in Sartre's terminology). Pure sensation, if it is intense enough and not disturbed, can then with exquisite pleasure be swallowed up by the "in itself" (*l'en-soi*). Yet this is not a form of mystical or pantheistic ecstasy. No Great Being or Nature is indispensable to such happiness. The sight of Lake Leman and the music of the bells are no doubt necessary, but other sights, under the chandelier of the theater and accompanied by other music, will result in equally perfect escapes. Hence it is wrong to see this happiness as a communion successful at last. In reality there is no communion, no "fusion" with contemplated nature. In the ravishing that results in the ultimate absence of consciousness, nothing is left but a body crackling with a powerful electrical charge. Initially sensation was immediate presence in the world, but now the moment of happiness is described as a total withdrawal from the world, with consciousness abolished and the entire body shaken by a cataclysm that leaves no room for "attention to pleasure."

In the instant of happiness, the self-directed gaze must perish or it is not true happiness. After confiding to his journal for 1805 a pleasure that "truly unhinged" him, Stendhal marks a difference by noting that "the pleasure of the Opera, with Martial, was of a lesser degree. I was not unhinged, I saw my happiness and had enough strength to analyze it."[11] What is true of happiness is also true of naturalness, which can be perfect only if all inward splitting is eliminated.

Stendhal observed that consciousness always brings duplicity and cunning. In his diaries he writes:

> It is very difficult to describe what was *natural* in you from memory. We are better at describing what is *artificial* or *feigned*, because the effort of *deception* that was required engraved it in memory. To practice remembering my natural sentiments is an exercise that can give me the talent of Shakespeare. We watch ourselves *playacting*; we have the *perception* of our performance. That sensation is easily reproduced by the organ of *memory*. But in order to remember *natural feelings*, we must begin by creating the *perception*.[12]

Thus the enemy of naturalness is not hypocrisy or sham but perception, which knows how to make itself necessary. We can escape from it only by furtive means. We are therefore condemned to sham; candor is impossible. Deliberate hypocrisy is merely a development of what is implicit in self-consciousness. In *De l'Amour* we find the striking statement that the sensitive man feels the immense weight that attaches to every word that he speaks to the beloved. It seems to him that his fate hangs on a word. How can he not strive to speak well? How, at any rate, can he fail to be aware whether or not he is speaking well? Whereupon there is no candor. Hence one must not claim candor, a quality that belongs only to a soul that does not look back upon itself. One is what one can be, but one feels what one is.[13]

The significance of Stendhal's liking for theater should now be clear. In the darkness of the theater, he is the object of no one's gaze. Hence he no longer needs to stand watch over himself. He no longer needs to think about the image others have of him. He belongs entirely to the scene that fascinates him. Pleasure in all its perfection is free to flourish. Self-consciousness is reduced to consciousness of the play. Watching a brilliant performance, he has no further need to perform for himself. Yet he does not withdraw from society. The play is a collective celebration, and the spectator's solitude is strangely encouraged by the complicitous presence of a crowd in thrall to the same ceremony. One can at least see without being seen, and above all without being obliged to see oneself.[14]

There is a voyeuristic side of Stendhal. At times he enjoys peering through keyholes. The scene absorbs him to such a degree that he becomes "all eyes," delivered from the need to subject himself to scrutiny. In this state of purely sensual curiosity, he feels that he is more natural, since he no longer needs to confront the gaze of others or the scrutiny of his own consciousness. On this point there is a very revealing passage in the diaries:

> Before going to bed I kept watch for a long time on the bedroom of a woman with whom I had supped and who seemed quite haveable. Her door was ajar, and I had some hope of catching a glimpse of a thigh or a bosom.
>
> A woman whose entire body in my bed would do nothing for me causes me to feel pleasant sensations when caught unawares. She is natural, *I am not caught up in my role*, and I am entirely invested in the sensation.
>
> My loves have always been somewhat disturbed by the concern to be agreeable, or, in other words, by my preoccupation with a role. These are circumstances in which one cannot be purely natural.[15]

Here, then, he describes a way of hiding so as to forget himself and at the same time heighten his "sensation." Seeking to avoid hypocrisy and the "concern to be agreeable," Stendhal further widens the distance between himself and the desired prey. The distances imposed by the conventions of gallantry are no longer sufficient. He prefers to disappear altogether. Thus he is delivered from the need to mask himself. But has he not also forsaken all possibility of ever meeting the woman behind the half-open door, whose life has for him become a pure spectacle? Having freed himself from self-consciousness, has he not simultaneously lost the *presence* of the woman he desires?

Naturalness is a promised land. Any way of achieving it is good, but initially every way is hypocritical, for naturalness is first of all that which is lacking; it is defined as an absence. The loss of naturalness is the only Fall known to this consummate atheist. At the outset Stendhal feels that he is condemned not to be himself and not to be happy. This initial situation must be overcome, but overcome by the resources of falsehood and hypocrisy, no other weapon being available. Stendhal thus appears in the guise of a man who resorts to hypocrisy in order to denounce and "demystify" the forced hypocrisy that he finds in himself and in society.

Stendhal's attitude toward language is revealing. For him, language is essentially arbitrary and inadequate compared to actual feeling. To speak is already to fail to coincide with oneself, to wear a mask. Words for Stendhal are conventional signs, not authentic means of expression. Between the emotion and the word there is a discontinuity, and the word is always second best. Between signifier and signified there is only a conventional relationship, as in algebra. Stendhal in the *Journal* invites the hypothetical reader to view what he writes as a mere "mathematical notation." Happiness, untranslatable into words, is always omitted, moreover. The more powerful the emotion, the more inadequate the words. Distance and dissonance are inevitable. Words and sentences are never thoughts and feelings but only abstract indices of thoughts and feelings, signs imperfectly attuned to the realities they designate. Thus when sentiment attains the extremes of exaltation and ecstasy, the conventions of language, relying as they do on the mechanisms of habit, will inevitably prove false. Better to remain silent. Stendhal's antilyricism is a refusal to accord any value to verbal intensity. Language is always at a distance from what it pretends to express. True expression can therefore take place only in spite of language, at certain moments when words fail, when the sentence suffocates in a communication made possible either by the annihilation of signs: "In passionate love, one often speaks a language that one does not understand. Soul makes itself visible to soul independent of the words used. I suspect that there is a similar effect in song." But such musical intimacy is exceptional, and it should not be counted on. Hence there is no choice but to reduce language to a firm algebra, a mathematical system, in order to make the best of the misunderstanding that is an essential part of language. (Stendhal's outrage at the "style of *Atala*," Chateaubriand's novel of pathos, clearly implies a philosophy of language.) Since we are condemned to act out what we think, it is important that we minimize the clumsiness of our acting. Unable to rely on always arousing the "musical" emotion that lies beyond language, Stendhal assembles a repertoire of ready-made phrases and gestures in order to maintain his poise vis-à-vis any person with whom he is engaged in conversation. The heroes of his novels behave and express themselves in the same way. The dissonance between language and intention then ceases to be a disadvantage. In his hands the powers of *deception* become an instrument of success; rather than become the plaything of duplicity, he avails himself of it. Hypocrisy converts an endured situation into a desired one.

Hypocrisy is therefore an inferior substitute for naturalness, to be practiced for want of anything better, until the lovely time of naturalness arrives. Stendhal justifies his behavior numerous times. He says that it is but a provisional tactical maneuver. Later, with the aid of music or passionate intensity or the confidence born of wealth, it will be easier for him to dare to be himself, and hypocrisy will vanish. But he also blames society:

> All my words of love for her were feigned. Not even one was natural. Everything I said to her was pure Fleury. I could almost point to the plays from which I took each gesture, and how much I loved them. Trust in appearances! But the reason was my confused notion that my love was too grand and too beautiful not to seem ridiculous in society, where all one's feelings must be truncated. My love was like Othello's before his jealousy. After I have enjoyed an income of 6,000 livres for six months, I shall be strong enough to be myself, even in love.[16]

What is this explanation worth? I have drawn attention to the inner reasons for Stendhal's seeking refuge in hypocrisy. He had only to feel that he was looked at in order for reflective splitting to occur, initiating a systematic duplicity. His tactical calculations and premeditated strategies are simply an aggressive transformation of an imposed division. How was society to blame? Is it not rather commonplace to blame social conditions for a self-chosen course of conduct? Stendhal wrote to Baron de Mareste: "It is this enormous, necessary hypocrisy that leaves me in despair."[17] But is it not true that Stendhal did everything he could to make sure that hypocrisy would be necessary? It is probable that others are not as hostile toward him as he imagines. Who is forcing him to defy them in a masked struggle? Is it not rather that, in his nostalgia for a long-lost "natural existence," he indulges himself in the myriad detours of perfect dissimulation? It feels good to say, even as he abandons himself to the pleasures of deception, that he is temporarily giving in to the rule of hypocrisy and that he is the victim of a harsh and nasty world. Sincerity will flourish only after a long struggle of one against all, but first he must conform to the obligatory laws of inauthenticity. Is this not a striking way of exonerating himself in order to persevere in crime? The deceiver regains grace in his own eyes by telling himself that he is merely living in a state of postponed sincerity, until he has won enough power to escape the constraints of society.

The case of Julien Sorel, in *The Red and The Black*, is the best example of this. In the provincial world of crooks like Valenod, the sensitive soul believes that immediate failure lies in store if it were naive enough to show itself as it really is. Overt solitary rebellion is tantamount to suicide. Instead one must conquer the possibility of being natural without being crushed. The commandment of sincerity cannot be obeyed unless it transforms itself into a commandment of success, and success requires deception. In a hostile world Ulysses cannot survive without a thousand ruses: "My name is Nobody." Thus Julien Sorel makes hypocrisy a temporary means, a provisional weapon, until such time as he is strong and rich enough to remove his mask and openly avow what he wants, what he thinks, and what he feels. The revelation of the true self is therefore simply postponed, delayed until success has been achieved. As we saw earlier, moreover, the Stendhalian hero achieves self-knowledge only by measuring himself against a scale of values defined in terms of *energy*, and only after engaging in perilous action. Thus there are two reasons to defer sincerity: one cannot know who one is until one has acted, and one may not show oneself as one is without obtaining power. One gains the right of self-discovery (in both senses of the word) only at the moment of success. (Whether or not authenticity is compromised by long familiarity with deceit is another question.)

Stendhal's rebellious heroes are therefore always involved in "high politics," because politics yields power. Since they do not accept the official values of the bourgeoisie, the Church, or the minor nobility, they are condemned always to play a double game. They can never openly defy society, but must murmur their challenge in the secrecy of the inner self, from the top of a tower or a lonely promontory. Yet it is presumably solely up to them whether or not to launch a frontal assault against the world they hate. Why not join the carbonari? Detest as they might the odious order they pretend to serve, Stendhal's heroes are not revolutionaries: they ask nothing of life but happiness. In 1820 the role of revolutionary offered no prospect of pleasure. Hence these heroes are content to sympathize with revolution, because its aim is to bring men the freedom that is a precondition of happiness. The Stendhalian hero is unwilling to link his fate to any person, not even for the most necessary of combats. He wants his own freedom, not that of others. Hence he will not fight to overthrow society, only to gain entry to it. His secret desire is to be accepted and recognized by men whom he can then turn around and despise openly. Living outside society, he seeks not to destroy it but to penetrate in order to dominate it. Knowing that society's high ground is invulnerable to frontal attack, the rebel shows his derision for the enemy by infiltrating its fortresses in the guise of a servant. After gaining control, he no longer cares about changing the order of things, since that order no longer oppresses him. He has outwitted all that threatened him: the police, public opinion, the temporal power of the clergy. Disrespect no longer runs the risk of incurring punishment, and for him that is enough. He has liberated himself; he does not seek to liberate others.

Success aside, Stendhal acted in just this way. How can he fail to be condemned to hypocrisy, since he places himself in a position where he cannot do without it? If he asks society to recognize him while holding it in contempt, he can only ask to be recognized for what he is not. This Jacobin needs to win a position on the Conseil d'Etat or a prefecture or a Legion of Honor in order to feel his strength, hence to merit his self-esteem and dare "to be himself." Thus he is condemned to play two separate games. He cannot win the wager of his inner life unless he immediately capitalizes on his winnings in the false social game. A man who thought of himself as a victim of an inner psychological division found in society conditions that encouraged and exacerbated his inner condition. He not only accepts those conditions but pretends to use them as a means for regaining possession of himself. He concentrates all the resources of his will, taking as his goal (or excuse) the need to prepare for the advent of an authenticity that he can finally avow.

Stendhal accuses society, but only because he first feels accused by it. From the first twinge of his timidity, the first moment of anxiety before the gaze of others, he feels condemned by a judgment brought in the name of "social values." He is ashamed not only of his body but of his common birth, his provincial bourgeois status. The stares of others bring home to him his social mediocrity, which he soon tries to deny by adopting an elegant style of dress and manner of life as well as a pseudonym with particule. Yet if he meets someone who knows of his Grenoble background, he feels dismally reduced to being no more than what he actually is.

Yet Stendhal lived at a time when it was not despicable to be bourgeois. On the contrary, the bourgeoisie was on the point of establishing itself in the highest positions, and soon it would erect itself as arbiter of the scale of social values. But Stendhal chose to be judged by an aristocratic society. It was by the nobility of the faubourg Saint-Germain that he felt himself condemned. Perhaps the explanation is to be sought in his childhood. In search of reasons to despise his father, he appealed to both Jacobin and aristocratic values. As a Jacobin he detested his father for his conservatism and legitimism. As an aristocrat, he could hate his father's pettiness, miserliness, and tedious moralism. Thus he was induced to play the noble lord, though well aware that he was far from belonging to the nobility himself and that, by his standards, most aristocratic salons were unbearably boring. Stendhal also exhibits a striking nostalgia for the libertine pleasures of the eighteenth-century nobility, which is to say, of a world in which he would have had no place. This was the world he revived when, ascribing anachronistic values to his own contemporaries, he felt that they judged him wanting in birth, prestige, and elegance. These were aristocratic values concerned exclusively with external appearances. There was no reason why they could not be simulated, since they were themselves a kind of sham. All that was needed was money and audacity.

Stendhal was thus led to shun his condition while dreaming of naturalness as of a promised land. The alienation he experienced initially he turned into a system intended to overcome all alienation. But such behavior required him to carry his distortion of self to an extreme, to the point where a kind of disintegration took place. There was tension in two directions. On the one hand, Stendhal had to become a stranger to himself in order to succeed in the world. On the other hand, he had to become a stranger to others, impenetrable to their gaze, in order to protect the secrecy of his inner life and of the demands he made on himself. If he needed a mask to play what he was not, he needed another mask to convince himself that he was not what he played. Stendhal hoped to convert this double discontinuity into a reconquered plenitude. The unity that he lacked initially was to be the reward for his masked activity. Through hypocritical action in which he shunned himself, he hoped to avoid external servitude. In this way he expected to "occupy a visible place" in the world while escaping the scrutiny of others. He would reconcile the pleasure of an external existence with that of exclusive possession of himself. (With exactly the same feelings and the same hopes, Julien Sorel is doomed to fail.)

Here we touch on an essential point concerning the psychology of masked existence, namely, that it is equivocal. The masked individual feels called to lose himself, to forget himself entirely, in the character he simulates; yet the mask enables him constantly to *feel* that he has another existence behind his appearance. Thus the hypocrite is conscious of being a person radically different from the person he appears to be. Just as we create an "interior" by erecting walls that separate us from the world, the masked man assumes possession of an inner life over which he alone has the right of scrutiny. He deepens his solitude, turning his inner life into an inviolable retreat. Hence, as Nietzsche was well aware, the mask is inextricably associated with individualism, which it serves as both an aggressive weapon and a defensive instrument. The more secretive the individual is, the more mysterious he sees himself become before the previously indifferent gaze of others. He ceases to be just anyone, and since others can no longer ignore his existence, he now feels able to approve himself. The actor, donning mask after mask, displays any number of different faces to the audience, but as a result he becomes acutely aware of the inner reality that he does not show. That reality is defined inwardly as an unlimited power to deny his mask, and through this negation the actor is violently restored to himself. (Rousseau, an accomplice in a persecution that obliged him to hide and to wear a mask, found therein all that he needed to satisfy the narcissism of "personal life.")

But the romantic individual, restored to himself, confirmed in his solitary singularity, protected by a mask that makes him impenetrable, suffers from being separated from the world and becomes an "unhappy consciousness," in Hegel's well-known terminology. He cannot persist in the haughty solitude that he had made his objective and must shed the hermetic identity that threatens to claim him for good. Once again he finds himself at odds with his desire. Having taken so much trouble to win the recognition of society, now he is obliged to count his success as worthless. He discovers that, having donned a mask in order to "arrive," he has gained recognition for being something he is not and is therefore constrained to accept the impossibility of revealing who he is; in the end his alienation remains. Reduced to his clandestine singularity, he cannot feel satisfaction. How can he escape this unhappy situation? Suicide (or a certain disdainful manner of seeking death) comes to represent the supreme disintegration of a freedom that shuns itself. The way in which Julien Sorel resorts to crime at the moment of his greatest success shows how intolerable to him that success really is. He achieves his truth and his triumph only in prison, where he is able to dominate both his own death and the world's vanity. At the moment of total rupture with the world, the imminence of death renders all masks futile; it supplants them. Finally it is possible for Julien to be himself—absurdly, magnificently himself. One might even say that his will to power reveals itself in the final moment as an absolute will to liberation. Having subjugated others, it can achieve fulfillment only by escaping its own domination and hurling itself joyfully into the jaws of death.

Stendhal's personal experience does not attain such extremes of violence, however. The sacrifice is carried out solely by the literary hero, via the detour of fiction. For Stendhal things take a different course. He is willing to allow the play to go on, alternating between escape and return to self. He deceives others by retreating into himself, and he escapes from himself by fleeing toward others. Hence he must again avail himself of the mask, sometimes to defend himself against others, sometimes to avoid being imprisoned behind the walls of the ego. The desire to be everyone constantly counterbalances the desire to be himself. Inner retreat offers but a momentary repose followed by renewed efforts to expand through the multiplicity of possibilities.

To be One, to be All: a double ambition that reveals a rivalry with

God. The hallmark of the creature's rebellion is that ultimately it claims individuality by rejecting all individuation: "My name is Legion," says the Rebel. Stendhal—in spirit the consummate atheist, regicide, and parricide—refuses incarnation in the Christian sense in order to become the master of his incarnations. As is well known, he liked to sign his letters Mephistopheles. Yet he was too tranquilly, too definitively an atheist to have persisted in his struggle against God. Stendhal's satanism never sheds its smile. He is not God's rival, for his real conflict is with society. In attacking priests and clerical institutions, he strikes out at the social figure of Christianity and insults God only through his temporal representatives. But other rebels will come for whom mask and metamorphosis will be indispensable, and this time for a savage struggle: "I am the son of man and woman, according to what people have told me. That astonishes me . . . I thought I was something more." The words are Maldoror's. He continues: "I cover my branded face with a piece of velvet as black as the soot in a fireplace. Eyes must not be witness to the ugliness that the Supreme Being, with a smile of impotent hatred, inflicted on me." And finally: "Metamorphosis never seemed to me in any way different from the great and magnanimous reverberation of a perfect happiness that I had long anticipated."[18]

Stendhal's mask threatens not God but the bourgeois order and the authority of Catholicism. Sometimes it is an instrument for unmasking the wickedness and greed of others. But above all it is a device that serves two contradictory ambitions: on the one hand to cling narrowly to the self, on the other to flee the self blithely. This an endless game, which seizes on each partial failure as an opportunity to begin anew. Both ambitions face insuperable obstacles, but each sustains the other and indefatigably recommences the experiment. Anyone who wishes to cling to himself eventually discovers that escape is inevitable, for the future is unpredictable and unavoidable. And he who wishes to flee himself must recognize that he can never succeed, because the past always catches up with him and reminds him of the unity of his life and his "history." Stendhal cannot sacrifice either his zest for the multiplicity of possibilities that beckon from the future nor his desire to find his "true" self. Hence he must *live* the contradiction. Through fiction, through dreams of possibilities, and through pseudonyms he will attempt to flee himself; yet he will never throw off the bonds that link him to an unsatisfactory identity. Through autobiography and intimate writings he will seek the formula of a durable unity without ever finding it. Alternately centrifugal and centripetal, this double movement achieves a rather surprising human success precisely because it is double. In the interval the mask offers an unfair advantage in the competition with time. It introduces a burst of discontinuity into life and makes it possible not only to possess an imaginary power but also to "breathe" an imaginary time. Therein lies yet another contradiction that gives zest to Stendhal's work (and life): in theory a mechanist and determinist, he uses the mask as a talisman that emancipates him from all determinations and "concatenations of causes." As a result Stendhal's psychology, far from being naturalist and realist, is perhaps one of the most magical in all literature.

Although each of the deep-seated tendencies in Stendhal is doomed to failure, the unwitting obverse of such failure is success. Each of his movements paradoxically culminates in his obtaining what the contrary movement desired. Escape from the self constantly leads back to quest for the self and vice versa. In trying to find himself, Stendhal was obliged to admit that somehow he always managed to slip away. Yet when he deliberately took flight, when he threw himself into the compensatory images of fiction, he found perhaps his deepest self, for his gaze was no longer focused inward. He who seeks to find himself is lost; he who consents to be lost finds himself. Stendhal's work lives on its paradox, which is to be both an effort of self-knowledge and a flight from self into "tender and mad" imagination; to be traversed by the contrary tendencies of alienation and knowledge, of metamorphosis and sincerity; and, finally, to be the work of a man who wished to be, more than is allowed, both inward and alienated.

4   The Critical Relation

The recent debate over critical method may have been salutary in that it obliged the participants to formulate their theoretical positions in clear terms. No one can complain about this sharpening of views, even at the price of the occasional polemical outburst. Any positive statement of position throws light, if not always on the fundamental problems, then at least on those contentious issues that, despite fashion or because of it, reveal the conflicts and perplexities of the moment.

Theory, method: two terms that, though not identical in scope, are rather too often treated as if they were interchangeable. Neither is perfectly unambiguous. *Theory*, in one sense, is a predictive hypothesis concerning the nature or internal structure of the object under investigation. Then it is correct to say that in the natural sciences theory necessarily precedes discovery. Yet in another sense, closer to the word's etymology, theory refers to the intelligent contemplation of a previously investigated whole, a general view of a system governed by some intelligible order. In the literary domain "theoretical" consideration of past production is therefore largely influenced by the equally "theoretical" project of work to come. We decipher the past in such a way as to make it culminate necessarily in a future preordained by our will. Wishing to continue and outdo the work of our antecedents, we ascribe to them an orientation in conformity with our wishes, indeed at times in conformity with our illusions. Thus history receives from us the meaning to which we claim to subordinate it. Critical *method*, on the other hand, refers sometimes to the careful codification of certain technical *means* and sometimes, in a broader sense, to a meditation on what the *ends* of criticism ought to be, without dogmatic insistence on the choice of means.

In any event, the current debate seems to me to come rather late in the day. If there is such a thing as "new criticism," it produced no manifesto to announce its arrival. It began by seeking to understand

and explain works of literature in its own fashion. Only after it had done so was it asked to explain itself. Both prosecution and defense issued statements of principle and discourses on method, couched in suitable tones of apology or accusation. Some distortion may have occurred. The theoretical manifestoes produced were not indispensable prerequisites of critical work but responses to a variety of contingencies (although it would not be wrong to see in those contingencies a hidden necessity). Their purpose was to make explicit or "thematize" rules tacitly observed in applied criticism. To be sure, such a posteriori legitimation and statements of principle have served as a stimulus. In our field, theorization of method can be seen as the fruit of long practical labors, hence as a prerequisite for further practical advance. There is a close relation between methodological reflection and active investigation; each supports, and is modified by, the other.

The foregoing remarks are intended to establish the place of methodological self-consciousness in literary criticism. For criticism to be successful, it is by no means essential that methodological rules be granted peremptory authority and unquestioned priority; a marginal role suits them just as well. As the study of texts progresses and results are obtained, methodological reflection accompanies the critic's work, illuminates it indirectly, is informed by it, and corrects its errors. But methodology can truly be made explicit only in epilogue, even if for expository or pedagogical purposes it sometimes usurps the place of the preface.

To be sure, the critic cannot confine his attention exclusively to the *particular case* of a body of work or an author. Critical discourse must educate itself, and it must adapt itself as circumstances require. Method is not simply an intuitive groping guided solely by guesswork and modified to suit the occasion. It is not enough to bring to each work the specific response that it seems to anticipate. To do so would be to limit criticism to the role of providing a sensitive echo, an intellectualized reflection of the work, docilely obedient to the uniquely seductive qualities of each individual text. Criticism, oblivious of the ultimate unity toward which it must strive, would thus abandon itself to the diverse blandishments of the many forms encountered along the way. It would merely take note of the diversity of literary works—regarded as so many worlds to be visited one after another—rather than elaborate a unitary vision within which that diversity would be available for comprehension as such. All good criticism has its share of verve, instinct, and improvisation, its strokes of luck and states of grace. But it cannot rely on them alone. It needs more solid principles to guide it (but without constraint), to point the way to its proper object. Even if those guiding principles are not part of a preexisting code, they are still necessary. They prevent wild deviation. They establish the *textual* point of departure. And they oblige the critic to adjust his step to the step before and the stride to come. Method is hidden in the style of the critical approach and does not become fully apparent until the journey is complete. In an apparent paradox, method cannot be formulated conceptually until it has discharged its function and become all but useless. The critic becomes fully aware of his method only when he retraces his steps. Here, by method I mean both meditation on the ends of criticism and codification of the means.

If criticism is knowledge (value judgments having been almost completely eliminated from today's criticism in favor of interpretive comprehension), then surely it must strive, beyond knowledge of the particular, toward generalization of its discoveries. Simultaneously it must achieve self-understanding or, better still, self-determination in view of its own ends. Each particular work on which it focuses attention is but a step toward a more subtle and comprehensive understanding of the universe of literary language. Criticism works toward a theory (in the sense of *theoria*, intellectual contemplation) of literature. The generalization of critical knowledge remains perpetually in flux, however. Criticism profits by recognizing that it is incomplete, by retracing its steps, by recommencing its efforts so as to ensure that every reading is an *unanticipated* reading, a simple encounter unencumbered by the shadow of any systematic premeditation or doctrinal preconception.

From naive reception to encompassing comprehension, from unbiased reading governed by the internal laws of the work to autonomous reflection upon the work and the history of which it is a part: there is no notion to which I cling more firmly than that of a *critical trajectory*—a trajectory that need not be inscribed in the critical work itself and may be located in the preparatory labors of which the critical work is the culmination. The critical trajectory traverses a series of sometimes discontinuous planes and touches many different levels of reality. Naturally I include under the notion of critical trajectory that of the "hermeneutic circle," which is simply a special case, albeit a particularly successful one.

I am not here advocating any particular method, if by method one means the automatic operation of a self-propelled mechanism. Every method offers a certain scope and thus establishes a plane of investigation for which it is best suited. Every method predetermines certain coordinates and assumes certain relations of homogeneity and congruence among the elements it envisions. For each plane of investigation there is a preferred method, and the fewer the number of auxiliary variables, the more rigorous the method: precision here is a direct function of limitation of scope. No matter what importance we may ascribe to certain techniques, we must concede that there is *no rigorous method for treating the transition from one plane to another*, that is, from the competence of one technique to the competence of another. Yet this transition is the crucial motor of the critical trajectory: it is controlled by the requirements of comprehension and totality. Thus philology is indispensable for establishing scrupulously accurate texts and determining precise definitions for words in their historical context. Any interpretation, no matter how ingenious, that fails to meet the requirements of philological rigor will be literally without foundation. Yet methods useful for establishing a text and working out the semantics of its vocabulary yield only primary information that must be subjected to further interpretive elaboration guided by methods whose orientation is quite different.

As critical work proceeds, in other words, the relation to the work changes. The fact I wish to emphasize is this: progress in research is not linked solely to the discovery of objective elements on any given plane; it does not consist exclusively in a scrupulous inventory of the parts of the work and analysis of their aesthetic interrelations. Beyond these things there must come a change in the relation between the critic and the work—a change thanks to which the work reveals its various aspects, and thanks to which critical consciousness conquers itself, moving from heteronomy to autonomy. Now change means flexibility. In each temporary *state* of the critic's relation to the work, awareness of the limitations of that state suggest the possibility of a new relation and consequently a different description of the work. A variable and flexible relation is by no means unstable or unsteady: all effort is directed toward gradual expansion of the scope of knowledge and range of intelligibility. And if, in the submissiveness of a naive reception, in the *empathy* of first hearing, I try to identify quite closely with the law of the work, what I learn from objective study of that law enables me to contemplate it from outside, to compare it to other works and other laws, and to formulate a discourse *about* the work that is more than a mere elaboration of the discourse immanent *in* it. Do I thereby estrange myself from the work? Of course, for I am no longer a docile reader, and my trajectory is no longer governed by that of the work itself: I detach myself from it, I swerve aside, in order to follow my own course. Yet my new course maintains a definite relation to the work with which I previously identified. The distance I have conquered can now be seen as a condition that must be satisfied if I am to meet the work rather than just acquiesce in it. A complete work of criticism always retains memory of the initial docility, but rather than adopt submissively the direction of the work being analyzed, it chooses a course of its own so as to *intersect* with the work at a crucial point. Where the two trajectories meet, a new light is born.

If critical reflection describes one kind of arc or trajectory, the literary work describes another. The shifting relations between a singular consciousness and the world establishes, through the medium of language, a system of variables that determines the trajectory of the work. Even for the naive reader, the work is *discourse* or *narrative thread* or poetic *flux*. It unfolds, according to its own inner proclivities and rhythms, between a beginning and an end. An event takes place in a series of linked sentences. But that event remains within the universe of words. Its specific mode of action, its intrinsic manner of acting, involves a "subsumption in words" (*disparition élocutoire*) of actions and passions. The fundamental paradox of literature is that it is a celebration (or profanation) of language—a kindled relationship, in other words, established by means of "elocutory" transposition, which implies the emergence, free and autonomous, of the element of pure language, hence also a *suspended relationship*. As soon as we isolate the substance of the word or sentence rather than try to apprehend its message, we cease to worry about our immediate interests and establish an interest of a different order, related to the exercise of the imagination. Thus there takes shape, in absence, a domain more remote than any other, yet endowed with the power to add to reality so as to move us more than any event in the world.

The unfolding of the language of the work produces an effect within the reader. As reader, I am immediately certain of that effect. My emotions, my internal sensations, my perplexity faithfully trace the work's current profile. Any subsequent description must preserve the memory of this primary fact, so as to bring to it, if possible, a supplementary clarity. To be sure, the work has an independent material consistency. It subsists on its own; it exists without me. Yet as Georges Poulet has so aptly remarked, it needs a consciousness in order to fulfill its destiny; it summons me to reveal its existence; it is predestined to find a receptive consciousness in which to realize its potential. It awaits actualization. Prior to my reading, the work is merely an inert object. Yet I am allowed to revert to the multiplicity of objective signs of which the work is composed, for I know that in them I will find the material basis for the sensations, perplexities, and emotions I felt while reading. Since I wish to understand the conditions in which my feelings were aroused, there is no reason not to turn to the objective structures that determined them. In order to do that, I need not renounce my emotion, but I must enclose it, as it were, in parentheses, for I am resolved to make an objective study of that system of signs whose evocative magic I have so far endured without resistance and without reflective examination. The signs have seduced me; they are the bearers of a meaning that has taken shape within me. Far from rejecting the seduction, far from forgetting the primary revelation of meaning, I seek to understand them, to "thematize" them for my own thought. My only hope of success is to establish a close connection between meaning and its verbal substrate, between seduction and its formal basis.

At this point it becomes useful to undertake an "immanent" study of the objective characteristics of the text: composition, style, images, semantic values. I may explore the work's complex *internal structure* and decipher as precisely as possible its order and law. I may examine the interdependence of structure and effect, the pragmatic pattern aimed at the reader. Contemplating the objective face of the work, I find that not even the most trivial detail, not even the most minor element of the text, fails to contribute in some way to the constitution of meaning. Significant relations turn up not only among values of the same kind (elements of style, composition, or sonority, say) but also between values of different kinds (elements of composition are unexpectedly confirmed by elements of style, and the latter, particularly in poetry, are obviously enhanced by their phonic substrate). Taken together, these sets of correlations—which one might call the *structure* of the work—constitute a system (or "organism") so laden with meaning that it would be idle to persist in distinguishing between "subjective" and "objective" components of the work. Form is not the external cloak of "content" or a seductive appearance behind which a more precious reality may be dissimulated. For the reality of thought consists in being appearance (*être apparaissante*): writing is not a dubious proxy for inner experience but the experience itself. Thus the "structural" approach helps to overcome a sterile antinomy: it makes us see meaning in its incarnation and "objective" material in its "spiritual" implications. It forbids us to abandon the *realized* work in order to search for the psychological experience behind it (the prior *Erlebnis*). Thus in recent structuralist criticism, the traditional dualism of thought and expression has been replaced by a monism of writing. A work reveals itself to us as a novel system of reciprocal relations defined by its "form," a system that appears to be closed to all that is not included within it; yet beyond a certain level of complexity it allows us to glimpse a combinatorial *infinity* of correlations, experienced by the reader as a kind of vertigo and revealed by the successive variations of the critical point of view (also virtually without limit). The task of criticism is then to stay with immanent analysis while striving to complete an impossible toting up of partial accounts, which are not to be left isolated but integrated to disclose the structural unity that governs the internal relations among the constituent elements of the work.

To proceed in this way is to treat the work as if it were a world governed by a law unto itself. It would be ill advised, however, to neglect for too long the fact that the work is a world contained within a larger world, and that it presents itself not only alongside other literary works but also in company with other realities and institutions not essentially literary in nature. Even if I decline to seek the *law* of the work outside itself (in its psychological sources, cultural antecedents, and so on), I cannot ignore how what is in the work implicitly or explicitly, positively or negatively, relates to the world outside. What is the nature of this relationship? A world within a world, the work may seem to be a microcosmic reflection of the universe into which it was born. The relations I discover within the work would then be reproduced faithfully outside it, in the larger world of which it is but one element. If so, I may feel convinced that the work's internal law is but a symbolic abridgment of the collective law of the moment and cultural milieu within which it was produced. Having grafted the work onto its context, I then look on as organic meanings burgeon, in the expectation that deciphering the work will reveal a "period style" and vice versa.

In some of its more radical manifestations, contemporary structur-

alism seems to admit this possibility, seeking to dissolve the work in
culture and society, not in order to discern behind all works a specific
determinism but to bring to light a *logos* or dialectical relation
common to all synchronic manifestations of a given culture or society.
As Sartre has observed, the result of this is a species of positivism
(almost a "Taine-ism") minus the causality, whose chief concern is to
substitute descriptive rigor for causal explanation, with description
drawing support from either formal codification or phenomenology.
Such a method may reasonably hope to succeed whenever it deals
with a stable, almost immutable culture, all of whose elements
maintain functional relations of a particular nature among themselves
in such a way as to perpetuate the established cultural equilibrium. In
other words, a radical structuralism is fully adequate only for
studying a disciplined literature in a disciplined society. Hence it
should come as no surprise that structuralism has yielded its most
satisfactory results in the study of primitive myths and folk tales.
Radical structuralism (by which I mean structuralism that "contex-
tualizes" works and society) proves inadequate the moment the
cultural equilibrium is disrupted. To see that this has happened, of
course, one has to know the nature of the disturbed equilibrium, and
structuralism can be of inestimable service in establishing the features
of an *order* prior to a change it has been unable to resist. The moment
philosophy arrogates to itself the right to question (not necessarily to
challenge) the foundations of institutions and traditions; the moment
that poetic language ceases to be confined by the rules of a well-
defined game, or ceases to be the exorcism of transgression and
becomes transgression itself; then culture acquires a historical dimension that cannot easily be accommodated even within the limits of a
generalized structuralism. The old normative criticism, which defined
genera dicendi, poetic genres, figures, and meters, attempted to
subject literature to the dominion of *rule*. But law, as the apostle Paul
said, presupposes sin, and rules presuppose the possibility of infraction.

When it comes to dealing with modern works, structuralism's more
sweeping cultural ambitions must perforce be limited, and its approach relativized. It is useful to study literary works as systems of
signifiers, wholes composed of cooperating parts. But works and
societies are not parts of the homogeneous texture of a single *logos*.

The language of a literary work and the language of the surrounding culture are not consubstantial and cannot simply be spliced together to make way for a unitary and coherent system of meanings. There is no need to point out that most great modern works relate to the world by declaring their rejection of it, their opposition or challenge to it. The task of "immanent" criticism is to discover within the literary text, in its "style" as well as in its explicit "thesis," the various signs of scandal, deviation, opposition, derision, and indifference that it may contain—in other words, all that makes the contemporary work of genius a monstrosity or exception from the standpoint of the culture that produced it and, later on, of the public that acclaimed it. We thus discover a striking multiplicity of meaning: elements that, through their relation to one another, contribute to the internal organic consistency of the work when viewed from another angle maintain an oppositional, polemical relation with previous literature or with the surrounding society. To say this is merely to recall a simple truth. *The Red and the Black*, for example, is both a work of art governed by formal, internal relations and a critique of French Restoration society. Elements that establish a *harmony* within the work are also sources of *disharmony*. It is important both to read the internal harmony and to recognize the extent of the writer's disharmony in the broader context established by the work and its "background." When we compare it with its surroundings, the work is a *concordia discors*, a compatibility of incompatibles, in which the positivity of the relations that constitute its material form is combined with a negativity aroused by its boundless expansiveness.

To put it another way, immanent structures are intertwined with a network of relations that set the work against an *exterior* that it transcends and by which it is transcended. The inner tensions that are the life of the literary object encompass "destructuring" forces, which can be understood only if the work is viewed in relation to its origins, its ultimate effects, and its milieu. Here, however, the principal clues do not come from outside but are found in the works themselves, provided one knows how to read them.

The "modern" writer in his work denies, transcends, and transforms himself, just as he contradicts the cogency of the surrounding reality on behalf of injunctions of desire, hope, and rage. To understand a work in its intrinsic intricacy therefore leads to questions about its differential relationship with its immediate context: by making himself the author of this work, a man made himself someone other than he was previously; in coming into the world, moreover, the work obliges its readers to alter their consciousness of themselves and of their world. Thus the "existential" dimension of the work is restored, the psychological and sociological dimension from which we abstracted in order to investigate the work's internal structure. We come back to this historical dimension now because the structure brings us back to it. Even though we have chosen not to look to psychology or sociology for *sufficient* conditions to explain the work of literature, we may still look to these disciplines for *necessary* conditions of the work's genesis and reception. The structured quality of the work implies a structuring subject, as well as a culture to which the work adds its own contribution, usually in the form of agitation or defiance. At the same time, we encounter problems traditionally treated by literary history. The quality of the work as *event* also reappears, an event arising from one consciousness and finding its fulfillment in other consciousnesses by way of publication and interpretation. Thus there is a transition to the work (inscribed, with greater or lesser clarity, in the work itself), just as there is also a transition from the work to the world. Though I know that I have no access to the author *prior* to his work, I have the right and duty to interrogate him *in* his work by asking the question, Who is speaking? And I must immediately ask myself to whom the work is addressed: to what real, imaginary, collective, unique, or absent audience. To whom or before whom are these words spoken? Across what distance? Over what obstacles? By what means? Only at this point does the work's full trajectory become apparent to me, because now I can supplement the textual trajectory with an *intentional trajectory* implicit in it. (Ancient rhetoric knew the essentials of this process.) The "structural" study of form—which brings to light the *how* of the work's construction—retains its central value, but it is no longer necessary to regard the work's internal structure as the only object of significance: the *fixed* elements of the book or page are traversed by a *flux*. In the very way in which spoken language (*parole*) relates to codified language (*langue*), I make out its relation to what is not yet or no longer language, before the work's inception or after its publication. Structuralism's purview is limited by the fact that this flux does not flow through the homogeneous and continuous "medium" of linguistic patterns. Points of discontinuity emerge, the most important of which is that of the transition from silence to language, the recourse to literature and to the imagination. There is no modern work that does not contain within it the sign or justification of its own coming into the world. (Proust's novel is here the prime example, but to an alert enough reader Montaigne's *Essays* are no less revealing.) One must decipher *within the work* the specific nature of a desire or power (or genius) that sought to discover itself and give proof of its existence by giving birth to the work. Again, this is a discontinuity that we can bring to light by viewing, as Leo Spitzer did, an author's personality in relation to a system of deviations and differences (syntactic, lexicological, etc.) relative to the "average" language of the cultural moment, deviations best exemplified in the exorbitant excess of certain extreme works, despite the fact that the culture later reclaims, or attempts to reclaim, these for the common language, most notably by way of critical interpretation. This raises the question of the work as *exception* (or *monster*), the sign of an individual asserting his unique and incomparable nature in a possibly irrefragable act of rebellion, which, because it resorts to language, also runs the risk of losing the benefit of its rebellion; of being tamed by interpretive understanding, which subsumes the exceptional under what Kierkegaard called the "general," that is, the order of what is rationally universalizable. For all their radical strangeness, perhaps even because of their radical strangeness, scandalous works become *exemplary*, paradigmatic.

This brings us back to a problem raised earlier. I said we did not want a literary criticism content to be only a plural echo of the plurality of literary worlds. But doesn't the *generalization* of critical discourse result in another kind of risk? In speaking of what is fractured and discontinuous in literary works, we develop the diaphanous and continuous discourse of knowledge. We smoothe things out. Turbulent irregularity, scandal, contradiction within and among works, the very strangeness of the literary chimera become themes of a calm and coherent discourse, which incorporates into a fabric of comprehension the very rips it reveals, thereby abolishing them. Critical discourse unifies the field it investigates, and the more it seeks a unity of its own, the more different it becomes from the multiple and fragmented reality it deals with. As Maurice Blanchot points out, given a choice between culture, which strives for the unification and universalization of rational discourse, and literature, which proclaims refusal and incompatibility, criticism customarily (and culpably) takes the side of culture. The great rebel works are thus betrayed. Through commentary and gloss they are exorcised, made acceptable, and added to the common patrimony. To be sure, the Hegelian tradition that still sustains us encourages us to regard the great acts of rebellion as so many moments in the becoming of spirit; by the very fact of having appeared, of not having been reduced to silence and obscurity, they cannot escape a gaze eager to embrace the whole of the real. But scrupulous critical comprehension does not seek to assimilate the dissimilar. It would not be comprehension if it failed to comprehend difference qua difference or if it failed to extend that comprehension to itself and its relation to other works. Critical discourse knows that in its essence it is *different* from the discourse of the works it investigates and explains. It is no more an extension or echo of the work than it is a rational substitute. By preserving consciousness of its difference from, hence its relation to, the work, criticism avoids the risk of monologue. Were it to extend the work, speak *like* the work, ratify its meaning, it would talk only to itself. Conversely, were it to substitute for the work or speak in its place, it would close upon its own coherence and never go beyond tautology, just as certain supposedly scientific techniques prove nothing more than that by starting from certain assumptions one infallibly obtains certain results. A tool that is capable of working only one material finds no material other than the one it is capable of working, thus creating the illusion that no other tool is conceivable.

The solitude of critical discourse is the great pitfall to be avoided. Too subservient to the work and criticism shares its solitude. Too independent and it follows a singular and solitary course, so that the critical reference ceases to be more than an accidental pretext, which in strict rigor ought to be eliminated. Idolizing scientific rigor, criticism is imprisoned by those "facts" that fit its chosen method. It becomes bogged down and ceases to progress. Each of these dangers can be defined as a loss of the critical relationship, of the duality and dialogue that can be achieved only if the critic's voice is clearly different. Paraphrase, autonomous "poem," and scrupulous inventory all reduce criticism to monody. Yet each of these dangers ceases to be a danger when it becomes a *moment* in the becoming of thought. The work must be listened to. We must make ourselves one with it and repeat it in ourselves. All objectifiable facts must be rigorously established (using whatever "techniques" are available). But those facts must then be freely interpreted, whereupon we become aware that for all their apparent objectivity, the facts are the product of a prior interpretive selection. Spontaneous sympathy, objective study, and free reflection are the three coordinated moments that allow criticism to profit from the immediate certainty of reading, the verifiability of "scientific" technique, and the rational plausibility of interpretation. The critical trajectory so far as possible runs the gamut between *accepting everything* (through sympathy) and *situating everything* (through comprehension). In this way we can be sure that the internal law of critical discourse remains closely related to the internal law of the work under analysis, moving from an admiring dependency to an attentive independence. Our autonomy (without which no explanation is possible) derives from our freedom to vary our relation to the invariant reality of the work, which doesn't preclude openness. Subjective estrangement is not incompatible with heightened interest and attention. Only if this condition is met can criticism wed the work and avoid becoming a "celibate machine." The acceptance of difference is the condition of any authentic encounter.

Admittedly the critic is never more than the prince consort of poetry, and the offspring of their union cannot inherit the throne. This marriage, moreover, is subject to the dangers of all marriages, and we know that there are several kinds of neurotic couples. Among them is the marriage in which the alleged beloved is not recognized in his or her truth, in his or her quality as a free and independent subject. The beloved is merely the object of projections of amorous desire that make him or her other than he or she really is. Another type of neurotic couple is one in which the lover is reduced to nothingness through fascination and absolute submission to the beloved object. Yet a third type is the couple in which love is directed not to the person of the beloved but to his or her circumstances and appurtenances: property, illustrious ancestors, what have you. In short, the work of criticism links two personal truths and is sustained by the preservation of their integrity.

Nevertheless, I must not forget that the work's mode of existence differs radically from my own. The work is a person only if I cause it to live as one. My reading must breathe life into the work so as to endow it with the presence and appearances of personality. I must bring the work back to life in order to love it; I must make it speak in order to respond to it. I must take account of the fact that many illustrious "works," such as Proust's late novels, are really nothing more than drafts. Hence one might say that the work always begins as "our dearly departed," awaiting resurrection through us, or if not resurrection then at least the most vivid possible evocation. The conjugal conceit that I used to describe the critical act failed to respect the intrinsic imaginary dimension of every literary work—so I shall fall back on the image of the Orphic quest, or of the Homeric *Nekuia*, in which the hero, standing near the blood of the sacrificial animal, conjures up shades that reveal their destiny and instruct him as to which route he must follow in order to realize his own. (Ulysses consults the dead in order to ensure that his own voyage will end happily.) Hermes, conductor of souls and patron of hermeneutics, is the god who crosses the divide between two worlds and restores to presence what had been swallowed up by absence or oblivion.

For the moment I am not speaking in particular of any of the currently controversial forms of criticism: sociological criticism, psychological criticism, thematic or phenomenological criticism, or linguistic criticism. These new approaches, which supplement rather than supplant the traditional historical approach, derive from the possibility and the need to extend to literature the various disciplines of the human sciences. Experiments with new critical methods have borne fruit in more than one way, not only because the human sciences approach literature from a new angle and reveal previously hidden aspects or implications, but also because in this area science is obliged to look not just at *average* group behavior but at what is freest and most inventive in man. Hence each discipline must test its explanatory powers through application to an extreme example, an exception, thereby revealing its strengths and weaknesses perhaps better than would be possible in any other way. Each investigator must question the validity of his arguments and proofs and the extent of his competence; he must ask if the causal factors he adduces are sufficient or merely necessary. And he must question the importance of the correlations he discovers within the context of the whole. In short, it is essential that the researcher learn to judge the relevance of his results and the degree to which they adequately characterize the object of investigation. Such judgment, I think, does not fall within the purview of scientific technique; it cannot be derived from any method. It is the user of the method who must decide—at his own risk and without benefit of any preestablished technique—whether or not the method has yielded satisfactory results, whether or not it has enabled him to explain the *meaning* of the work.

In the most rigorous scientific disciplines, methods are transformed and refined only because they are criticized in unforeseen ways as a result of experience or of conflict between theories. If the new methods prove valuable in the study of literature, the ability to furnish a critique of method will prove even more valuable. Therein lies the purest manifestation of the critical spirit. Once again, vigilance must be exercised at more than one level. Beyond the primary critique of method, aimed at perfecting a given tool, a freer, more sovereign form of critique is also needed. Its job is to assign to each specialized tool its proper role in order to secure the desired unity of knowledge. One might call this job of ordering "philosophical"; it requires comprehensive consideration of all aspects of the work using all the specialized tools available. Then each work can be studied by the means appropriate to it. Rather than attempt to impose the same approach on all literature, we can let each poem or book indicate the most suitable means of access. The more truly cultivated a critic is, the better he is able to recognize the changes that the very notion of a literary work has been subjected to over the course of history. The status of the work is of course a primary fact, and any interpretation of the work should be appropriate to it.

If I had to define the ideal criticism, I would say it was one that combined methodological rigor (based on verifiable techniques and procedures) with reflective openness (free of all systematic constraint). Technique, by nature repetitive, carves out homogeneous slices of the work and reveals what might be called its "objective face." Each technique yields an incomplete picture of the work. Once perfected, techniques are readily taught; they can be mastered by anyone who wishes to devote the necessary effort to learning them. They are common property, and so are the results obtained with their help. As far as technique is concerned, one trained investigator is as good as another. Technique "depersonalizes" scrupulous users. "Teamwork" is not only possible but desirable, for it permits a more rapid accumulation of information. In theory a technique can be reduced to a mechanical procedure; all or part of the work could in principle be carried out by a machine. The work of the assistant is then qualitatively no different from that of the master. The disciple can take over at any point without compromising the result.

The work of choosing and modifying techniques, and even more

of interpreting the facts brought to light by using them, is another
thing entirely. It is a matter of *reflection* and aims for a far broader
kind of generality than that obtainable through technical craft.
Reflection also seeks to establish a more specific relation with each
work studied. It aims to be both more comprehensive and more
subtle. It is willing to start at a more humble place, from zero
knowledge, total ignorance, in order to arrive at a broader
comprehension, for which the material and formal aspects revealed
by technique are but fragmentary data, incomplete findings in need
of interpretation. What reflection perceives and elaborates it
communicates, but it cannot inculcate; it makes use of rational
persuasion, contradiction, and discussion—but no one can claim,
except by a kind of imposture, to continue the thought of another
critic, to carry on his research. Free reflection is condemned,
precisely because it is free, always to begin anew. Teaching in this
respect consists not so much in the transmission of a certain body of
instrumental technique as in the exhortation to make use of a liberty
that must in each case be reinaugurated. Far be it from me, however,
to suggest the absurd notion that criticism is a kind of Sisyphean
labor, always to be recommenced. The commencement of free
reflection is an *enlightened* beginning. In theory no prior research or
technical result is ignored; the critic need not begin ex nihilo.

Yet even so, reflection must find its own way, invent its own
procedures, from beginning to end. One can inherit results accumulated by means of "objective" techniques, but one's guiding concept
is inherited from no one, not even oneself. A critical inspiration is
required, and its source and development cannot be predicted. If
criticism is to be up to all of its tasks, if it is to be a comprehensive
discourse about works of literature, then it cannot remain within the
confines of verifiable knowledge. It must become a work of literature
in its own right, and incur the risks associated with any such work.
Hence it will bear the stamp of a personality, but a personality that
has been subjected to the impersonal ascetic discipline of "objective"
knowledge and scientific technique. It will be knowledge about
language incorporated into a new language of its own, an analysis of
the poetic "event" that becomes an event in its own right. By delving
into the material substance of the work, by exploring the details of its
construction, its formal makeup, its inner harmonies and extrinsic
relations, criticism enhances its capacity to recognize the trace of an
action. Rehearsing that action in its own way, it judges and thereby

bestows upon it a heightened meaning, a product of its internal truth and external correlations, its explicit content and implicit consequences. Criticism thus becomes an action in its own right. It makes a statement, it communicates, so that in the posterity it creates it may receive an answer in the form of other actions still more limpid and sovereign.

5   Psychoanalysis and
Literary Understanding

In 1907 Freud published in the first issue of *Schriften zur angewandten Seelenkunde* his study of "Delusions and Dreams in Jensen's *Gradiva*." In a period when the principal elements of psychoanalytic theory were still being worked out, psychoanalysis had already turned its attention to literary works. Was the intention initially to use the analytical method as a "disinterested" tool of literary criticism? Certainly not. Freud was more interested in giving new proofs of the validity of his theory. Having begun with an explanation of hysteria and moved on to the study of dreams, slips of the tongue, puns, and sexuality, he had developed a unified doctrine subject to subsequent modification but already applicable, in Freud's view, to the normal human being as well as the neurotic. Psychoanalysts, with Freud leading the way, became convinced very early on that they held the key to a general interpretation of culture. They therefore sought to demonstrate the value of their method by applying it in all fields where psychological explanation seemed necessary: to works of art, myths, religions, primitive societies, and daily life in modern countries. No human activity or institution, no product of the imagination, was in principle beyond the reach of a science that traced human behavior back to its source, to its first causes, and claimed to provide unsurpassed understanding of the reasons for men's actions.

Jensen's short novel *Gradiva* is full of dreams. Freud undertakes to show that these dreams can be interpreted by means of psychoanalysis and that the sequence of their development makes it seem that the novelist intuitively understood the dream processes first set forth in Freud's *Traumdeutung* (1900). Fiction is thus called to testify on behalf of psychology. This testimony is particularly valuable because actual collusion was impossible. Even though Jensen knew none of Freud's writings, he nevertheless established between dream images and latent desires the very relation, at once dissimulating and revealing, to which Freud had so forcefully called attention. Thus the truth of psychoanalysis found one more confirmation. It proved its "operational" value in a field quite remote from the psychiatric clinic. Psychoanalysis therefore profited from this demonstration as much as literature. The same can be said of Freud's applications of his method to problems of anthropology and sociology. He showed that he could throw new light on the evolution of society or on the contemporary crisis of civilization. Along the way he borrowed from sociology and ethnology concepts that he would later incorporate into psychoanalytic theory. The notion of the "primitive horde" (which specialists today consider rather debatable) soon ceased to be a thing *to be explained* and became in Freud's eyes the archaic principle of a *historical (phylogenetic) explanation* of the Oedipal adventure, to be repeated in the development of each individual (ontogeny recapitulates phylogeny). Thus, when psychoanalysis began to look for areas outside its own domain (neurosis and hysteria) to which its theories might apply, it was not content simply to propose explanations and suggest interpretations. Rather, it borrowed material to be incorporated into its own edifice. It enriched itself, *instructed itself*, at least as much as it shed light on the foreign object.

In considering what psychoanalysis might contribute to literature, we are therefore led to turn the question around, to ask instead what elements psychoanalysis might have borrowed from literature and incorporated into its own doctrine. If, to however limited a degree, literature was one of the sources of psychoanalysis, then psychoanalysis, in becoming an instrument of literary criticism, was only paying literature its due. It would then not be (as has been alleged) an outside intruder, but neither would it have the right to arrogate to itself, as it so often does, the authority of scientific knowledge. It would speak the language of literature without being aware of it.

It would be childish to question the originality of psychoanalytic thought. What intellectual movement is without sources, antecedents, and precursors? Even the most revolutionary systems when looked at closely often turn out to have done little more than effect a bold reorganization of elements scattered among several disciplines.

In fact, psychoanalysis stems from a cultural climate in which it is difficult to isolate literature from a context of scientific ideas and ideas about science. Antimetaphysical in tendency, those ideas were nevertheless formulated at such a level of generality that they tended to become a substitute philosophy. It is impossible to overstate the influence of Darwinism, particularly (in German-speaking countries) in the form in which it was presented by Haeckel. So powerful was the lure of science, so seductive the doctrine of evolution, that someone like Ferdinand Brunetière (in France) could think that the first task of literary science must be to trace the evolution of genres. In Freud's work, evolutionary theory served as a historical background for a genetic psychology of the emotions. Freud hoped that in the realm of the "psyche" he would be the one to further the Copernican revolution that Darwin had wrought in zoology. He wanted to add to human knowledge, whatever the cost might be to human pride. At the end of a lengthy history, Darwinism was thus enriched by the addition of a new idea, that of the unconscious. It had of course previously played an important role in Jansenist psychology as well as in the psychology of Leibniz. The concept was not absent from the philosophy of the Enlightenment, though it was given greater emphasis by the enemies of the Enlightenment, namely, the German romantics and, later, Schopenhauer, von Hartmann, and Nietzsche. Throughout the nineteenth century, moreover, the unconscious and subconscious were continually invoked by physicians and psychologists interested in hypnotism, secondary states, and alterations of personality. Some would argue, not without reason, that psychoanalysis was one of the greatest products of nineteenth-century romantic literature. Yet it must be said at once that Freud's "romanticism" is constrained by a heavy armature of positivist rationalism. He confronts us with a doctrine of singular complexity, in which epistemological optimism (the progress of science and growth of knowledge) is combined with a pessimistic metaphysics (the primitive forces that move us are obscure, blind, barbarous, violent, and insatiable). Lucidity is possible, but the ultimate ground of things is irrational. There is no certainty that life will triumph. This view of the world is in fact intrinsic to the postromantic positivism of the second half of the nineteenth century, and Freud's conviction is strikingly similar to Renan's, which caused him to say (to the dismay of the young Paul Claudel) that "the truth is perhaps sad."

A great deal could be said about this curious coexistence of the joy of discovery with the tragic feelings aroused by the somber aspect of the discovery. We are not far from a certain form of pessimistic quietism, or impotent contemplation of evil, typical of many fin-desiècle works. Think, for example, of the climate of literary naturalism. Yet Freud, tempted though he may have been, avoids such morose delectation. From the first he is a practitioner interested in the success of his "cures" and unwilling to resign himself to an attitude of unarmed comprehension. Knowledge, must bring increased power. By speculating on the obstacles, failures, and resistances encountered in his therapeutic endeavors, he develops a theory in the hope of increasing the pragmatic efficacy of his treatment. Convinced of the decisive importance of instinct, psychoanalysis seeks to transform it, to educate it, to deceive it, to compromise in such a way as to bring individual life into harmony with the requirements of both nature and culture. The ostensible aim is to create a living unity, a person gifted with vital energy as well as knowledge, in whom the contradiction between the clarity of rational knowledge and the dangerous opacity of the energy that knowledge finds lurking in the depths will have been attenuated.

The "intellectual style" of Freudianism is therefore characterized by a sharp division between the joyful imperative of knowledge and the black evidence of instinct, a division that might be overcome through a kind of *practice*. Here one cannot fail to be struck by the similarity in the approaches of Freud and Marx. Determined to work as scholars, both men set out to discover in man, in society, a *latent* depth, something hidden or disguised but essential: the elementary substance, the raw material, the material bonds that link man to the world and to his fellow men. Unveiling this hidden depth reveals, beyond the misleading superstructures, something simple, universal, and apparently ignoble: need, either in its economic or "instinctual" sense. For Marx and Freud, the error of nineteenth-century civilization was to deceive needful man (*homo economicus, homo natura*) by giving him false answers. Civilization ought to satisfy man's elementary need and thus transform it (or sublimate it, in Freud's terminology). Instead it frustrates this need, so that instead of being transformed it remains harsh and raw, a dangerous source of potential disorder beneath the reassuring semblance of a well-ordered world. Hence it is essential to denounce the scandalous discrepancy between appearance and reality, between the superstructure and the "real forces," between consciousness and unconscious drives. And it is necessary to change man or to change society, not in order to give free rein to instinct or to make society an instrument for satisfying elementary needs, but rather to raise at last that instinct and need, finally satisfied, above the level of the elementary, enabling man to know plenitude (I almost used the theological term *pleroma*) instead of division. Clearly one can go some distance by describing Marxism and Freudianism in the same terms, arriving, as might be expected, at secularized religious formulas.

Since we are discussing secularized religious themes, I shall take care not to omit an influence to which Freud, in his autobiography, ascribes his medical vocation.[1] Shortly before his graduation from high school he had been impressed by a text on nature, thought to be by Goethe. But this famous text, which Haeckel cites at the beginning of his *Natürliche Schöpfungsgeschichte* was written not by Goethe but by the Swiss theologian Ludwig Tobler.

It is worth pausing a moment to glance at this text, which owed the prestige to the incorrect attribution. The vision of nature it expresses is of a mythical order. Employing a series of antitheses, it makes us feel that man is immersed in nature, subject to her law, yet excluded from nature by conscious reflection, which is powerless to grasp secrets inscribed in the uttermost depths of organic life.

> Nature! We are enveloped by her, absorbed in her, incapable of escaping from her yet just as incapable of penetrating more deeply within her. She leads us unaware in a merry dance, carrying us with her until, exhausted, we drop from her arms.
>
> She creates eternally new forms. Present reality has never existed before. Past reality will never return again. Everything is new, yet the old force has not changed.
>
> We live in her bosom, and we are strangers to her. She constantly converses with us and never betrays our secrets. We work tirelessly to vanquish her, yet we have no power over her.

In eo movemur et sumus. Here we have the image of a Nature that is omnipresent but refuses to give herself to man. Her generative power is the supreme meaning, the supreme reason, but our reason has no access to it. Nature leads us astray and enlightens us with a revelation that remains obscure. Through us she seeks her own satisfactions: "She gives needs, because she loves movement . . . Each need is a boon, quickly satisfied, quickly reborn. If she creates yet another, it is a new source of pleasure. But she quickly achieves equilibrium."

One would like to be able to cite and compare texts at greater length, so numerous are the concordances between the lyrical enthusiasm of this 1780 text and Freud's "metapsychological" speculations. For Ludwig Binswanger, Freud's thought, despite its "positivist" appearances, secretly remained subject to the influence of powerful images of natural energy, images glorified by the philosophers and poets of the "age of genius" (and their Romantic heirs). Binswanger goes so far as to say that Freud remained a lifelong admirer of this text, which he read in his adolescence. He never renounced his sacred reverence for a Nature mythical and all-powerful but veiled and mysterious.[2]

The nature evoked by Tobler is not unlike that described in Diderot's *Rêve de d'Alembert*. Freud was indeed a great admirer of Diderot, to whom he was grateful for the frankness with which he recognized the reality of desire and instinct. On several occasions Freud mentioned that the whole theory of the Oedipus complex was prefigured by a passage in the *Neveu de Rameau*:

> If the little savage were left to himself, if he preserved his imbecility and combined the lack of reason of the child in his cradle with the violent passions of a man of thirty, he would wring his father's neck and sleep with his mother.

These lines can also be found in the article on Hobbes in the *Encyclopédie*. What sounds like an anticipation of Freud is in reality a commentary on Hobbes' famous formula: *Ita ut vir malus idem fere sit quod puer robustus, vel in animo puerili.*[3] The wicked man is a strong and sturdy child. Thus neither Freud nor even Baudelaire was the first to assert that childhood is not innocent.

With this brief investigation of the philosophical sources (or context) of Freud's thought out of the way, I may now mention certain key features of his psychology. These will become clear as I attempt to define the intentions of the analyst (and of Freud first and foremost) in applying psychoanalysis to the study of literature. The first thing to notice is the determination to subject art to a positivist, rationalist interpretation (perhaps reduction would be a better word).

Although Freud was always careful to pay homage to the writers and artists who showed him the way, he was also careful to mark the distance between his work and theirs, a distance he insisted on maintaining in order to safeguard the scientific nature of his project. Commentators often cite a remark he made on the occasion of his seventieth birthday, after a speaker had hailed him as the discoverer of the unconscious: "Poets and philosophers discovered the unconscious before me. What I discovered was the scientific method that makes it possible to study the unconscious."[4] This remark is important in more than one respect. If by any chance we were tempted to see psychoanalysis as an effort *on behalf of the irrational*, such a statement would remind us that for Freud the important thing was not simply to assert the existence of the unconscious, much less to proclaim its primacy and claim for it an unlimited right of expression. His fundamental wish was to subject the unconscious to methodical exploration, to accumulate as much rational knowledge about it as possible. The unconscious, a universal fact of human life, is thus called to witness before an objectifying consciousness, which does not, however, construe itself as a tribunal. Consciousness for once does not seek to abolish desire but is concerned rather to respect it and shed light on its object. Freud discovered the inner darkness, but he did so with the intention of illuminating it and inspecting its construction. His purpose was to reduce the mystery, not heighten it, but only after devoting the most ample attention to the obscure aspects of personality.

In short, the aim of psychoanalysis is to build a clear scientific discourse out of the confused murmurs of the unconscious and the id, out of inner conflicts lurking in silence and darkness. It is to make audible the whispers of the psyche. Its rhetoric plays on the contrast between what appears and what remains hidden; metaphors of light and darkness occur frequently. Now we can understand where the boundary falls between the respective domains of the scientist and the artist. Poets give voice—eloquent voice—to the vagaries of desire but without clarifying its inner law. They offer the "scientist" invaluable material to the extent that their work accentuates the movement of desire or invests it with exemplary value. Thus literature becomes the purveyor of paradigms to be exploited in creating the vocabulary of psychoanalysis: narcissism, sadism, masochism, and the Oedipus complex are not fully intelligible without knowledge of the myth, author, or literary work designated as archetypes for certain modes of behavior.[5] Poetic language is located in the gap that separates the scientist from an enigmatic nature whose instincts must be deciphered. The poet is comparable to the dreamer, awake or asleep. But he is more gifted than other men in the power to reveal the life of the emotions, a privilege, Freud is convinced, that makes him a mediator between the obscurity of instinct and the clarity of systematic, rational knowledge. Through his gift of experience, the result of a temporary or permanent elimination of certain inner resistances, he is much closer than less gifted human beings to "unconscious sources." And through his eminent gifts of expression he is able to express in figurative form the *meaning* that the scientist, having deemed himself the sole possessor of discursive logical truth, would like to be able to state in clear prose.

Is this humiliating for the poets? Surely this grant of superiority to "scientific discourse," this manner of reducing the poet to the role of a purveyor of murky "raw material" for exegesis, seems to imply a prejudice against poetic language and in favor of the argumentative language of psychology. Seen in this way, the poet is nothing but a producer of dreams and fantasies, no different from any other dreamer, neurotic, or man in the street. It is paltry compensation to add that if psychoanalysis depoeticizes art, it poeticizes daily life in return and speaks after a fashion of a poetry "made by everyman," since everyone dreams. But there is another way of looking at the matter. Poets have declared themselves to be the "mouth of shadow." They have described themselves as mere instruments, through which courses a mysterious power. They have been pleased to describe poetry as words spoken by one in the name of all. "When I speak of myself, I am speaking to you about you. How can you not feel it? O fool, you think I am not you!"[6] "The essence of surrealism is to have proclaimed the total equality of all normal human beings in the subliminal message, to have argued constantly that this message is a common heritage from which each person has only to claim his due."[7] Freud, therefore, is doing nothing other than taking the poet (especially the romantic poet) at his word. If the poet is a voice of *nature*, the psychologist, provided he takes certain precautions, can apply to poetic language the investigative methods of his own discipline, which he believes to be a part of natural science.

In fact, the rationalist labors of psychoanalysis, whether directed toward dreams or neurotic symptoms, and thus a fortiori when directed toward the reveries of poets, may be described as labors of interpretation and translation. It is a question of going from one language to another, from the enigmatic language of symbols to the clear language of interpretation. To do so requires a technique for decoding or deciphering, sustained by knowledge of the vocabulary, grammar, syntax, and rhetoric of the language in which desire is expressed in the interval between consciousness and the unconscious. As this interpretation progresses, the size of the mystery decreases. Everything has a meaning. There is nothing accidental in psychic life. In the final analysis everything can be reduced to the operation of elementary forces. Analysis pursues the exegesis of meaning beyond the provisional appearances of nonsense, absurdity, or wonder. Sometimes the results are disappointing. At their best, however, Freudian analyses are not reductions of the complex to the elementary, the noble to the ignoble: they lay bare numerous and complex intentions, relations, and aims. It remains true, however, that Freud sought to unravel the symbol, contrary to the advice of Goethe, who recommended that the symbol be allowed to live as such. Because Freudianism classes symbols together with hysterical symptoms (both being "compromise formations," material translations of desire diverted from its actual object by the effects of censorship), the ultimate aim of analysis is "desymbolization." For analysis the symbol is an "oblique expression" behind which the primitive sense of desire, its initial direction and purpose, can be made out.

Thus, after the analyst has uncovered, accepted, or provoked the mythical and symbolic expressions of personality, he endeavors to dissolve them by revealing the true intentions behind the veiled forms of expression. Freud encourages the analysand to yield to the promptings of the unconscious, but only within the carefully defined limits of the analytic process, with its techniques of free association and narration of dreams and fantasies. Subsequent work is devoted entirely to recovering consciousness from the unconscious, a labor that Freud compares to the draining of the Zuyderzee. In practice, free expression of fantasy is desirable, but only to provide the text or pretext for an explanatory interpretation, which by unraveling the strands of the dream gradually brings the dreamer face to face with the reality of his unknown desires. Accordingly, Freud was never particularly interested in surrealism, which claimed him as its precursor (on the basis of an inattentive reading or a misunderstanding).

Emile Benveniste made the profound observation that the expressive stratagems Freud ascribes to repressed desire are strikingly similar to the stylistic figures and tropes of classical rhetoric. "The symbols of the unconscious derive both their meaning and their

difficulty from a metaphorical conversion."[8] Analytic interpretation
of metaphor involves reduction of figurative language to literal
language. No sooner is a metaphor identified than it is traced to its
origin. Condensation is uncondensed, displacement replaced, inversion set on its feet, and so on. The psychoanalyst, an expert in the
rhetoric of the unconscious, does not wish to be a rhetorician himself.
He plays the role Jean Paulhan assigns to the terrorist in *Les Fleurs de
Tarbes*: he wants people to speak clearly. He has learned the language
of the obscure in order to effect a conversion from obscurity to
clarity, just as eighteenth-century Jesuit missionaries learned to
perform pagan rites in order to convert pagans. A skeptic would no
doubt ask whether the language ascribed to the unconscious, with its
own peculiar grammar and rhetoric, might not be simply the imprint,
shadow, or superimposed figure of the analyst's interpretive procedure.

   Freud initially asked nothing of literature but to provide illustra-
tions and confirmations of his clinical hypotheses. Later he turned
more boldly to the creative process itself in the hope of grasping the
central secret of the work of art. His late writings, however, suggest
something of a retreat, as if he had been frightened by statements
made by some of his disciples. He seems anxious to circumscribe the
application of his method, to set limits on its use. He begins his study
of "Dostoevsky and Parricide" by distinguishing four aspects of
Dostoevsky's personality: the poet, the neurotic, the moralist (*der
Ethiker*), and the sinner. He quickly adds: "Unfortunately analysis
must lay down its arms before the poet!"[9] Psychoanalysis declares
itself incompetent to define the essence of the work of art. It can speak
only of the personality of the author, that is, of a psychological reality
that underlies or precedes the work but knowledge of which is
insufficient to illuminate all its aspects. "Now we can see how many
features of the work were conditioned by the personality of the
man . . . Such research shows what factors stirred him and what kind
of raw material was imposed by fate. To study the laws of the human
psyche as they affect extraordinary individuals is a particularly
attractive task."[10] Freud thus retreats into his own domain—the laws
of the human psyche—while deliberately leaving "creative genius"
unexplained. (Certain of his heirs came to believe that he therefore
left a gap in his theories for them to fill.) Even if we learn to see the
prehistory of a work of art more clearly, we learn nothing about how
to understand and judge its quality as art. The aesthetic quality added

to the psychological material cannot be explained, except by its results; it has a cathartic effect on the reader's emotions, creating a "pleasure premium."

Freud thus limited the competence of psychoanalysis, but on condition that the scope of art be correspondingly limited. What he appears to have wanted was a sort of armistice or nonaggression pact. Analysis would not infringe upon the domain of literary genius, but in return art must not set itself up as a rival of psychoanalysis on its own terrain. In the *Introductory Lectures on Psychoanalysis* he oddly enough mentions art, philosophy, and religion as potential adversaries of science. "Art is almost always inoffensive and beneficial. It aims for nothing other than illusion. With the exception of a few people who are as it were possessed by Art, the latter does not attempt to infringe upon the domain of reality." Thus art is banished from the domain of reality, as though its "unconscious source" were not part of reality. Why? Because in Freud's eyes art is the expression of a desire that declines to seek satisfaction in the world of tangible objects. It is desire diverted or sublimated toward the realm of fiction, and in virtue of a very constricted definition of reality. Freud therefore attributes to art a mere power of *illusion*. Art is the substitution of an illusory object for a real object that the artist is incapable of attaining.

Apparently Freud never abandoned his theory of art as compensation, indeed almost as an inferior alternative to something better. In his 1909 essay "Literary Creation and Daydreaming" he writes: "The writer behaves like the child at play: he creates a fantasy world which he takes quite seriously." Art is a ludic activity of a regressive, narcissistic type. In *Totem and Taboo* art is compared with magic, for both rely on the omnipotence of thought to obtain the satisfaction of desire. But Freud's clearest and bluntest statements on the ersatz nature of aesthetic pleasure are to be found in the *Introduction to Psychoanalysis:* the artist, incapable of confronting reality directly and taking from it the benefits he desires, seeks refuge in a world of fantasy, which enables him to avoid action. If the work meets with success, the artist will have obtained in a roundabout way what he could not get directly: "Honor, power, and the love of women." In simplified form, Freud is bluntly telling us what others have expressed more subtly: that the work of art often performs a mediating function between the artist and his contemporaries, that it is an indirect way of relating to others, that it originates with an experience of failure, and that it develops apart from the world in the realm of imagination. Art, at least since romanticism, is perhaps an attempt to repair an unhappy relationship with persons and things, a deferred revenge.

Why did Freud carry the positivist interpretation of art to this degree of harshness? Now I want to try my own hand at psychoanalysis to explain Freud's ambivalence toward the artist. The reason is this: Freud, who wanted to do rigorous scientific work, was aware of the fragility of his own position. Psychoanalysis had no choice but to propose its anthropological *model* in the form of an edifice of words, and Freud knew that he was quite vulnerable to the charge that he was nothing more than a man of letters, a "poet." He wished to mark his distance from the artist, and there was no better way to do this than by adopting a condescending stance toward the poet. His apparent disdain for art would then be a defensive mechanism intended to mask and repress a "literary complex" associated with the very inception of psychoanalysis.

Psychoanalysis saw itself as conscious, rational discourse about the irrational, the unconscious, and the nondiscursive. We have no grounds for challenging the sincerity of this intention. Now, however, we have come to suspect that psychoanalysis is itself a form of *mythopoesis*, a language that is if not mythological then at least figurative or metaphorical. Among the antecedents of psychoanalytic thought was a mythical image of nature that Freud shared with the romantic poets.

Even if Tobler's text had only anecdotal importance in shaping Freud's thought, a glance at Freud's language should be enough to convince us that it is predominantly figurative, that space is treated, in spite of cautious admonitions, no less allegorically than in the *Roman de la rose*, and that the drama of consciousness was one that Freud not only described but also experienced. Recall the terms that Freud borrowed from the realm of literature or coined in the course of reflection on literature. There is no question of impugning his methods on a matter of vocabulary. After all, he was perfectly free to use the myth of Narcissus or the story of Oedipus as psychological symbols. He was well aware of what was arbitrary and approximate in resorting to such words. Freud examined the issue and readily acknowledged that his terminology was mythological: We are obliged, he writes to operate with the scientific terms at our disposal, that is to say, in our case with the figurative language (*Bildersprache*) peculiar to psychology (or, more precisely, to depth psychology). We could not otherwise describe the processes in question at all, and indeed we could not have become aware of them. The deficiencies in our description would probably vanish if we were already in a position to replace the psychological terms by physiological or chemical ones. It is true that they, too, are only part of a figurative language; but it is one with which we have long been familiar and which is perhaps a simpler one as well.[11]

The admission is important. It suggests (and a closer examination would show even more clearly) that the mythological element in psychoanalysis resides not only in its vocabulary and terminology but in its very syntax and rhetoric. It is not only the verbal material that is essentially metaphorical but the very structure of psychoanalytic discourse. The passage cited above puts us in an embarrassing situation, and Freud was here less prudent than usual. The figurative language of psychology (with its mythical elements, literary allusions, and above all its allegorized representation of psychic "sites" and its "economic" theory of the distribution of libidinal energy) is *in fact* the only language capable, according to Freud, of describing affective phenomena; *in principle*, however, it ought to be replaced, as soon as possible, with the purely quantitative language of physiology and chemistry. Now, at the same time, Freud tells us that not only the description of phenomena but the discovery of their very existence would have been impossible without the figurative language—the mythological language—that he uses. However sincere Freud's desire to recover the *literal* meaning of desire beneath the images and symbols used to disguise it, he cannot avoid reverting to an image-laden language even for the purposes of his own research. His "metalanguage," which is supposed to be rigorously scientific, is contaminated by its object. As a result, a close cooperation is established between psychoanalytic rhetoric and the phenomena that become the object of psychoanalytic research and interpretation. One therefore cannot speak of a provisional description or of a metaphorical language as the best available in the circumstances. Inevitably the question arises whether the phenomena discussed by psychoanalysis are not *constituted* by the very way in which it elaborates its discourse.

Admittedly this kind of situation is frequently found in today's science, except that science relies on experimental controls and bows before the verdict of measurement. Psychoanalysis wants to be a scientific discourse in an unquantifiable language. The only possible reference is to "clinical" experience, which is always unique and not reducible to precise coordinates. Hence it is impossible to think of replacing the language of psychoanalysis without thereby causing the disappearance of the object to which that language is supposed to correspond, namely, the topic of personality and the economics of psychic energy. The phenomena designated by psychoanalysis with the aid of the figurative language that is its research instrument therefore disappear as soon as another language is substituted. This new language will be concerned with and perhaps constitutive of correspondingly new phenomena.

Therein lies the central difficulty: psychoanalytic discourse, which was supposed to be scientific discourse about man's affective life, cannot avoid becoming an expressive dramaturgy, constantly in danger of being carried away by the intrinsic inventiveness of its own rhetoric. One thing no doubt compensates for another. Ever since Freud, psychoanalysis has faced two complementary dangers: that of accentuating its rationalist, objective side at the price of narrowing its focus and stifling its inventiveness; and that of letting its figurative rhetoric run away with itself, transforming the discipline into a literature of speculation that readily bends the malleable language of metaphor to its own purpose. Freud, always careful to avoid both the scientific dryness and the garrulous inventiveness of some of his followers and to engage in constant dialogue with his patients, maintained his mythology midway between the expressive language of poetry and the highly conventionalized quantitative language of science.[12]

These ambiguities account for Freud's appeal both to critics interested in doing scientific criticism and to writers (surrealists) eager to liberate man's deepest language. The reservations I have just expressed, which prevent me from confronting literary works purely and simply as a psychoanalyst, do not prevent me from recognizing the value of the psychoanalytic contribution or from acknowledging my debt to psychoanalysis—in which I find, especially in the work of Freud, a lesson in exegetical technique.

In both the therapeutic relation with a patient and the examination of a literary work, there must be an initial phase, a phase of experience. In vigilant neutrality the gaze goes out to meet the reality presented to it without undue haste to identify definitive structures, for the danger is great that it would simply impose its own. As far as possible, one refrains from interpreting and simply takes in data useful for later interpretation. With the literary work everything is present from the first, and nothing can be added. By contrast, in treating an analysand, the psychoanalyst can approach the subject again and again, seek new associations, overcome resistances. Evident as these differences are, literary criticism can benefit from adhering to the psychoanalytic principle of "free-floating attentiveness"—a sort of vigilance in suspense, a watchful benevolence. Little by little certain themes, certain similarities, will stand out. Attention is drawn to what the work passes over in silence, as well as to the quality of its intonation, its rhythms, its verbal energy and organization. Structures, connections, and "networks" (Mauron) begin to take shape as if of their own accord, as the work develops a complex presence whose organic structure must be identified.

Psychoanalysis casts the old problem of the relation between the life and the work in a new light. It forbids us to settle for biography that is nothing more than a collection of anecdotes. A man's "inner" history is the history of his relation with the world and with others. For psychoanalysis it is the history of the successive stages of desire. Biography thus becomes the history of those actions through which the developing individual (body and consciousness) creates himself by seeking what he lacks. At this level a continuity is established between work and life, because the work, sustained by the individual who produces it, is itself an act of desire, a revealed intention. Since life and work are no longer incommensurable realities, psychoanalysis confronts us with a significant entity, an expansive, continuous melody that is at once life and work, destiny and expression: the life takes on the value of expression, and the work takes on the value of destiny. To explain the work in terms of the life becomes inconceivable, since everything is work and at the same time everything is life.

Even so, psychoanalysis itself advises against completely eliminating the boundary between life and work, for in the work desire lives a singular life: an indirect life, in which reality is transposed into image and image into reality. Even if we do not entirely accept the facile theory of compensation, it is still true that desire detaches itself from the world in order to become desire of the work and to a certain

extent desire of desire, desire of itself. Each work serves a different
function with respect to its author and in its indirect relation with the
world. Psychoanalysis encourages us to search for the work's vital
function, that is, what in the work the writer wished to reveal or hide
or protect or simply chance.

We should, to be sure, be suspicious of a psychoanalysis that
would be satisfied to show us the antecedents of the work, a world
of memory filled with details of the past. Such an approach would
decipher symbols in a regressive direction, working back from the
present to the antecedent, from the literary expression to the
underlying desire, as if the literary were a mask to be torn away.
That kind of psychoanalytic criticism simply follows the artist's path
in reverse. It thinks it has explained the work when in reality all it
has done is to reveal certain of its necessary preconditions. Only by
nullifying Baudelaire's work through such regressive analysis can
one speak, as René Laforgue has done, of "Baudelaire's failure."
Such a method limits itself to seeking the previous instrumental and
material cause of the work while neglecting the final cause—its
actual *project*, to use a word much in fashion. As a result, one loses
sight of the work and becomes caught up in a "background" world.
One hypothetically reconstructs the author's prior experience and
early wishes. Mistaking the shadow for the substance, one is all too
likely to overlook the fact that work is itself part of experience, and
often the only part of the author's experience to which we have
access. Of course it is good, when we are granted access to it, to
know the inner history that precedes the work, which can be useful
in deciphering the work's purpose. But great literary works are so
clear about their purpose, about their intentional axis, that it is
enough to read them with an eye to the meanings with which they
are replete, even when the author hesitates between several
competing versions. Their meaning lies ahead of them because it lies
entirely within them.

Meaning abounds; one must know how to gather it in. Psychoanalysis deserves credit for pointing out that in psychic life nothing is
accidental and that a perspicacious observer can make rich sense of
accidents that someone less observant would very likely dismiss as
meaningless. Symbols emerge and hitherto unsuspected connections
become obvious.

The famous distinction that Freud makes in the *Interpretation of
Dreams* between latent and manifest content is, I think, unlikely to be

fruitful in literature if interpreted as a distinction between the hidden and the apparent. If we reject the manifest meaning of a work of art in favor of a supposed latent meaning, we must perforce deal with what is no more than a conjectural prehistory or subhistory. The analyst must settle for using biographical incidents to reconstruct a coherent (perhaps too coherent) sequence of desires, fixations, repressions, and sublimations. He speaks in place of the work. He deprives the work of its reality and regards it as a screen, bestowing the force of reality upon what is actually no more than a tissue of hypotheses. Rather than latent it is better to say *implicit*: what is present *in* the work, not *behind* it, but which we were unable to decipher at first glance. The latent content is evidence that needs to be made evident. This is what Merleau-Ponty had in mind when he wrote: "Phenomenology and psychoanalysis are not parallel. Far better than that: both are directed toward the same latency."[13] In criticism, the convergent operation of phenomenology and psychoanalysis might be called stylistics. Even if Freud is right that the symbol is what dissimulates or disguises an underlying desire, it is also what reveals or designates desire. It is not clear why the symbol must be dispelled (as if it were an intervening screen) in order to let us enter a region prior to or beyond the work of literature. Let us grant the symbol the right to live a life of its own. By so doing we give ourselves a chance of providing a truly complete interpretation: the work would not cease to represent a current experience, the text would retain its legitimacy, and the critical gaze could investigate the forms that reveal themselves in the pages of the book. To be sure, the work includes in its meaning the writer's past and personal history. But it is a transcended history, a history that we must not forget is directed toward the work, a history that is intertwined with the work itself, a past become inseparable from its implicit or explicit representation in the vital present of a work wherein a future is already being invented. Understood in these terms, the work is dependent on both a past destiny and an imagined future. To choose the past alone (say, childhood) as the only explanatory dimension is to make the work a consequence, when for the writer it is very often a way of anticipating his own future. Far from being constituted solely under the influence of an original experience or prior passion, the work must be seen as an original act in itself, a point of discontinuity, in which an individual, throwing off the shackles of the past, undertakes to invent with his past a fabulous future, a timeless construct.

*   *   *

At the conclusion of a project of analytic research, the question arises whether *comprehension* has been achieved. Karl Jaspers, for whom comprehension is in principle incomplete and unattainable, criticizes psychoanalysis for giving the illusion of having understood everything, when in fact it has merely reduced and translated all problems into the terms of a preordained vocabulary. At best this can be no more than a hypothetical comprehension (*als ob Verstehen*). Yet one could reply, with Binswanger, that it is a question of hypothetical experimentation, whose purpose is gradually to bring to light the significant relations among the facts turned up (or revealed) by analysis.[14] Eventually this results in an adequate understanding, an encounter with the living meaning.

Is the requirement of intelligibility as rigorous in literary criticism as in the clinical analysis of neuroses? In the case of literature should there not be an inviolable residue of "mystery?" Many have argued as much. I do not honestly see why knowledge of literary works should be more discreet, hesitant, or cautious. If I condemn the excesses of analysts who treat the work as a symptom, it is not to join those who regard the work of literature as an absolute without a history, a product of immaculate conception. If anything distinguishes literary criticism, is it not the desire to know more and not to stop where psychoanalysis does? It is not enough to know man as a natural and social being prior to the work of art. We need to know man in his faculty of transcendence, in the forms and creative acts whereby he alters the destiny he must endure as a natural being, whereby he transforms the situation assigned him by society, and whereby in the long run he alters society itself.

Some would say that it is harmful to want to know too much. Is it not dangerous to press too far in methodical exploration of a reality that poets say is accessible only to inspired divination? In psychoanalysis and criticism is there not a rationalist presumption inimical to the true interests of the spirit?

The answer must be in the language of myth, to which psychoanalysis itself is not afraid to resort. Psyche, unable to bear not knowing her monstrous husband's face, gives in to overwhelming curiosity and bends over the sleeping body of Eros. Her crime is cruelly punished: exiled into the desert and the kingdom of the dead, she is condemned to endure endless trials, absurd labors, and above all separation. But the myth ends with a luminous reconciliation and a definitive marriage. Psyche is forgiven because she has not ceased to love. The gaze of knowledge is also the gaze of love. The myth of Psyche is in this respect the inverse of the myth of Actaeon.[15] The hunter's gaze upon Diana in her bath is one of sacrilegious indiscretion and nothing more. No love—Actaeon's gaze is aggression. Thus Actaeon, transformed into an animal, is torn to pieces by his own dogs. Critics and analysts, keep Psyche's lamp burning, but remember the fate of Actaeon!

6 Hamlet and Oedipus

Returning from vacation on 21 September 1897, Freud in Vienna wrote a letter to Wilhelm Fliess in which he serenely set forth a negative assessment of his results. He could no longer accept the early seduction hypothesis, which had been the basis of his theory of hysteria. "Now I do not know where I am, as I have failed to reach theoretical understanding of repression and its play of forces."[1] Yet his self-analysis was proceeding well, and he was not discouraged. "It is curious that I by no means feel disgraced, though the occasion might seem to require it." Freud was eager to see Fliess and talk to him. He grasped at the first opportunity to make the long trip to Berlin. "If during this slack period I slip into the North-West Station on Saturday night I can be with you by Sunday midday and travel back the next night. Can you make the day free for an idyll for two, interrupted by one for three and three-and-a-half?"

A little later in the same letter is a reference to Hamlet: "To go on with my letter, I vary Hamlet's words: *To be in readiness.* Cheerfulness is all. I might be feeling very unhappy." Freud is citing from memory. The exact text is: "The readiness is all." A slip? What does it prove other than that Freud knew the English text well enough to risk citing from memory? If there is something odd here, it is that Freud, prior to the much-desired interview with Fliess, repeats the words that Shakespeare's hero utters prior to his fatal duel with his fraternal enemy, Laertes.

We do not know what Freud and Fliess discussed during their "idyll" on the last Sunday in September 1897. Immediately after this meeting, however, Freud let it be known that he had made rapid progress in his self-analysis. His discoveries were of considerable importance: "Later (between two and two-and-a-half) libido toward *matrem* was aroused."[2] The next letter is dated 15 October 1897; it precedes by eight days the first anniversary of the death of Freud's father. This letter, the most important of all Freud's letters, establishes the analogy between the feeling that he uncovered in his childhood and Sophocles' *Oedipus Rex*. Thus, as soon as he discovered the story of his personal desire, Freud hastened to find the same desire expressed in impersonal, collective form in tragedy and myth. This identification was his warrant for crystallizing and giving structure to a psychological theory only posited a few days earlier. The mythical paradigm serves both as a corollary of the new hypothesis and as a warrant of its universality. Reasoning in a manner similar to Aristotle's, Freud ascribes the gripping effect of tragedy to its exact representation of a passion (traditionally referred to as imitation or *mimesis*). Tragedy works because of its aptitude for arousing sympathy. To participate intensely in a represented passion is to expend the energies associated with that passion and hence to eliminate them. The man who, together with Breuer, had recently proposed a *cathartic* treatment of hysteria could not have been unaware of the Aristotelian theory of catharsis to which a relative of his wife's had devoted a philological study. Now the release of passion while viewing *Oedipus Rex* was so profound only because it was associated with the return of the repressed:

> I have found love of the mother and jealousy of the father in my own case too, and now believe it to be a general phenomenon of early childhood, even if it does not always occur so early as in children who have been made hysterics . . . If that is the case, the gripping power of *Oedipus Rex*, in spite of all the rational objections to the inexorable fate that the story presupposes, becomes intelligible . . . Greek myth seizes on a compulsion which everyone recognizes because he has felt traces of it in himself. Every member of the audience was once a budding Oedipus in fantasy, and this dream-fulfillment played out in reality causes everyone to recoil in horror, with the full measure of repression which separates his infantile from his present state.

Recognition! Aristotle saw this as a crucial moment in any tragic work: the opening up of a meaning associated with the appearance of an identity. But classical recognition took place on stage, between characters in the drama, whereas Freud is here proposing the outline of a theory of recognition involving the spectator. For the spectator, to recognize himself in Oedipus was to expand his conscious identity by actually becoming the mythical hero, at the same time deciphering the language of instincts that predates the moment of recognition.

Loss (the ego of the spectator absorbed by Oedipus loses possession of the psyche) coincides with recovery (as the spectator recognizes in Oedipus his own obscure past, his unconscious).

The letter of 15 October 1897 has yet another surprise in store. Without transition Freud moves from *Oedipus* to *Hamlet*. Consider the paragraph that immediately follows the one just cited:

> The idea has passed through my head that the same thing may lie at the root of *Hamlet*. I am not thinking of Shakespeare's conscious intentions, but supposing rather that he was impelled to write it by a real event because his own unconscious understood that of his hero. How can one explain the hysteric Hamlet's phrase "So conscience doth make cowards of us all," and his hesitation to avenge his father by killing his uncle, when he himself so casually sends his courtiers to their death and despatches Laertes so quickly?[3] How better than by the torment roused in him by the obscure memory that he himself had meditated the same deed against his father because of his passion for his mother—"use every man after his desert, and who should 'scape whipping?" His conscience is his unconscious feeling of guilt. And are not his sexual coldness when talking to Ophelia, his rejection of the instinct to beget children, and finally his transference of the deed from his own father to Ophelia's father, typically hysterical? And does he not finally succeed, in just the same remarkable way as my hysterics do, in bringing down his punishment on himself and suffering the same fate as his father, being poisoned by the same rival?[4]

Thus in Freud's early research the figure of Hamlet is closely associated with the discovery of the child's desire for its mother and with the generalization of the results of Freud's self-analysis using the Sophoclean model. For Freud, *Hamlet* immediately evokes the symptomatology of hysteria. We find ourselves at the confluence of self-analysis, cultural memory, and clinical experience.

Recall the theoretical problem that preoccupied Freud at this stage in his research. He refused to interpret neurosis and hysteria as effects of diminished mental energy. Janet's notion of "psychasthenia" was difficult to accept. If Hamlet was, as Goethe and Coleridge believed, a man too weak to carry out his assigned task, did he not become an emblematic figure of "psychological weakness"? By substituting the dynamic image of repression for the simple draining away of energy implied by asthenia, Freud laid down the basis for a new interpretation of *Hamlet*: the prince's inhibitions are no longer a sign of psychological weakness but the result of an inner conflict involving extraordinarily violent forces. Hamlet does not lack for energy, but he is not in control of the energy he expends, which is almost entirely used up in the depths of his psyche. A new hero is born within the enigmatic hero of old, namely, the unconscious. Furthermore, since the interpretation of *Hamlet* follows that of *Oedipus Rex*, the "content" (or meaning, if you prefer) of unconscious energy is identified as the Oedipal drive. The prince of Denmark is not entirely exonerated of the charge of weakness, but his weakness is deciphered to mean something quite specific. It is not simple inadequacy but rather inability to overcome guilt feelings provoked by the return of an infantile desire now cast as a crime by the words of the ghostly father and the actions of the incestuous uncle. Hamlet's inaction is the obverse of terrifying action within.

Let us look in greater detail at the place Freud accorded to Shakespeare's work. As we saw earlier, Shakespeare was on his mind ("the readiness is all") in the final stages of uncertainty preceding the discovery of what would later come to be known as the Oedipus complex. No sooner did he give the crucial formulation of his idea, moreover, than he turned to a discussion of the case of Hamlet, which sticks to the Oedipal paradigm like a shadow. The two tragedies are linked throughout Freud's work. Hence it may be of some interest to gather here the various texts that restate the intuition first formulated in Freud's letter of 15 October 1897.

  1. Fliess did not immediately respond to the hypothesis put forward by his friend. Worried and anxious for confirmation, Freud again broached the subject in a letter dated 5 November 1897:

> You have not said anything about my interpretation of *Oedipus Rex* and *Hamlet*. As I have not said anything about it to anyone else, because I can imagine in advance the hostile reception that it would get, I should be glad to have some short comment on it from you. Last year you turned down a number of my ideas, with good reason.[5]

Apparently Freud was prepared to retreat on this issue. His hypothesis was at the mercy of his friend in Berlin. Some months later, however, on 15 March 1898, Freud presented the plan for the *Interpretation of Dreams* to Fliess along with his observations on

Oedipus Rex, the story "Talisman," and perhaps *Hamlet.*[6] In the interim he had read Georg Brandes's book on Shakespeare.

2. In the *Interpretation of Dreams* (1900) *Oedipus Rex* is discussed in chapter 5 ("The Material and Sources of Dreams"), section D ("Typical Dreams"), subsection b ("Dreams of the Death of Beloved Persons"). Rather than reveal the key role that the Oedipal theme already played in his thinking (as he would do in subsequent texts), Freud conceals its importance by including it in a descriptive catalogue of dream topics.[7] *Hamlet* is still discussed in connection with *Oedipus* in a lengthy footnote. In later editions of the *Interpretation of Dreams* the text from the note is incorporated into the body of the work. Since this note is the starting point of Ernest Jones's work, it deserves to be quoted in full:

> Another of the great creations of tragic poetry, Shakespeare's *Hamlet,* has its roots in the same soil as *Oedipus Rex.* But the changed treatment of the same material reveals the whole difference in the mental life of these two widely separated epochs of civilization: the secular advance of repression in the emotional life of mankind. In the *Oedipus* the child's wishful fantasy that underlies it is brought into the open and realized as it would be in a dream. In *Hamlet* it remains repressed; and—just as in the case of a neurosis— we only learn of its existence from its inhibiting consequences. Strangely enough, the overwhelming effect produced by the more modern tragedy has turned out to be compatible with the fact that people have remained completely in the dark as to the hero's character. The play is built up on Hamlet's hesitations over fulfilling the task of revenge that is assigned to him; but its text offers no reasons or motives for these hesitations and an immense variety of attempts at interpreting them have failed to produce a result. According to the view which was originated by Goethe and is still the prevailing one today, Hamlet represents the type of man whose power of direct action is paralyzed by an excessive development of his intellect. (He is "sicklied o'er with the pale cast of thought.") According to another view, the dramatist has tried to portray a pathologically irresolute character which might be classed as neurasthenic. The plot of the drama shows us, however, that Hamlet is far from being represented as a person incapable of taking any action. We see him doing so on two occasions: first in a sudden outburst of temper, when he runs his sword through the eavesdropper behind the arras, and secondly in a premeditated and even crafty fashion, when, with all the callousness of a Renaissance prince, he

sends the two courtiers to the death that had been planned for
himself. What is it, then, that inhibits him in fulfilling the task set
him by his father's ghost? The answer, once again, is that it is the
peculiar nature of the task. Hamlet is able to do anything—except
take vengeance on the man who did away with his father and took
that father's place with his mother, the man who shows him the
repressed wishes of his own childhood realized. Thus the loathing
which should drive him on to revenge is replaced in him by
self-reproaches, by scruples of conscience, which remind him that he
himself is literally no better than the sinner whom he is to punish.
Here I have translated into conscious terms what was bound to
remain unconscious in Hamlet's mind; and if anyone is inclined to
call him a hysteric, I can only accept the fact as one that is implied
by my interpretation. The distaste for sexuality expressed by Hamlet
in his conversation with Ophelia fits in very well with this: the same
distaste which was destined to take possession of the poet's mind
more and more during the years that followed, and which reached
its extreme expression in *Timon of Athens*. For it can of course only
be the poet's own mind which confronts us in Hamlet. I observe in
a book on Shakespeare by Georg Brandes (1896) a statement that
Hamlet was written immediately after the death of Shakespeare's
father (in 1601), that is, under the immediate impact of his
bereavement and, as we may well assume, while his childhood
feelings about his father had been freshly revived. It is known, too,
that Shakespeare's own son who died at an early age bore the name
of "Hamnet," which is identical with "Hamlet." Just as *Hamlet*
deals with the relation of a son to his parents, so *Macbeth* (written
at approximately the same period) is concerned with the subject of
childlessness. But just as all neurotic symptoms, and, for that matter,
dreams, are capable of being "overinterpreted" and indeed need to
be, if they are to be fully understood, so all genuinely creative
writings are the product of more than a single motive and more than
a single impulse in the poet's mind, and are open to more than a
single interpretation. In what I have written I have only attempted to
interpret the deepest layer of impulses in the mind of the creative
writer.[8]

The interpretation that Freud set forth in his letter to Fliess has
been reproduced in full, with two additions, one pertinent to the
history of civilization,[9] the other to the supposed connection between
the tragedy of Hamlet and the life of Shakespeare. Today, knowing as
we do the biography of Freud and the genesis of the Oedipal theory,
we are able to perceive a fact that went totally unnoticed by the first

readers of the *Interpretation of Dreams*: in stressing the chronological relationship between the death of Shakespeare's father and the writing of *Hamlet,* Freud is telling us in veiled words that Shakespeare's poetic creation came about in circumstances similar to those in which Freud conceived the Oedipal theory, which he hit upon in the course of analyzing dreams that occurred in the months following his father's death. In the realm of knowledge the *Interpretation of Dreams* is thus supposed to be the equivalent of what *Hamlet* was in the development of Shakespeare's theatrical oeuvre. The poet is a dreamer who has not analyzed himself but who has nevertheless abreacted dramatically; Freud is a Shakespeare who has analyzed himself. The citation in which Freud for a moment jokingly entered into the role of Hamlet ("the readiness is all") is thus extended by Freud's circumstantial identification with Shakespeare, not in the realm of literature but in his aptitude for making symptoms speak or for deciphering a universal human fact buried in the subconscious. The frequent citations from *Hamlet* found in Freud's correspondence are, I think, not simply the mark of a cultivated man with an admirable knowledge of the classics but evidence of Freud's profound fascination with the Shakespearean character. To Arnold Zweig Freud wrote: "Wasn't our Prince Hamlet right when he asked whether anyone would escape a whipping if he got what he deserved?"[10] And when he left Vienna in 1938 he ended a letter to his brother with the words: "The rest is silence."[11]

3. In the *Introductory Lectures on Psychoanalysis* (1916) Freud still treats *Hamlet* as a satellite theme of the Oedipal myth. In the meantime the first version of Jones's study as well as Rank's had appeared. Freud took some account of Jung's hypotheses about the "retrospective fantasy" (*Rückphantasieren*), which necessitated a more subtle theory of interpretation:

Mother-incest was one of the crimes of Oedipus, parricide was the other. It may be remarked in passing that they are also the two great crimes proscribed by totemism, the first socio-religious institution of mankind. But let us now turn from the direct observation of children to the analytic examination of adults who have become neurotic. What help does analysis give towards a further knowledge of the Oedipus complex? That can be answered in a word. Analysis confirms all that the legend describes. It shows that each of these neurotics has himself been an Oedipus or, what comes to the same thing, has, as a reaction to the complex, become a Hamlet. The

analytic account of the Oedipus complex is, of course, a magnifica-
tion and coarsening of the infantile sketch. The hatred of the father,
the death-wishes against him, are no longer hinted at timidly, the
affection for the mother admits that its aim is to possess her as a
woman. Should we really attribute such blatant and extreme
emotional impulses to the tender years of childhood, or is analysis
deceiving us by an admixture of some new factor? It is not hard to
find one. Whenever someone gives an account of a past event, even
if he is a historian, we must take into account what he unintentionally puts back into the past from the present or from some
intermediate time, thus falsifying his picture of it. In the case of a
neurotic it is even a question whether this putting back is an entirely
unintentional one; later on we shall have to discover reasons for this
and have to do justice in general to the fact of "retrospective
fantasying." We can easily see, too, that hatred of the father is
reinforced by a number of factors arising from later times and
circumstances and that the sexual desires towards the mother are
cast into forms which must have been alien as yet to a child. But it
would be a vain effort to seek to explain the whole Oedipus complex
by retrospective fantasying and to attach it to later times. Its
infantile core and more or less of its accessories remain as they were
confirmed by the direct observation of children.[12]

Freud would again make the same point in a note belatedly added
to a reprinting of his "Three Essays On Sexuality": recognition of the
Oedipus complex remained "the Shibboleth that divides proponents
of psychoanalysis from its adversaries."[13] As set forth by Freud,
however, the Oedipus complex appeared to be an unstable amalgam
of an "infantile core" (visible to the external observer but not
accessible to the patient's conscious mind) and a retrospective
fantasy.[14] This confluence must be reached, moreover, by the words
of the interpreter, which resonate like those of the father and which,
in a transference situation, excite the retrospective fantasy and
reactivate the infantile core. To read Freud is to listen to this
interpretive language, addressed first to Fliess, then to the readers of
the *Interpretation of Dreams* and the *Introduction*, as it lays out the
Oedipal theme in its conceptual form (and which before long will be
picked up by the patient).

The distinction between the infantile core and the retrospective
fantasy should help us get a better grasp on the situations in *Oedipus*
and *Hamlet*. If we begin with the idea first proposed by Freud (and
later taken up by Karl Abraham and Jung) that myths are the

collective equivalent of dreams, then clearly the Oedipal myth corresponds to the "infantile core." Whatever the role of the "retrospective fantasy" that transforms Jocasta into a spouse and consummates incest in the form of matrimony, we feel that the story unfolds at a primary level, prior to which there is nothing else to look for.

The unconscious is not only language. It is dramaturgy, that is, staged speech, spoken action (ranging between the extremes of clamor and silence). *Oedipus*, mythical drama in its pure state, is instinct revealed with a minimum of retouching. Oedipus has no unconscious because he *is* our unconscious, by which I mean one of the principal roles assumed by desire. He does not need any depth of his own because he is our depth. Mysterious as his adventure is, its meaning is complete, without gaps. Nothing is hidden: there is no reason to delve into Oedipus' ulterior thoughts or motives. To attribute a psychology to him would be foolish: he is already an instantiation of psychology. Far from being a possible object of psychological study, he becomes a functional element in the creation of a psychological science. In this case Freud did not reject the notion of an archetype, but it is an archetype limited to a single character, Oedipus.

There is nothing behind Oedipus because Oedipus is depth itself. *Hamlet*, on the other hand, compels us to ask in a thousand ways the irritating question, "What lies behind Hamlet? his motives, his past, his childhood, and everything else that he dissimulates or is unconscious of?" The spectator or reader feels that something is missing. He even wonders if the author did not deliberately write a play whose tragic effect is related to the representation of a universe—cosmic, political, and psychological—filled with holes. Shakespeare's play was in fact written in a period when the traditional image of the cosmos was disintegrating. It was born at a time when subjectivity was beginning to establish its separate kingdom, inaccessible in principle: "Nobody but you knows whether you are cowardly and cruel or loyal and devout. Others do not see you, but divine you" (Montaigne, *Essays* 3.2). Appearance and reality do not coincide. Such is the scandalous affliction denounced by Hamlet; yet he is contaminated by it. One of his defensive weapons is the mask of madness, a form of dissimulation; and his first offensive weapon is a form of simulation—theatrical representation. Appearance is a universal poison that is killing society, the state, and the individual.

Appearances are deceiving. But cannot the hidden truth be ferreted out by causing the crime to be played out in a fictional spectacle before the criminal deceivers? Cannot theater, which draws upon the resources of appearance, compel reality to reveal itself? Hamlet chooses the theater, that orchestration of appearances, as the scene of a trial: he sets out both to test Claudius and to assure himself that the apparition of his father's ghost was neither a trick of the devil nor a fantasy of melancholy. Nowadays a critic of psychoanalytic bent would no doubt make even more of what might be called the circulation of poisoned language. In "The Death of Hamlet's Father," for instance, Jones makes much of the scene in which poison is poured into the sleeping king's ear—a symbol, he says, of homosexual aggression. Yet one should not neglect the apparently more superficial allegory in which Hamlet, by heeding the word of a dead man, spreads the influence of the venom through his own discourse. Thus the orchard scene narrated in act one by the Ghost is the replica of a supposedly antecedent literary model, "The Murder of Gonzago," which Hamlet presents to the royal couple in a dual representation, first as silent pantomime, then as spoken action. The theatrical representation in its unreality and brutality is the very image of the crime committed by the incestuous couple. With the aid of modifications introduced by Hamlet—a new tirade added to the preexisting text—the staged fable is no longer simply a prior model but a posterior imitation of Claudius' crime. The criminal is supposed to feel surrounded. A dizzying play with time mingles the independent literary work ("The Murder of Gonzago"), the words of the Ghost, the fantasies of Hamlet, and the crime of Claudius. Hamlet, here both stage director and playwright, has not forgotten the traditional metaphor according to which the theater is the *mirror* of life. In his advice to the actors (which Freud cites, incidentally, in "Wit and Its Relation to the Unconscious"), he declares that the purpose of the theater "both at the first and now, was and is, to hold, as 'twere, the mirror up to nature; to show virtue her own features, scorn her own image, and the very age and body of the time his form and pressure."[15] Thus the play within a play is a stratagem to "catch the conscience of the king." Hamlet would like the theater to be for Claudius what the Ghost was for him: the herald of truth. He even hopes that the truth will touch Claudius in the depths of his soul and cause him to confess his crime on the spot. In the event Claudius gives himself away by the precipitous manner in which he leaves the theater. Hamlet is certain that Claudius is guilty, but he also knows that words alone will never get the better of him.

If the king's guilty conscience did not altogether fall for the trap set by "The Murder of Gonzago," the conscience of posterity was caught in another way by *Hamlet*. It was unable to break free of the pathetic series of apparitions, representations, actions first hindered and suddenly carried through, and endless, repeatedly interrupted meditations. "The Murder of Gonzago" was a mirror painting, in which Claudius was supposed to recognize his own criminal actions, preserved by repetition. By contrast, *Hamlet* develops an intricate intertwining of fragmentary action and discourse in such a way as to create at its center a reflecting surface, empty but capable of reflecting the image of the spectator, whoever he may be: a mirror is held up. From century to century, generation to generation, Hamlet's appearance has changed with each new spectator or reader. In the history of major literary types, such a fate is rarer than one might think. Is it not striking, therefore, that an equal variety of exegesis has been devoted over the centuries to another character who is almost an exact contemporary of Hamlet, namely, Don Quixote? In both men there is a void that fascinates, a void that we attempt to fill with our thoughts (or our subconscious). Even if Shakespeare's play were, as some have said, an incoherent patchwork hastily cobbled together out of disparate materials, it nevertheless deprives us of our rest, and its effect, unlike that of pictorial "anamorphoses," depends not solely on the spectator's point of view but also on the projections infallibly stimulated by the very richness of its content. Even if it were throughout its length similar to the mad Ophelia's incoherent babbling, it would share the strange power of her speech:

> Her speech is nothing,
> Yet the unshaped use of it doth move
> The hearers to collection. They aim at it
> And botch the words up fit to their own thoughts.[16]

Oedipus' tragedy has the plenitude of symbolism; it overwhelms us with its symbolic efficacy. By contrast Hamlet, it must be said, moves us and captivates us because he strives for symbolic plenitude without ever achieving it, remaining a "hemisymbol." In the Oedipus tale, we feel that (in Freud's terms) a *common* infantile core has been linked to a *common* retrospective fantasy. The two parts of the symbolic tessera fit together to form a whole. In the case of *Hamlet*, however, we are confronted with a series of events, speeches, and monologues that seem to yield up only a part of the global meaning required by the logic of coherency. Nowadays we may be inclined to resign ourselves to this partial withholding of meaning or even to regard it as yet another beauty of the text, for many recent works have accustomed us to divining the essence of their "message" in what is kept from us, in what is mutilated or fractured. It is legitimate to assert that the metaphysical theme of *Hamlet* is the divorce between consciousness and a wicked "world," and it is clear that the play would not fully attain its goal if consciousness, disillusioned by the world and shunted off toward the infinite question mark that it represents for itself, were to allow itself to be fully understood.

Yet most commentators since the end of the eighteenth century have wanted to restore the incomplete meaning, interrogate the underlying space, define the hidden substance of the work, and unite the text with its elusive complement. To us Hamlet seems to behave as if his torment were unfathomable. He appears to have a singular psychology, a mysterious profundity, of which we see only the bizarre effects and whose causes we are curious to know. Generations of interpreters have wanted to penetrate behind the curtain, unafraid of being treated like Polonius since Hamlet wields only a fictitious sword. The fascination with what might lie "behind" is so intense that the perspective expands to a dizzying degree. Behind Hamlet are his literary prefigurations, his mythical prototype (in the history of Saxo Grammaticus), his resemblance to Orestes or to Brutus. Others will argue that behind Hamlet are his dissimulated reasons, his method of inquiry, his plans, themselves subverted at a more profound level by his madness, his unconscious. And behind that unconscious? Shakespeare's intentions. Ultimately Shakespeare himself seems to elude our grasp. What lies behind him? his jealousies and torments, his childhood, his unconscious, his genius, or in other words the voice of creative nature? And so Shakespeare is reduced to nothing but a front: behind him stands someone else, another writer, a grand personage, who writes with Shakespeare's pen.

It is probable that spectators in Elizabethan times were less curious than we are when confronted with an incoherent pattern of behavior and that they accepted the absence of a single, permanent psychological mechanism. The great debate among interpreters and commentators did not erupt until a century and a half later, when it became impossible for people to accept that a hero who interested them as Hamlet did could be without an inner principle capable of accounting for and unifying all his contradictory words and actions. It was no longer enough that the play should hold us in thrall by dint of its imperious necessity; it needed a perfect causal clarity as well. So long as that causality remained enigmatic, the text seemed like the first term of an equation whose second term had yet to be formulated.

The sequence of Oedipus' acts is guided by necessity, and no question arises as to the psychological causes of his behavior. Oedipus is fulfilling the oracle, and the oracle is *both* necessity and causality. In modern terms, Oedipus is instinct or, rather, its figurative counterpart. In the case of Hamlet, who has the three-dimensional character of a living person rather than the opaque, residueless plenitude of a psychic image—necessity, which erupts in the fatal denouement, appears to be thwarted throughout the action by a proliferating gratuitousness; necessity works in subterranean fashion, moved by hidden causes.

Freud's bold hypothesis is not only that gratuitousness can be dispelled and that, through the elucidation of hidden causes, everything can be shown to be necessary and meaningful, but also that *the* hidden cause is the Oedipus complex, the quintessence of necessity. *Hamlet* fulfills its meaning in and through Oedipus. Freud treats the universal interest in *Hamlet* as a sign. Such interest can scarcely be accounted for by the individual peculiarities of Hamlet's "neurosis." Rather, it is explained by the presence in Hamlet of the universal theme, Oedipus. But someone may object that if the Oedipal theme is acknowledged to be universal, where can it *not* be found? To which Freud would simply reply that Oedipus is present in Hamlet with unusual artistic mastery and intensity.

Oedipus does not need to be interpreted; he is the controlling figure of interpretation. By contrast Hamlet's words and actions (or inaction) are treated as symptoms and subjected to interpretation. To say that Hamlet does not fill the role that Oedipus fills is also to say that Shakespeare's play is not the equivalent of a collective dream and that we do not see it as a common retrospective fantasy coupled with a common infantile core in the unity of a symbol. In Hamlet the two pieces of the token or symbolic tessera remain forever separate. For who here can assume responsibility for the retrospective fantasy? Not

Hamlet, who exists solely in the discursive space created for him by Shakespeare. And not Shakespeare, who proposes no lateral interpretation of Hamlet. Hence it must be the interpreter, who, treating the speeches of the characters in the drama as a *result*, reconstitutes a prior history by extrapolation and looks toward a source, a primary "core" that belongs at once to himself, to Hamlet, and to Shakespeare. The retrospective fantasy is thus the responsibility of the interpreter, who relies on the similarity between the behavior of Hamlet and that of neurotics treated by psychoanalysis in real life. In the interpreter's discourse, the imagined unconscious of Hamlet, the imagining and imagined unconscious of Shakespeare, and the thoughts of the reader converge on a common point, where the figure of Oedipus looms, dispelling the mystery of the melancholy prince by flooding it with the light of an etiological myth.

Thus the fluidity of possible interpretations. For Ernest Jones, who was consciously elaborating Freud's central thesis, Hamlet was a quasi-person equipped with his own conscious, unconscious, instincts, superego, and so on—in short, with all the psychic apparatus corresponding to his personal history. Shakespeare, that prodigious imitator of reality, created not a role but a complete man. But if we shift our attention from Hamlet to Shakespeare, the character Hamlet becomes only a partial instantiation of the poet's consciousness, a momentary fantasy. So much is clear from the interpretation given by Ella Sharpe, who psychoanalyzes not so much Hamlet as Shakespeare's unconscious through the principal characters of the tragedy. Hers is an allegorizing interpretation, in which *distribution* takes on the value of a topic and *action* that of an economics. The status of the characters becomes mythical: rather than have depth they are depth, rather than have instincts they are instinct. Yet it is not the collective myth—Oedipus—that unfolds before our eyes, even if that myth remains visible in the background, as a warrant of the universal dissimulated in the particular. We witness the creation of what Charles Mauron calls a "personal myth," elaborated in conjunction with the analyst.[17]

4. In his *Autobiographical Study* (1925), Freud, again drawing on the classical tradition (in particular the contrast between Euripides and Aeschylus), contrasts *Hamlet* and *Oedipus* as the "tragedy of character" versus the "tragedy of destiny." This contrast is an analogue of the relation between the primary model of the Oedipal drive and its neurotic variant:

A number of suggestions came to me out of the Oedipus complex, the ubiquity of which gradually dawned on me. The poet's choice, or his invention, of such a terrible subject seemed puzzling; and so too did the overwhelming effect of its dramatic treatment, and the general nature of such tragedies of destiny. But all of this became intelligible when one realized that a universal law of mental life had here been captured in all its emotional significance. Fate and the oracle were no more than materializations of an internal necessity; and the fact of the hero's sinning without his knowledge and against his intentions was evidently a right expression of the *unconscious* nature of his criminal tendencies. From understanding this tragedy of destiny it was only a step further to understanding a tragedy of character—*Hamlet*, which had been admired for three hundred years without its meaning being discovered or its author's motives guessed. It could scarcely be a chance that this neurotic creation of the poet should have come to grief, like his numberless fellows in the real world, over the Oedipus complex. For Hamlet was faced with the task of taking vengeance on another for the two deeds which are the subject of the Oedipus desires; and before that task his arm was paralyzed by his own obscure sense of guilt. Shakespeare wrote *Hamlet* very soon after his father's death. The suggestions made by me for the analysis of this tragedy were fully worked out later on by Ernest Jones. And the same example was afterwards used by Otto Rank as the starting-point for his investigation of the choice of material made by dramatists. In his large volume on the incest theme he was able to show how often imaginative writers have taken as their subject the themes of the Oedipus situation, and traced in the different literatures of the world the way in which the material has been transformed, modified, and softened.[18]

5. In the unfinished *Outline of Psychoanalysis* (1938), the same ideas reappear but in a more apologetic guise. Literary historians and critics had not shown themselves to be very appreciative of Freud's interpretation of *Hamlet*. Freud's reply is worth citing at length, even at the risk of some repetition:

One may hear it objected, for instance, that the legend of King Oedipus has in fact no connection with the construction made by analysis: the cases are quite different, since Oedipus did not know that it was his father that he killed and his mother that he married. What is overlooked in this is that a distortion of this kind is inevitable if an attempt is made at a poetic handling of the material, and that there is no introduction of extraneous material but only a skillful employment of the factors presented by the theme. The ignorance of Oedipus is a legitimate representation of the unconscious state into which, for adults, the whole experience has fallen; and the coercive power of the oracle, which makes or should make the hero innocent, is a recognition of the inevitability of the fate which has condemned every son to live through the Oedipus complex. Again it was pointed out from psychoanalytic quarters how easily the riddle of another dramatic hero, Shakespeare's procrastinator, Hamlet, can be solved by reference to the Oedipus complex, since the prince came to grief over the task of punishing someone else for what coincided with the substance of his own Oedipus wish—whereupon the general lack of understanding on the part of the literary world showed how ready is the mass of mankind to hold fast to its infantile repressions.[19]

Thus in all of Freud's work from 1897 to 1938 Hamlet continues to figure as the *second* great dramatic figure, not simply as one literary character among others. The Hamlet character belongs to the category of prototypes, of exemplary themes. If Oedipus expresses through transgression and punishment the universal law that presides over the genesis of moral being, a moment that must be experienced and transcended, Hamlet exhibits through his specific inhibition and nontranscendence the anxious, masked remnant of infantile tendencies. Freud gives a name—Oedipus—to what Hamlet stubbornly conceals, to what all his loquaciousness hides.

6. And that is not all. Freud, who is remarkably knowledgeable about Shakespeare's play, offers in the remainder of his work scattered elements of a broader interpretation. In his "Notes on a Case of Obsessional Neurosis" (1909) he writes:

The doubt corresponds to the patient's internal perception of his own indecision, which, in consequence of the inhibition of his love by his hatred, takes possession of him in the face of every intended action. The doubt is in reality a doubt of his own love—which ought to be the most certain thing in his whole mind; and it becomes diffused over everything else, and is especially apt to become displaced on to what is most insignificant and small. A man who doubts his own love may, or rather *must*, doubt every lesser thing.[20]

In a footnote Freud cites, in English, "Hamlet's love poem to Ophelia" (act 2, scene 2):

Doubt thou the stars are fire,
Doubt that the sun doth move,

> Doubt truth to be a liar,
> But never doubt I love.

This literary souvenir, slipped into a clinical essay, throws additional light on a whole other aspect of *Hamlet*. Love has been proclaimed indubitable, but it will turn cold and dry up. It is not only the queen who fails to keep the promise of boundless love she made to the late king. Hamlet is also unable to maintain his love for Ophelia (or at any rate his professions of love). And Ophelia herself, too obedient to the advice of her father and brother, too ready to assume the false role thrust upon her, renounces her initial sentiments. Doubt, along with the confusion that follows fatally in its train, establishes its dominion over love. The biting cold of the first nocturnal scene on the ramparts spreads throughout the entire play, and the mournful refrain "Good night!" is heard continually. Ophelia, having lost all that she loved, even love itself, dies in a frigid pond. The observation also holds good for *Othello, Lear,* and *The Winter's Tale* (in which death is followed by resurrection), had Freud wished to pursue his studies. But clinical work on neurosis took priority.

7. Shakespeare's play contains yet another lesson. Hamlet, paradigm of neurosis, is also a model of the man who knows how to keep a secret. Freud is therefore able to point to him as a particularly eloquent example of the resistance of the neurotic, particularly to attempted manipulation by clumsy amateurs. In *On Psychotherapy* (1905) he attacks self-taught psychoanalysts:

> Reports reach my ears that this or that colleague has arranged appointments with a patient in order to undertake a mental treatment of the case, though I am certain he knows nothing of the technique of any such therapy. His expectation must be therefore that the patient will make him a present of his secrets, or perhaps that he is looking for salvation in some sort of confession or confidence. I should not be surprised if a patient were injured rather than benefited by being treated in such a fashion. For it is not so easy to play upon the instrument of the mind. I am reminded on such occasions of the words of a world-famous neurotic—though it is true that he was never treated by a physician but existed only in a poet's imagination—Hamlet, Prince of Denmark. The King has ordered two courtiers, Rosencrantz and Guildenstern, to follow him, to question him and drag the secret of his depression out of him. He wards them off. Then some recorders are brought on the

stage and Hamlet, taking one of them, begs one of his tormentors to play upon it, telling him that it is as easy as lying. The courtier excuses himself, for he knows no touch of the instrument, and when he cannot be persuaded to try it, Hamlet finally breaks out with these words: "Why, look you now, how unworthy a thing you make of me! You would play upon me . . . you would pluck out the heart of my mystery, you would sound me from my lowest note to the top of my compass; and there is much music, excellent voice, in this little organ, yet you cannot make it speak. 'Sblood, do you think I am easier to be played on than a pipe? Call me what instrument you will, though you can fret me, you cannot play upon me" (act 3, scene 2).[21]

And again it is a speech from Hamlet ("Words, words, words") that Freud ascribes to the "impartial observer" who resists the arguments of the analyst and refuses to accept the validity of psychoanalysis ("On the Question of Lay Analysis").[22]

Yes, Freud was sufficiently intimate with the prince of Denmark to refer to him as "our Hamlet." Note too that Shakespearean *wit* is closely related to the *Witz* (joke) as explicated by Freud. Who but Hamlet, master of the double-edged pun, could have suggested to Freud one of the fundamental rules of wordplay: Thrift, Horatio, thrift! The same rule of economy is also recommended by "garrulous old Polonius," whose sententious advice Freud does not neglect to cite.[23]

It would be impossible to overstate the value of Hamlet as a *model* for Freud's thinking, a model no less important even than Oedipus himself. If the Oedipus myth establishes the *normal* infantile orientation of the libido, Hamlet is the prototype of an *anomaly*, namely, the failure to emerge triumphant from the Oedipal phase.

The letters to Fliess reveal a striking coincidence between Freud's still hesitant moves to investigate childhood and his interpretation of two masterpieces of Western drama. Freud's thought appears to have been elaborated through a combination of clinical experience, reading (or memory of having read) literature, and retrospective interpretation of his own past. The result of this confrontation of different kinds of experience was first expressed in a *letter* to his faraway friend and colleague—hence in a situation of "transference"—couched in the free language of analogy and metaphor: "Might it not be like . . ."

For Freud the enigma, the sphinx, was hysteria; it was neurosis. Hamlet, who from the beginning of the play speaks in enigmas (intentional riddles, double and triple meanings, decipherable at first but ultimately, by virtue of their sheer number, undecipherable), openly offers himself to all the would-be interpretations that seek to get at the neurosis of which he is the emblem. After Freud himself, he is the second experimental subject, and the experimentation is conducted not *in anima vili* but *in anima nobili*. Something of Hamlet would remain in psychoanalysis, every neurotic becoming a prince of Denmark, an honor in some cases perhaps excessive.

As I have already suggested, the hallmark of Freud's genius lies in his manner of linking together *recognitions*, as the term is used in Aristotelian poetics to denote the discovery, by the characters in a tragedy, of a hitherto obscure identity, their own as well as that of others, usually in a moment of reciprocal illumination. Freud carried over the central recognition in Sophocles' tragedy to what he had recently divined in the darkness of his own childhood, in such a way that the dimly perceived *scene* was illuminated and structured by the dramatic poem. The Oedipus story coincides exactly with the archaic history of the personality, thus constituting the truth of the rediscovered past.

Freud's intellectual method has two components. A tendency rediscovered in the history of childhood (the "libido oriented toward *matrem*") is made explicit and universal through the Oedipal myth, whereas the Sophoclean tragedy takes on the guise of a dream and is seen as the realized desire of a subjectivity identical with that of humanity itself. Through recourse to the Oedipean model, (Freud's) subjectivity is objectified, whereas the "ancient myth is subjectified" (as the expression of a universal *psychic* law). Thus the inner core of personal subjectivity, the lived past, can finally yield up its secret and reveal its meaning only if it is given structure (in the mind of the investigator-subject) by a model, one of the most powerful works of language in the cultural "heritage." If Freud's research involves retrospective fantasy, clearly the armature of that fantasy, the seed of its crystallization, is the language of the myth. Otherwise why all the Latin terms in the letter to Fliess of 3 October 1897: "libido oriented toward *matrem*"? Leave aside the term libido, which is the "scientific" translation of desire. But is it out of modesty that Freud writes *matrem*? Or to seem "scientific"? Or because indecencies are always couched in Latin? None of these hypotheses can withstand scrutiny.

Only a term borrowed from a *dead* language could bestow upon the mother the necessary mythical image, the "Jocastian" features.

Once the Oedipus story became a crucial part of psychic ontogenesis, it was inevitable that it would also take on the hypothetical status of a primitive phylogenetic stage. It represents a bygone phase covered up by the subsequent evolution of culture. Repression is not simply an individual accident. It is a law of history and an imperative for every individual, a norm of historical origin. In other words, the history of the species is not solely a matter of additions and acquisitions but also a question of negations, rejections, and repressions. For the species as well as the individual, the condition of progress is that the repressed should not retain an excessive amount of autonomous energy.

Now we are in a position to trace more clearly the series of recognitions that mark the progress of Freud's thought. He began with the hypothesis, I am like Oedipus. Immediately this proposition was stood on its head and formulated as a universal historical truth: Therefore Oedipus is all of us. Self-understanding through self-analysis is possible only through recognition of the myth, and the myth, thus internalized, is subsequently read as the drama of an instinct. But Freud's boldest recognition is this: Hamlet is also Oedipus, albeit masked and repressed, and Oedipus remains too active in the shadows to permit Hamlet, to advance by so much as a single step. And Freud's final recognition is this: Hamlet is the neurotic, the hysteric with whom I must deal every day. In other words, it is as if the transition from Oedipus to Hamlet had to take place before Freud could interpret the unconscious of his patients as he had interpreted his own past. Oedipus and Hamlet are mediating images between Freud's past and Freud's patients: they are guarantors of a common language.

This series of recognitions must therefore be seen as essential stages in the progress of analytic thinking itself rather than as applications of psychoanalysis to other fields. The satisfaction that Freud expresses in his letter of 15 October 1897 at unraveling the mystery of Hamlet's inhibition does not concern literature. It is simply a provisional essay, a symbolic trial application of the Oedipal "law" that would eventually be used to decipher the words not of dramatic characters but of real flesh-and-blood patients.

This was a bold stroke on Freud's part, and it is hardly surprising to discover that he was anxious about Fliess's response. For Freud had extended the Oedipal schema to a case that seemed to stand in sharp contrast to that of Oedipus. Hamlet is not his father's murderer but his avenger. Only he is a hesitant avenger who, beset by anxiety and tempted by suicide, repeatedly postpones the act of vengeance. Freud makes what is essentially a grammatical or logical move, showing that a double negation is the degraded, ghostly equivalent of an affirmation: Hamlet did not murder his father, but neither has he managed to take action against the man who did. Hence unconsciously he always *desired* his father's death. The ghost-father continues to be the object of a ghost-murder that remains forever uncommitted. Hamlet therefore sees himself darkly in the real murderer: hence the anxiety, which results in a specific paralysis that prevents Hamlet from punishing himself by ending his life and from punishing himself in Claudius who is but a substitute for Hamlet. Freud therefore interprets Hamlet's "procrastination" as a case of isolated motor paralysis. After "Studies in Hysteria" this is one of the first cases in which no organic conversion takes place and in which the symptoms remain intrapsychic. Thus Hamlet contributed in some way to the differentiation of "pure" neurosis from hysteria or conversion neurosis.

When Ernest Jones elaborated upon what had been a mere footnote in the *Interpretation of Dreams*, the focus of research shifted radically. Not that Jones was in the slightest degree unfaithful to Freud's teaching: his interpretation of Hamlet's character is identical to Freud's. But for Freud that interpretation was a step toward the creation of psychoanalysis, a stage in the creation of analysis and its conceptual equipment. In other words, Freud read *Hamlet* while working toward what would become psychoanalysis. Jones reread the play with the completed structure of psychoanalysis as his starting point. Arguing against rival interpretations and offering new proof in support of the Oedipal interpretation, Jones offers an example of *applied* psychoanalysis. The method is given, not tested. It is simply a question of showing that it works. It allows some freedom in the manner of its use, as shown by the work of Jones and, later, Ella Sharpe, Norman Holland, and André Green.

Although Freud was given to repeating that "Prince Hamlet suffered from an Oedipus complex,"[24] there is no question that his interpretation of Shakespeare's play always had, in his eyes, a propaedeutic function. It was valuable as a model, a way of imparting understanding that would find its ultimate application elsewhere.

When the Swiss psychiatrist Ludwig Binswanger visited Freud for the second time in February 1910, he attended one of Freud's weekly seminars, the subject of which happened to be *Hamlet*. One paper analyzed two scenes "along the lines of the well-known note in the *Traumdeutung* of 1900." Then:

> A second participant read a paper which presented a rather uncritical and very confused analysis of Hamlet's relationship to his father, still along the same lines and especially taking up the *Traumdeutung*'s suggestion about the division of one person into several figures. Thus, in the present case, the "paternal complex" was divided between the stepfather and Polonius. A younger participant compared the change in the characters in the drama as so vividly portrayed by Shakespeare with the change of scene in the dream. Freud himself remarked that in the theme treated that day, it was simply a question of making things more or less plausible (*ein mehr oder weniger Plausibelmachen*) and not of discovering immutable facts (*um Auffindung feststehender Tatsachen*)! At the same time he stressed the training function of such research.[25]

This testimony accords fully with several statements in which Freud expressed himself with great caution. In 1930, when a translator of Shakespeare asked him if Lear might not also be considered a hysteric, Freud answered that "one has no right to expect a poet to give a correct clinical description of a mental illness. It is enough that our feelings not be affronted in any way and that what can be called our popular psychiatry allow us to follow the person described as abnormal through all his twists and turns."[26] Limits of general plausibility are thus set up around the psychoanalytical interpretation of literature. When a character does not represent a disease in all its details, psychoanalysis for its part must not pretend to give an exhaustive explanation of the work.

Perhaps the most striking indication of Freud's attitude, however, is to be found in a note added to his *Autobiographical Study* in 1925, where he approves the hypothesis of J. T. Looney according to which the true author of the works attributed to Shakespeare is Edward de Vere, Earl of Oxford. Another note on the same subject, added to the *Outline of Psychoanalysis* (1938),[27] mentions briefly that de Vere "had lost, while still a child, a beloved and admired father, and that he had completely broken off relations with his mother, who had entered into a new marriage shortly after her husband's death."[28]

This new line is pregnant with consequences. As long as Hamlet remained the work of the Stratford actor whose father died in 1601, *Hamlet* and psychoanalytic theory were united by a kind of twinship, for both were born in similar circumstances. Now this twinship is denied or, rather, established on another basis. Did Freud hope thereby to cover his own tracks? I don't think so. It can of course be argued (anything can be argued) that by this late date Freud felt the situation of the son less keenly than before, that he had definitively accepted the role of the father, of Moses, indeed of the father who "died prematurely." This is the role he is assigned in the often guilty fantasies of his heirs: "Remember me!"

7 The Interpreter's Progress

This essay, in which I analyze an episode in Rousseau's *Confessions*, leads to a theory of interpretation. A close reading provides the materials I need to develop my own views on critical reading. The *explication de texte* that I take initially to be my goal ultimately becomes a means for interpreting and understanding my interest in the text. In this way I draw out the necessary connection between interpretation of the object and interpretation of self, between discourse on texts and the ground of my own discourse.

I

The Style of Autobiography

The biography of a person written by the person himself: this definition of autobiography determines the inherent nature of the task and thus establishes the general (or generic) conditions of autobiographical writing. We are not dealing, however, with a literary genre in the proper sense. Autobiography, reduced to essentials, requires first that the narrator be *identical* with the hero of the narration and second that there be *narration* and not description. A biography is not a portrait. More precisely, even if it can be described as a portrait, it must include elements of duration and movement. The time span of the narrative must be long enough to allow the course of a life to emerge. Provided these conditions are respected, the autobiographer is clearly free to confine his narrative to a single page or to extend it over several volumes. He is free to "contaminate" the narrative of his life with events he witnessed remotely, in which case he becomes a memoirist as well as an autobiographer (like Chateaubriand). He is also free to ascribe precise dates to the various stages of his writing and to direct his attention inward as he writes; autobiography is then contaminated by elements of the private diary, and the autobiographer at moments becomes a "diarist" (once again like Chateaubriand). Plainly, the defining criteria of autobiography do no more than establish a rather ample frame within which a wide variety of particular styles may be practiced and exhibited. Hence we must be careful to avoid speaking of a style or even a form of autobiography, for there is no obligatory style or form. In autobiography even more than in other forms of literature, style is an individual affair. It bears emphasizing, however, that the writer who wishes to develop an autobiographical style must respect the defining criteria set forth above. Indeed style might be defined as the way in which each autobiographer meets the general requirements of autobiography—requirements of an ethical and "relational" order, which simply call for truthful narration, leaving it up to the writer to choose a particular mode, tone, rhythm, extent, and so on. In a form of narrative in which the narrator's theme is his own past, the individual mark of style takes on a special importance, adding to the explicit self-reference of the narrative the implicit self-reference of a personal mode of expression.

Style is linked to the present of the act of writing. It is a result of the freedom offered by language and literary convention and of the use made of that freedom by the *scriptor* (by which I mean the author of an autobiography considered independent of his quality as writer). Style as self-reference relates to the writer at the moment of writing, to the present "self." This "presentness" of self-referentiality may in fact impede accurate understanding and precise reproduction of past events. In considering Rousseau or Chateaubriand, critics have often held—independent of the substance of the facts described—that the perfection of style casts doubt upon the content of the narrative and imposes a screen between the truth of the past and the present of the narrative situation. Any stylistic originality implies a redundancy that appears to perturb the message itself. True, the past can never be evoked except from the vantage of the present: the "truth" of bygone days is truth only for the consciousness that, in calling up the image of the past here and now, cannot avoid imposing a form and style of its own. All autobiography, even that which purports to limit itself to pure narration, is self-interpretation. Style is here the sign of the scriptor's relation to his own past, but at the same time it manifests a specific way of revealing oneself to others, which is a project directed toward the future.

The misunderstanding described above is largely the result of ideas about the nature and functions of style. Given the representation of style as a "form" added to a "content," it is reasonable to cast a suspicious eye on qualities of style in an autobiography. "Too beautiful to be true" becomes a principle of systematic mistrust. Furthermore, common experience in the use of language suggests a constant risk of slipping unwittingly from truth into fiction. Not only is it possible for the autobiographer to lie, but the "autobiographical form" may conceal fictional invention at its most unconstrained: "pseudo-memoirs" and "pseudo-autobiographies" exploit the possibility by narrating purely imaginary stories in the first person. In such cases the narrative "I" is not "existentially" assumed by anyone. It is an "I" without a living referent, which refers exclusively to an invented image. Yet the "I" of fiction is indistinguishable from the "I" of "sincere" autobiographical narration. It follows that, despite the desire for sincerity, the "content" of autobiographical or confessional narrative can escape or wander into fiction; just as there is nothing to prevent this transition from one level of narrative to another, so too there is nothing to reveal its existence unmistakably. By accentuating the *present* of the act of writing, the original quality of the style seems to encourage arbitrariness of narration rather than fidelity of reminiscence. Style is not so much an obstacle or screen as a source of distortion and falsification.

If, however, we set aside the conception of style as a form (or cloak or ornamentation) added to a content, and consider instead the definition of style as disparity or deviation (*écart*), originality of style in autobiography, far from seeming suspect, offers a revealing system of symptomatic traces or features. Redundancy of style is an individualizing characteristic: it sets the writer apart.[1] Was not the notion of style as deviation developed as a way of approaching the psychic singularity of the writer?[2] We thus come back (with a slight distortion of meaning) to the celebrated statement of Buffon: "Le style c'est l'homme même." The style of an autobiography can now be seen to embody at least a *current* truthfulness. However doubtful the facts related, the writing will at least offer an "authentic" image of the writer's personality.

At this point it may be useful to interject a few more general remarks on the implications of the theory of style. Style in the sense of "form added to content" will be judged primarily in terms of its inevitable lack of fidelity to a *past reality*: the content is held to be prior to the form, and the theme of the narration, a story completed in the past, will inevitably occupy the position of anteriority. By contrast, style interpreted as deviation will be viewed primarily in terms of *fidelity to a present reality*. Here, the very notion of style is secretly governed by a set of organic metaphors, according to which expression arises *with no discontinuity* out of experience, much as a flower is the result of the flow of the sap and the growth of the stem. The form-plus-content representation implies discontinuity, that is, the opposite of organic growth, in its very formulation; it suggests a mechanical operation, an instrumental intervention applied to material of a different nature. The image of the *stylus* or sharpened point then tends to take precedence over the image of a *hand* guided by the writer's inward animation. (No doubt what is needed is an idea of style that encompasses both the stylus and the hand—the stylus guided by the hand.)

In his study of "tense relations in French verbs," Emile Benveniste draws a distinction between *historical* statements, "narratives of past events," and *discourse*, "statements presupposing a speaker and a listener and an intention on the part of the former to influence the latter in some way."[3] Benveniste observes that, in French, narration of past facts in historical utterance generally uses the tense known as the *passé simple* (or aorist, as Benveniste calls it), whereas (in contemporary French) discourse avoids this tense and uses the *passé composé* instead. A glance at recent autobiographies (such as those of Michel Leiris and Jean-Paul Sartre) is enough to show, however, that characteristics of discourse (or utterance associated with a speaker who says "I") coexist with characteristics of historical narration (use of the aorist tense). Is this an archaic mannerism? Or might it be that autobiography is a mixed entity, what might be called *historical discourse*? Surely this hypothesis deserves examination. The traditional form of autobiography strikes a balance between two extremes: third-person narrative and pure monologue. Third-person narrative is familiar from Caesar's *Commentaries* or the second part of La Rochefoucauld's *Memoirs*: it is narration not distinguished from history by its form. We must possess external information in order to know that the narrator and the hero are one and the same. Generally a procedure of this sort is used to trace a series of important events in which the writer himself plays a major role. The self-effacement of the

narrator (who assumes the impersonal role of historian) and the
objective presentation of the protagonist in the third person[4] emphasize the *event* and secondarily reflect upon the protagonist the glory of
the actions in which he takes part. A form of apparent modesty,
third-person autobiographical narrative adds the luster of event after
event to the glory of a hero who declines to speak in his own name.
The interests of personality are here bestowed upon a "he," or "she,"
who effects a solidification through objectivity. The pure monologue
is the exact opposite: the emphasis is on the ego rather than the event.
In extreme forms of written monologue (which escape the realm of
autobiography and come close to lyrical fiction), the event is none
other than the unfolding of the monologue itself, independent of the
"facts" related, which become a matter of indifference. Here the
process is the reverse of what takes place in third-person narrative:
the exclusive affirmation of the "I" favors the interests of the "he"
who has apparently vanished; the impersonal event is secretly para-
sitic on the "I" of the monologue, which it drains of color and
depersonalizes. A glance at some of the prose of Samuel Beckett is
enough to show how the repetition of the first person amounts to the
deployment of a "nonperson."

Autobiography is certainly not a disciplined genre, but it does
require that certain conditions be met, most notably conditions of an
ideological (or cultural) nature. For instance, a certain importance
must be attached to personal experience, and there must exist
opportunities to offer others a sincere account of those experiences.[5]
These conditions establish the legitimacy of the "I" and authorize the
subject of the discourse to choose its past existence as its theme. What
is more, the "I" is confirmed in its role as permanent subject by the
presence of its correlate "thou," which establishes the motivation of
the discourse. Here I am thinking of the *Confessions* of Saint
Augustine: the author addresses God with the intention of edifying
his readers.

God is the direct addressee of the discourse. By contrast, men are
named in the third person as indirect beneficiaries of the effusion they
are allowed to witness. Thus autobiographical discourse takes shape
by conjuring up almost simultaneously two addressees, one addressed
directly, the other obliquely called upon to bear witness. Is this an
unnecessary luxury? Is it possible that the invocation to God is here
merely a rhetorical device? Not at all. To be sure, God has no need of
receiving Augustine's account of his life, because God is omniscient

and takes in all of time in a single view: he receives prayers and thanksgiving, and he is thanked for bringing his grace to bear upon the destiny of the narrator. He is the present interlocutor only because he was the master of the narrator's whole prior history: he put the narrator to the test, rescued him from error, and ever more imperiously revealed himself. By openly taking God for his interlocutor, Augustine dedicates himself to absolute *veracity*. How could he distort or hide anything whatsoever from one who sounds the depths of human existence? Hence the content of the discourse is approved by the most unimpeachable of witnesses. By virtue of the divinity to whom the confession is addressed, the perils of distortion that beset ordinary narratives are averted. But what is the function of the secondary recipient of the confession, the human audience obliquely invoked? Its assumed presence legitimizes the *discursivity* of the confession. It is not God but the human reader who needs a narration that will exhibit the sequence of events as they unfold in time.

The double destination of discourse—God and the human audience—renders truth discursive and discursivity truthful. The instantaneousness of divine knowledge is somehow coupled with the temporality of the explanatory narration required by human intelligence. Thus the edifying motivation and the transcendent finality of confession are reconciled: the speech addressed to God may convert or comfort other men.

Yet another element needs to be considered. There would have been no good reason to write a biography had there not been a radical change or transformation in the writer's prior existence, namely, conversion, the beginning of a new life, the sudden advent of grace. If the narrator had not changed in his life, he might have painted a portrait of himself once and for all. Then all change would have been limited to external events, and only these would have been suitable for incorporation into a narrative: the conditions of what Benveniste calls *history* would then be satisfied, and there would be no need for a first-person narration. By contrast, the inner transformation of the individual (and the exemplary character of that transformation) provides material for a narrative discourse in which the "I" is both subject and object.

Interestingly, it is because the past self is *different* from the present "I" that the latter can truly claim all its prerogatives. The "I" will tell not only what happened to it in *another* time but even more how *another* person came to be itself. Hence the discursivity of the narration is further justified, this time not by its recipient but by its content. It is a question of exploring the origins of the current situation, the antecedents of the moment from which the present discourse begins. A chain of episodes traces a path, a sometimes sinuous course culminating in the current state of recapitulative knowledge.

The difference established by autobiographical reflection is therefore twofold: it is both a temporal difference and a difference of identity. In language, however, the only evidence is temporal. The personal reference (the first person, the "I") remains constant. This constancy is ambiguous, for the narrator then was different from what he is today. But how could he fail to see himself in the other person he once was? How could he refuse to accept responsibility for his errors? Confessional narration accentuates the difference of identity, renouncing past errors, but it does not deny the responsibility borne permanently by an unchanging subject. The invariant pronoun is the vector, as it were, of this permanent responsibility: the first person is the basis of both present reflection and the multiplicity of bygone states. Changes of identity are indicated by *verbal* and *attributive* elements. They are perhaps still more subtly expressed through the contamination of *discourse* by traits specific to *history*, namely, the treatment of the first person as a quasi third person, justifying the use of the historical aorist tense. The aorist tense assigns a certain coefficient of otherness to the first person. Note too that the famous "twenty-four-hour rule" was generally respected in the eighteenth century,[6] and that the use of the *passé simple* was all but indispensable for remote or unique events (except for the occasional use of the "historical present"). Finally, it is the narrator's statements themselves, their specific *tone*, that make fully explicit the distance between the narrator and his sins, errors, and tribulations. Here, the figures of traditional rhetoric (especially those that Fontanier calls "figures of expression through opposition," such as preterition, irony, and so on) have their role to play, lending each autobiographical style its particular coloration.[7]

Here I shall again use Rousseau as an example. The presence of an imaginary addressee is striking in the *Confessions* as early as the preamble: "Whoever you may be, whom my destiny or my confidence has made arbiter of the fate of this notebook."[8] More striking still, in the third paragraph of book 1 we find the dual addressee (God and men) whose function I discussed in connection with the Augustinian prototype:

> Let the last trump sound when it will, I shall come forward with this work in my hand, to present myself before my Sovereign Judge . . . I have bared my secret soul as Thou thyself hast seen it, Eternal Being! So let the numberless legion of my fellow men gather round me, and hear my confessions. Let them groan at my depravities and blush for my misdeeds.[9]

To guarantee the veracity of his words, Rousseau, like Augustine, summons the presence of the divine gaze. But Rousseau summons it once and for all, as a preliminary. In the body of the narrative there are almost no invocations of or apostrophes to God. The *reader* is a diffuse presence, and Rousseau sometimes engages in imaginary dialogue with him, but this possible witness is usually reduced to nothing more than the indefinite general pronoun *on*: *On pensera que*, *On dira que* (It will be thought, It will be said). Rousseau habitually entrusts to this imaginary interlocutor the function of raising the objections of common sense and social convention.[10] He also ascribes to the reader the *suspicion* with which he feels himself surrounded. He seeks to persuade us of the absolute veracity of his account as well as of the persistent innocence of his intentions. The fact that there is no direct relationship between Rousseau and God as there is between Augustine or Theresa of Avila and God inevitably affects the status of truth. We sense that the preliminary invocation is not sufficient. Truth must be truth in every instant, and Rousseau does not invite the divine gaze to scrutinize every instant of his existence. It is Jean-Jacques's *inward sentiment* or *conscience* that inherits some of the functions ascribed to God in traditional theology. Hence the veracity of the narration is subject to the scrutiny of conscience in the very moment that feeling is communicated through writing. The charge of a transcendent recipient is replaced by the pathos of faithful expression. Hence it is hardly surprising that Rousseau borrows from Montaigne and the Latin letter writers the *quicquid in buccam venit* in order to attribute to it, this time, a quasi-ontological value: the spontaneity of the writing, in principle patterned after the spontaneity of present feeling (which yields itself up as old emotion relived), guarantees the absolute authenticity of the narration. Style, Rousseau himself assures us, then takes on an importance that goes beyond the mere use of language, the mere technical quest for effects; it becomes emphatically "self-referential," insisting that it points infallibly to the author's inward truth. In asserting that he has reexperienced past emotions, Rousseau wants to make the present of narration directly dependent on past "impressions":

> For what I have to say I need to invent a language as new as my project, for what tone, what style to take in order to bring clarity to the immense chaos of sentiments so diverse, so contradictory, often so vile and sometimes so sublime that constantly agitated me . . . Hence with respect to style as with respect to things, my decision is the same. I do not seek to make it uniform. I will always have whatever style comes to me; I shall change it without scruple according to my mood; I shall say each thing as I feel it, as I see it, without straining for effect, without embarrassment, and without worrying about the mixture of colors. By surrendering to the impression received and to the sentiment of the moment, I shall paint the state of my soul twice over, at the moment the event occurred and at the moment I wrote it down. My uneven and natural style, sometimes rapid and sometimes diffuse, sometimes sage and sometimes mad, sometimes grave and sometimes gay, will itself become part of my story.[11]

Among the diverse styles to which Rousseau here lays claim, the reader of the *Confessions* is struck by two particularly significant "tonalities," one elegiac, the other picaraesque.

The elegiac tone (employed, for example, in the celebrated opening lines of book 6) expresses a lament for lost happiness: living in a climate of affliction and menacing shadows, the writer takes refuge in the memory of the happy days of his youth. Looking back fondly on his sojourn at Les Charmettes, he revisits the scene in his imagination and once again savors bygone pleasures. He thus *fixes* on the page a moment in his life toward whose refuge he would like to flee in thought. He is certain that he will never be granted such happiness again:

> My imagination, which in my youth always looked forward but now looks back, compensates me with these sweet memories for the hope I have lost forever. I no longer see anything in the future to attract me; only a return into the past can please me, and these vivid and precise returns into the period of which I am speaking often give me moments of happiness in spite of my misfortunes.[12]

Clearly the qualitative accent favors the past over the present. The time in which writing occurs is the time of disgrace. The earlier period that Rousseau hopes to recapture through writing is a lost paradise.

By contrast, in the picaresque type of narration the past is a time of weakness, error, errancy, humiliation, and expedients. Traditionally the picaresque tale concerns a character who, having achieved a certain level of comfort and "respectability," casts his mind back upon an adventurous past and marginal beginnings: *then* he did not know the world, he was a stranger who made his way as best he could and usually not very well. Hence he became familiar with all the abuses, all the oppressive powers, all the insolence of the mighty. He misbehaved when misbehavior was profitable. For the picaresque narrator, the present is the time of rest finally deserved, of knowledge finally achieved, of successful integration into the social order. He is able to make fun of the obscure, needy person who plunged headlong into the world and all its illusions. Hence he will speak of his past with irony, condescension, pity, and good cheer. Frequently this narrative tone requires an imaginary addressee, a confidant, who is presented as an indulgent accomplice amused by the jocular skill with which the most heinous crimes are retold. (The *Lazarillo of Tormes*, prototype of the picaro, confides in a character designated simply as *vuestra merced*. Humorously inverting the pattern of Augustinian confession, he declares his wish "not to be more holy than my neighbors" [*confesando yo no ser mas sancto que mis vecinos*]. Lazarillo's expressed wish to begin at the beginning—*por el principio*—is not unrelated to the method of the *Confessions*. Like Jean-Jacques, Lazarillo claims to give a complete image of his character: *por que se tenga entera noticia de mi persona.*[13])

Although there are a good many purely picaresque episodes in the first six books of the *Confessions*, it is not rare to find episodes in which the elegiac and picaresque tones are closely intertwined, with very rapid transitions from one to the other. This is perhaps the narrative embodiment of an important aspect of Rousseau's "system," a replica of his philosophy of history. Primitive man, he argues, possessed happiness and innocence. Compared with that primitive felicity, the present is a time of degradation and corruption. But primitive man is also a "brute" deprived of "light," whose reason still slumbers. Compared to this initial obscurity, the present is the time of *lucid reflection* and expanded consciousness. Hence the past is by turns an object of nostalgia and an object of irony. The present is experienced by turns as a morally degraded state and an intellectually superior state.[14]

I I

The Dinner at Turin

Irony interprets the difference between past and present to the benefit of the present: the ironist does not wish to belong to his past. Conversely, nostalgia interprets the difference between past and present to the benefit of the past: the nostalgic cannot bear to be the captive of the present. These two narrative tonalities are obviously governed by an interpretive act, often implicit, which shifts the accent along the time scale so as to modify the relative value of past and present.

Here the important text is found in book 3 of the *Confessions*:

> Mademoiselle de Breil était une jeune personne à peu près de mon âge, bien faite, assez belle, très blanche avec des cheveux très noirs, et, quoique brune, portant sur son visage cet air de douceur des blondes auquel mon cœur n'a jamais résisté. L'habit de cour, si favorable aux jeunes personnes, marquait sa jolie taille, dégageait sa poitrine et ses épaules, et rendait son teint encore plus éblouissant par le deuil qu'on portait alors. On dira que ce n'est pas à un domestique de s'apercevoir de ces choses-là; j'avais tort, sans doute, mais je m'en apercevais toutefois, et même je n'étais pas le seul. Le maître d'hôtel et les valets de chambre en parlaient quelquefois à table avec une grossièreté qui me faisait cruellement souffrir. La tête ne me tournait pourtant pas au point d'être amoureux tout de bon. Je ne m'oubliais point; je me tenais à ma place, et mes désirs même ne s'émancipaient pas. J'aimais à voir Mademoiselle de Breil, à lui entendre dire quelques mots qui marquaient de l'esprit, du sens, de l'honnêteté; mon ambition bornée au plaisir de la servir n'allait point au-delà de mes droits. A table j'étais attentif à chercher l'occasion de les faire valoir. Si son laquais quittait un moment sa chaise, à l'instant on m'y voyait établi: hors de là je me tenais vis-à-vis d'elle; je cherchais dans ses yeux ce qu'elle allait demander, j'épiais le moment de changer son assiette. Que n'aurais-je point fait pour qu'elle daignât m'ordonner quelque chose, me regarder, me dire un seul mot; mais point. J'avais la mortification d'être nul pour elle; elle ne s'apercevait pas même que j'étais là. Cependant son frère qui m'adressait quelquefois la parole à table, m'ayant dit je ne sais quoi de peu obligeant, je lui fis une réponse si fine et si bien tournée

qu'elle y fit attention et jeta les yeux sur moi. Ce coup d'œil qui fut court ne laissa pas de me transporter. Le lendemain l'occasion se présenta d'en obtenir un second et j'en profitai. On donnait ce jour-là un grand dîner, où pour la première fois je vis avec beaucoup d'étonnement le maître d'hôtel servir l'épée au côté et le chapeau sur la tête. Par hasard on vint à parler de la devise de la maison de Solar qui était sur la tapisserie avec les armoiries. *Tel fiert qui ne tue pas.* Comme les Piémontais ne sont pas pour l'ordinaire consommés dans la langue francaise, quelqu'un trouva dans cette devise une faute d'orthographe, et dit qu'au mot *fiert* il ne fallait point de *t*.

Le vieux comte de Gouvon allait répondre, mais ayant jeté les yeux sur moi, il vit que je souriais sans oser rien dire: il m'ordonna de parler. Alors je dis que je ne croyais pas que le *t* fût de trop, que *fiert* était un vieux mot français qui ne venait pas du nom *ferus*, fier, menaçant, mais du verbe *ferit*, il frappe, il blesse; qu'ainsi la devise ne me paraissait pas dire, *tel menace*, mais *tel frappe qui ne tue pas*.

Tout le monde me regardait et se regardait sans rien dire. On ne vit de la vie un pareil étonnement. Mais ce qui me flatta davantage fut de voir clairement sur le visage de Mademoiselle de Breil un air de satisfaction. Cette personne si dédaigneuse daigna me jeter un second regard qui valait tout au moins le premier; puis tournant les yeux vers son grandpapa, elle semblait attendre avec une sorte d'impatience la louange qu'il me devait, et qu'il me donna en effet si pleine et entière et d'un air si content que toute la table s'empressa de faire chorus. Ce moment fut court, mais délicieux à tous égards. Ce fut un de ces moments trop rares qui replacent les choses dans leur ordre naturel et vengent le mérite avili des outrages de la fortune. Quelques minutes après, Mademoiselle de Breil levant derechef les yeux sur moi me pria d'un ton de voix aussi timide qu'affable de lui donner à boire. On juge que je ne la fis pas attendre, mais en approchant je fus saisi d'un tel tremblement qu'ayant trop rempli le verre je répandis une partie de l'eau sur l'assiette et même sur elle. Son frère me demanda étourdiment pourquoi je tremblais si fort. Cette question ne servit pas à me rassurer, et Mademoiselle de Breil rougit jusqu'au blanc des yeux.

Ici finit le roman; où l'on remarquera, comme avec Madame Basile et dans toute la suite de ma vie que je ne suis pas heureux dans la conclusion de mes amours. Je m'affectionnai inutilement à l'antichambre de Madame de Breil; je n'obtins plus aucune marque d'attention de la part de sa fille. Elle sortait et rentrait sans me regarder, et moi j'osais à peine jeter les yeux sur elle. J'étais même si bête et si maladroit qu'un jour qu'elle avait en passant laissé tomber son gant; au lieu de m'élancer sur ce gant que j'aurais voulu couvrir de baisers, je n'osai sortir de ma place, et je laissai ramasser le gant par un gros butor de valet que j'aurais volontiers écrasé. Pour achever de m'intimider je m'aperçus que je n'avais pas le bonheur d'agréer à Madame de Breil. Non seulement elle ne m'ordonnait rien, mais elle n'acceptait jamais mon service, et deux fois me trouvant dans son antichambre elle me demanda d'un ton fort sec si je n'avais rien à faire? Il fallut renoncer à cette chère antichambre: j'en eus d'abord du regret; mais les distractions vinrent à la traverse, et bientôt je n'y pensai plus.

Mademoiselle de Breil was a young lady of more or less my own age, well formed, rather handsome, extremely fair with jet black hair, and, though a brunette, she had that sweet expression which one finds in blondes, and which my heart has never been able to resist. Court dress, so flattering to the young, brought out her pretty figure, revealed her breast and shoulders, and made her complexion still more dazzling, since at that time mourning was being worn. It may be observed that it is not a servant's business to notice such things. I was at fault, no doubt. But still I did notice them, and I was not the only one to do so. The steward and the valets discussed her sometimes over table with a crudity which I found deeply distressing. My head, however, was not so turned as to make me absolutely in love with her. I did not forget myself, I stayed in my place, and even my desires remained under control. I loved to see Mademoiselle de Breil, to hear her say a few words that displayed her wit, her good sense, and her modesty. My ambition was limited to the pleasure of serving her, and went no further. At table I was always on the look-out for chances of asserting my rights. If her footman left her chair for a moment, I took up my place there immediately. At other times I stood facing her, following her eyes to see what she might want and watching for the moment when I could change her plate. What would I not have done for her to give me a single order, a single glance, a single word! But no. To my mortification I meant nothing to her. She did not even notice that I was there. Her brother, however, did sometimes speak to me at table, and on one occasion, when he said something to me that was pretty uncivil, I gave him so neat and smart an answer that she noticed it and threw me a glance. That glance was short enough, but it threw me into transports of delight. The next day I had the opportunity of earning another, and availed myself of it. They were giving a grand dinner, and on that occasion, to my great astonishment I saw the steward for the first time waiting with his hat on his head and his sword at his side. The conversation chanced to turn upon the motto of the house of Solar, which was embroidered on the tapestries around the coats of arms: "Tel fiert qui ne tue pas." As the Piedmontese are not as a rule perfect masters of French, someone discovered a spelling mistake in this motto, and said that the word *fiert* did not require a *t*.

The old Count de Gouvon was about to reply when, glancing at me, he saw that I was smiling, though I dared not say anything, and he ordered me to speak. Whereupon I said that I did not consider the *t* superfluous, that *fiert* was an old French word which did not come from *ferus*, fierce, threatening, but from the verb *ferit*, he strikes, he wounds; so that the meaning of the motto appeared to me to be not "some threaten" but "some strike and do not kill."

They all looked at me and at one another without saying anything. Never had such astonishment been seen. But what flattered me more was to see a look of pleasure on Mademoiselle de Breil's face. That haughty young lady condescended to throw me a second glance, every bit as precious as the first; then, turning towards her grandfather, she seemed to wait almost impatiently for him to give me the praise which was my due, and indeed he did compliment me so generously and whole-heartedly, and with such an air of pleasure, that the whole table hastened to join in the chorus. That moment was short, but it was in every respect delightful. It was one of those rare moments that replace things in their natural order, repair the slights on true merit, and avenge the outrages of fortune. Some minutes later Mademoiselle de Breil lifted her eyes to me again and asked me in a shy but friendly voice to give her something to drink. Of course I did not keep her waiting. But when I came to her I was seized with such a trembling that I overfilled her glass, spilling some water on her plate, and over her. Her brother stupidly asked me why I was trembling. This question did not help to put me at my ease, and Mademoiselle de Breil blushed to the whites of her eyes.

Here the romance ended, with the same ill fortune as my affair with Mme. Basile and others throughout my life; from which it will be observed that I am never lucky in the conclusion of my amours. I haunted Madame de Breil's anteroom, but to no purpose. I received not one further mark of attention from her daughter. She came in and went out without looking at me, and I scarcely dared to glance at her. I was so stupid and awkward indeed that one day when she had dropped her glove in passing, instead of dashing to recover that object, which I should have loved to smother with kisses, I had not the courage to move, but left it to be picked up by a great lout of a valet whom I would gladly have throttled. Then, to complete my discomfiture, I discovered that I had not the good

fortune to please Mme. de Breil. Not only did she never give me
orders, but she never accepted my services; and twice when she
found me in her antechamber she asked me very coldly whether I
had nothing to do. I had to renounce that dear antechamber. At first
I regretted it, but distractions intervened, and soon I never gave the
matter a thought.[15]

The episode is striking for its neat closure, which separates it from
its context. Is it not an abbreviated "romance" (the very word used by
Rousseau)? If so, it is a romance in rudimentary form, a parody of a
romance: for Rousseau's use of the word is ironic, Don Quixotesque.
The nonchalant "and soon I never gave the matter a thought" that
concludes the adventure interposes oblivion; it seems to be a farewell
without regret. It is possible that the accent is placed on the
interruption and incompleteness of Rousseau's timid lovemaking in
order to heighten the "reality effect."[16] The concluding phrase is in
every way written in the historical key as defined by Benveniste. The
negative statement here designates only the adolescent of Turin. The
elderly author of this autobiographical *discourse* has retained a very
vivid memory of Mademoiselle de Breil and the dinner at Turin. He
still thinks about it and has a very detailed image of the occasion, and
he admits to having recalled the episode when the first thoughts began
to stir in him of the character who would become Julie.

By the time the reader of the *Confessions* comes to this passage, he
knows Rousseau from all that has gone before. Mademoiselle de
Breil, on the other hand, is present solely in these lines. She reigns over
a very brief period in the narrative. Rousseau's art is to confer,
through the intensity of his own emotion, a powerful presence upon
this brief feminine apparition.

The episode consists of three stages, whose succession constitutes
an abbreviated romance: first distance, followed by exploit and
abolition of distance, followed by reestablishment of distance, separation. Arrayed around the central couple are secondary figures
whose functions are clearly indicated: the young lady's grandfather, a
beneficent personage who facilitates and encourages the hero's exploit; the girl's mother, a malevolent character who intervenes in
phase three of the story to signify a permanent prohibition; the
brother, who periodically goads Jean-Jacques to action; and finally
the guests, who represent the universal witness, like the chorus of an
opera. The analogy with the first part of *La Nouvelle Héloïse* is
striking, both in regard to the three phases of the love story and the

distribution of roles. To be sure, in the novel it is Julie's mother who is favorable to the hero, whereas her father puts obstacles in his way, a situation more in keeping with the tradition of paternal authority. It is also true that Julie has no brother (her one brother is dead) and that her companion is her charming (female) cousin. In terms of *functions*, however, the similarities outweigh the differences: the hero wishes to attract the attention and win the love of a heroine who is socially out of his reach; there is a parental dyad, with the two parents taking radically different attitudes toward the hero and hostility winning out in the end; there is also an "acolyte," whose intervention does not determine the outcome directly but whose words (close at times to buffoonery) provoke the hero indirectly and oblige him to reveal himself; and finally there is public opinion, which examines the hero, his merits, and his illicit loves sometimes with favor, sometimes with suspicion. Should we be surprised by these analogies? The three phases of the story of Mademoiselle de Breil reflect, it seems to me, an emotional archetype in Rousseau, an archetype present in everything that bears the stamp of his imagination. What is more, the distribution of roles fits the structural pattern of the myth of the "forbidden princess." (Think of the story of Turandot and the role of the riddles.) One has the sense that this is Rousseau's personal interpretation of a timeless mythological situation.

In the Turin dinner scene, desire, heightened by improvised resources of wit (the response to the brother) and knowledge (the interpretation of the motto), brings about an extraordinary metamorphosis in social and emotional relations. It provokes an event and, through that event, an emotion that temporarily changes the world, or at any rate the color of the world. But the metamorphosis does not last: the "brief but delightful" moment is delightful only by reason of its brevity. This is the law that governs Rousseau's imagination at all times and in all places. He begins in a state of separation and anxiety, seeks to alleviate the pain of distance (whether social or amorous), reestablishes presence, and in order to fully savor the intoxication of the feast and the transparency of hearts is willing to lose these prizes immediately after winning them, to have them snatched away after a brief but jubilant moment of triumph. He is then plunged back into separation and aridity but not without the bittersweet pleasures of memory and hope. Mademoiselle de Breil recedes; Jean-Jacques, occupied with other thoughts, forgets her, mentions her only once more in the *Confessions*, until he falls into a period of nostalgic reverie at the Hermitage, where her image comes back to him along with many other forgotten faces during the confused outpouring of emotion that precedes the writing of his great novel.

To each of the phases sketched in rudimentary form in the Turin dinner scene, the novel would give ultimate and finished expression: Julie surrenders, Julie dies—none of which happens with Mademoiselle de Breil. But it makes little sense to view the novel as a mere "compensation." In it the energy of desire is employed in the service of a far more profound and prolonged metamorphosis than that whose limits are so quickly attained in Turin. By attaching a fatal meaning to the final separation, the novelist establishes in imagination a religious communion in which nothing can henceforth be lost. That is why the Turin episode, with its ironic conclusion and collapse into oblivion, has the value of an "apprenticeship tale." Many Mademoiselle de Breils—apparently forgotten only to be rediscovered later on—are required to make one unforgettable Julie.

Extreme temporal condensation is needed to permit the development of the "abbreviated romance." The three phases of the narrative sequence must be compressed into the briefest of intervals and still retain their distinct values. The composition seems to consist of just three scenes. The background is a habitual situation (indicated by the use of the imperfect tense). In the first scene, at table, we have the response to the brother: this is narrated in the perfect tense, but without being definitely situated in time. The second scene, the formal dinner, unfolds in a setting more or less identical to the first, virtually confounded with it. Yet its time is more precisely specified, for we are told that it takes place on *the day after* the reply to the brother. It ends with the story of the overfilled glass. The first draft contains a significant variant: the incident with the glass takes place on the day after the little philological triumph. In the final version, however, Rousseau found this delay intolerable, and he wrote "a few minutes later." Not only is the episode of the glass once again precisely situated relative to the previous event; now the unit of measurement has shifted from days to minutes. The temporal indications become more precise as we draw closer to the moment of climax, marked by the shared emotion of the two protagonists. The concentration of time culminates in a focal point. Finally, the last phase of the story, though composed of a series of incidents, has a unique setting: Madame de Breil's antechamber. Temporal indications are relaxed, stretched out, and once again made indeterminate: words like "one day" and "twice" separate events and make no close connection between them. This is the fall, which follows the moments of glory and happiness.

Thus the episode that is temporally most sharply situated, whose *definition* (in the optical sense of the term) is finest, corresponds to the peak of the amorous adventure: the shortening of temporal intervals brings pent-up emotion rapidly to a head. The emotional crescendo and decrescendo dictate a gradual compression and decompression of time. At first all intervals become shorter and shorter and more and more specific. They culminate in the strange communion of the trembling servant and the blushing mistress. But in the end distance reasserts itself. The temporal rhythm of the tale is secretly governed by the law of desire.

Note, moreover, that the events of the abbreviated romance all take place in an instant, in the blink of an eye. Attention is immediately drawn to the matter of brevity in the recital of unavailing attempts: "If her footman left her chair for *a moment*," "watching for the *moment* when I could change her plate." Subsequently Rousseau enumerates Mademoiselle de Breil's glances: the first following his answer to her brother, the second after he is praised by the Count de Gouvon—"That moment was short, but it was in every respect delightful." The crucial events stand out in the extreme luminosity of a moment, associated with the bestowal of a glance. The spilling of the water, trembling, and blushing again define momentary thresholds, sudden excesses. Even the negative episode of the glove evokes the *instant* of the fool, the precious seconds in which Jean-Jacques, inhibited, allows himself to be overtaken.

The three clearly specified locales—servants' hall, table, and antechamber—correspond to the three main areas of a footman's service. In objective terms these places reflect the sequence of distance, proximity, and distance that embodies the story's meaning. In addition to objective space, however, there is also a moral (or symbolic) space. Here this second kind of space is evoked primarily through the (French) noun *place* and verb *replacent* (as opposed to *lieu* or *endroit*).

Compare the following sentences:

1. "I stayed in my place (*place*)." Here the word *place* is symbolic, referring to the respectful *distance* that a servant is supposed to maintain vis-à-vis his betters.

2. "It was one of those rare moments that replace things in their

natural order." This is an intervention of the author, a substitution of discourse for history, in which we recognize the epiphonema of classical rhetoric in a sentence marked by the pathos of a claim. All Jean-Jacques's servile efforts to please Mademoiselle de Breil were therefore the expression of a violent order, contrary to "nature," yet as the original version somewhat perversely observes, an order in which the young servant "felt an extreme passion for the pleasure of [his] condition." The word *replace* (with its prefix suggesting return or reestablishment) has a meaning quite different from that of *place* in the first sentence. The reference in this case is to the *natural order* (explicitly named) as opposed to the social order in which Rousseau a moment earlier seemed resigned to occupy "his" place, namely, the inferior role assigned to him along with its derisory "rights." The pairing of *place-replace* and the gap between the two senses of *place* establishes a spatial symbolism suggesting a reversal, a revolution, a transition from exclusion to inclusion, from periphery to center. Rousseau had been unnoticed; now he is recognized. He had made his way respectfully around the table; now he has become the master of his masters, their acclaimed hero. The whole relation between self and others changes its sign in a momentary readjustment. Emotion, which is both sudden and fleeting, reveals itself in the affective and moral experience of space, in the *recentering* of an initially *eccentric* individual.

Another repetition of terms, perhaps less striking at first glance (because there is no semantic variation affecting the word itself), serves to produce an identical effect of reversal. The word *astonishment* occurs twice in statements of antithetical significance:

1. ". . . to my great astonishment I saw the steward for the first time waiting with his hat on his head and his sword at his side."

2. "Never had such astonishment been seen." Astonishment thus changes sides. In the first sentence, Rousseau is gripped with astonishment at the sight of the solemn rites of aristocratic society: his reaction is that of the naive stranger confronting the novelty of an unknown world. By contrast, in the second sentence he is the object of astonishment. The use of metonymy and the amplification achieved through hyperbolic negation ensure that the noun occupies all of space. The nominalized collective reaction is the sole complement of the verb (*On ne vit de la vie un pareil étonnement*, "Never had such astonishment been seen").

The device of repeating a word in two sentences of contrary

meaning is worth noting. In another instance the repetition takes place within a very small interval, yielding an important reversal of status or position. I am thinking of the moment when Jean-Jacques first speaks, first dares to open his mouth. Within one line we read: "I dared *not say* anything . . . Whereupon I *said*." In this episode of the "romance," which leads up to the moment of shared emotion, this is the central reversal. The other oppositions that we have noticed to this point symmetrically enclose this turning point of the story, the moment when the neglected hero reveals his prowess, following the mythological pattern that underlies the entire episode. Now it is the turn of the others present, of the noble dinner guests, to be reduced to silence: "They all looked at me and at one another without saying anything."

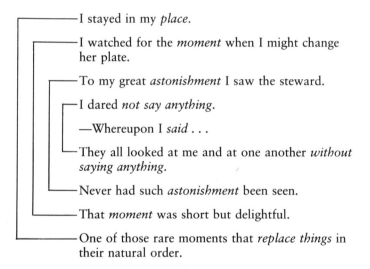

I stayed in my *place*.

I watched for the *moment* when I might change her plate.

To my great *astonishment* I saw the steward.

I dared *not say anything*.

—Whereupon I *said* . . .

They all looked at me and at one another *without saying anything*.

Never had such *astonishment* been seen.

That *moment* was short but delightful.

One of those rare moments that *replace things* in their natural order.

What we have here is a system of repetitions structured in such a way as to indicate a permutation, a qualitative reversal, an inversion of roles.

To be sure, not all the repetitions in this text suggest reversal. Indeed the episode in question does not bring about any lasting change in Rousseau's status. Only his flight from Turin and the return to Mme. de Warens marks a true liberation from his humiliating dependency. That is why the vocabulary of *domesticity* (words such as *serve* and *service* on the one hand and *order, request,* and *bid* on the other) is so evident in this passage, establishing its fundamental texture. Let us turn our attention once more to the point at which the reversal takes place. The actual turning point is in the phrase "he *ordered* me to speak." The neglected servant opens his mouth and achieves his momentary glory only *when ordered* to do so by his master. For him, speaking does establish a new order of things, but the count's injunction simultaneously maintains the old order, the old subordination.

A domestic provokes the admiring astonishment of his masters. The social hierarchy is temporarily effaced. High and low briefly cease to matter; only "merit" counts. Here we would do well to recall Erich Auerbach's important observations concerning the relation between the hierarchy of styles and the social hierarchy.[17] In this passage we expect to find a mingling of the elevated style and the low style called for by the "content." And indeed we do find juxtaposed and almost mixed together two distinct tones: that of the sentimental novel (in the tradition of noble romance established by d'Urfé, Magdeleine de Scudéry, and La Calprenède), and that of the picaresque in the tradition of Lesage. The first two sentences, with their fine musical cadence, might well be mistaken for sentimental romance (but for a few details). Elements of romance-like style are scattered through the remainder of the text: in the extreme value attached to the gaze, for example; in the excessive emotion caused by a mere glance; in the flights of eloquence, extending even to a pathetic reference to the "outrages of fortune"; and in the fetishism of the glove, which the hero wishes he could "smother with kisses." The romantic tonality is also evident in passive forms that express the fatality of feeling (forms so often found in Prévost): "which my heart has never been able to resist," "threw me into transports of delight," "I was seized with such trembling."

Yet "vulgar" objects and individuals—the chair, the plate to be changed, the glass, the rough company of the other servants— establish the presence of trivial reality and remind the servant who has begun to fall under the spell of the noble damsel of his humble condition. Doubtless it is no accident that the attractiveness of the heroine, described to us as if she were a bust, is followed almost immediately by mention of the crude words spoken in the servants' hall. The extremes are set down at once: the lovely but inaccessible figure of the girl, the uncouthness of the servants. The contrast, moreover, is heightened by the opposition between the fine cadences of the romantic style and the monosyllabic concluding phrases of the sentences ending "I was not the only one to do so" and "for sure": *pas le seul, tout de bon.* The most common effect of these abrupt endings is *trivialization.* They contribute to the animation of the narrative, as does the occasional use of parataxis and juxtaposition of short sentences (asyndeton).

We are struck, however, not only by the contrast between the elevated romantic style and triviality but also by their fusion and mixture carried to the point of equivocation. To be sure, even in the most traditional picaresque fiction, the reader's interest is piqued by the use of expressions appealing to the tender feelings. The pathetic relative "which made me suffer cruelly" is a cliché that might be found in Lesage as easily as in *Cleveland.* What is more striking is the use of terms relating to *knightly service* to denote what is in fact mere *table service.* The text plays several times on the ambiguity of the referent. A writer of seventeenth-century heroic romance might well have a suitor say "what would I not have done for her to give me a single order, a single glance, a single word." But this is a question of changing a dish! Note, moreover, that the hyperbolic thought in this passage, so closely associated with a great outpouring of sentiment, is in several places constructed from elements of the common language. The free use of adverbs and circumstantial complements that gives this text its pathos allows for the use of ready-made and rather homely phrases that would have been perfectly suitable for comedy: "never had such astonishment been seen," "blushed to the whites of her eyes." I am inclined to regard this as a synthesis of the elevated romantic style (with its hyperbole and signs of excess) with the verve of low style. (Recall that Rousseau's style was criticized for its *commonness* by many contemporary critics, most notably Buffon.[18])

Having considered the contrast between the noble romantic style and the picaresque realistic style in relation to the social significance of our passage, I now want to reconsider it in the light of the narrator's relation to his past. The time has come to return to a question I raised earlier concerning elegiac and ironic narration.

Here again I shall want to consider the minute details of the writing. Look at the opening sentence that offers us a physical portrait of Mademoiselle de Breil. A series of adjectives modified by adverbs stretches out a simple ascriptive proposition in the imperfect.

The sentence broadens out in surprising fashion with the elliptical concession "though a brunette" followed by the present participle (*portant*) and a relative clause in the compound past (*auquel mon coeur n'a jamais résisté*). The value of this compound past tense, in light of the imperfect that precedes it, is considerable: it suggests an ample expanse of time both before and after the dinner in Turin; it states a preference that continues to be felt at the present time. This compound past belongs to the realm of *discourse* rather than *history*. It is moored to the present, as it were, to the recent act of narration. As a result, the evocative writing makes a quasi-present of the remembered figure, bridging the interval of time by the deictic designation ("that sweet expression") of the cause of Rousseau's unvarying and still-present sentiments toward blondes. Hence Mademoiselle de Breil's individuating features (her "fair" skin and "jet black hair") are drawn by decree of desirous memory into the indeterminate community of *blondes*, the object of Rousseau's favor. She becomes the elder sister of Julie d'Etanges, a true blonde, an unreal image forever exempt from the ravages of time. We can go so far as to say that the figure of Mademoiselle de Breil, set at the beginning of the sentence in the distance of a bygone time, becomes by the end a vivid presence associated with a timeless sentiment. As she becomes "plural" she also draws nearer or, if you will, Rousseau has moved closer to her.

It should come as no surprise that the next sentence is even clearer, even more fraught with erotic implications: the text has provided an *object* for amorous desire. Elegiac diction is so effective that it can render with magical power the presence of beloved individuals. Yet they are still lost, and the illusion of proximity lasts only an instant. So it is with our text. No sooner is the image of the beloved conjured up than a voice of prohibition is raised, a voice attributed by Rousseau to an unidentified source representing the rules of social convention: "It may be observed that it is not a servant's business to notice such things." Foreseen and evaded, this external intervention serves as a reminder of the social taboo that a noble maiden cannot be the object of a servant's desire. This judgment, a call to order, is formulated from the standpoint of strict conformism: the man of inferior rank is denied the right of belonging to the same branch of humanity as his masters. The use of the future tense (*on dira*) and an imaginary interlocutor interrupt the flow of the narration and forcibly command our attention. The illusory proximity is suddenly abolished, and social and temporal distance are simultaneously restored. Above all, a distance is suddenly established between the narrator and the person he was, who ceases to be "I" and becomes "a servant." This way of seeing oneself as someone else, an objectification through the assumed gaze of others, is one of the chief characteristics of irony. The relation is no longer one of solidarity or identity but one of exteriority. What is more, it is quite clear that the scandalized interlocutor and the writer who admits that "I was no doubt at fault" momentarily occupy a position of superiority relative to the insignificant servant whose head is filled with confused reveries: at this point it is no longer the *past* that is qualitatively favored but the *present*—the present of the narrative act, in which knowledge, experience, and notoriety justify the writer in evoking his ignorance, indiscretions, and timidity with an air of amused condescension. In an abrupt turnabout, the past goes from being a scene of lost happiness to one of seemingly humiliating dependency. Mademoiselle de Breil's image has been summoned up through passionate contemplation only to be lost again as the result of an anonymous decree (*on dira*) that points out the obstacle and accuses the amorous design in its very source: to gaze upon this *object* is not allowed. Yet in his reply to the scandalized observer, Rousseau pretends to accept the accusation only to counter it immediately by setting passion against oppressive law. The portrait of Mademoiselle de Breil is the mark of an audacious curiosity, an insolent transgression. We now know that despite a prohibition still accepted in principle, the pleasure of admiring Mademoiselle de Breil has been illicitly stolen. The narrator enjoys repeating the theft and giving it the value of a challenge: "But I did notice."

From this point on Rousseau will play constantly on the two registers—irony and nostalgia—with wonderful skill. The ability to play freely over two emotional registers is an objective aspect of what a criticism limited to "impressions" alone would call the verve of this romance in miniature. More precisely, it is a sign of the freedom used by the narrator first to surrender and then to free himself from a past with which he would like to identify but from which he nevertheless feels separated by his whole painful and glorious destiny. The aging man who is writing his *Confessions* knows that his literary success has liberated him and carried him far beyond any hopes that the house of Solar might have fostered in the young servant's mind. That is why the tone of the narration is so extraordinarily full of joy. Not only is Rousseau aware that his success has amply compensated for whatever humiliations he may have endured, but he is now able to mock what would have been his patrons' highest favors. At best he might have become the private secretary, secret agent, and factotum of a noble family involved in the affairs of the Piedmontese court. Now he is able to smile at all that. He would never have achieved *universality* of thought or developed his unique *personality*. He is an unhappy man but an absolutely independent one, who speaks of a happy youth during which he was temporarily the prisoner of social bonds.

That is the important fact demonstrated in this passage. The relation to the past, alternately elegiac and ironic, and the free play of sentimental and picaresque tones are marks of a writer who is master of his literary powers and who easily dominates resources that permit him to *tell all*, and to tell it as he wishes. He has dared to claim and has earned the right to omit none of the movements of his "heart" (although at the time Rousseau wrote the *Confessions* he was under compulsion not to publish in France). What is Jean-Jacques's situation at the beginning of the "romance"? He is obliged to keep silent, even doubly silent. He has his orders from above ("It may be observed that it is not a servant's business to notice such things"). But at the same time, the other servants speak of their desire in a tone that Rousseau is unable to share. Theirs is the language of servile desire, expressed with a "crudity which I found deeply distressing." He does not accept the language of the base servant class, and he is unwilling to covet Mademoiselle de Breil with a "proletarian eye," to sully with words that which cannot be attained. Crude gossip, far from bridging the gap between social ranks, preserves and widens that gap. Pretending to be irreverence and liberty, it actually reinforces degradation; it is the self-confirmation of inferiority. Thus Rousseau's solitude is total. He cannot communicate with either those at the top or those at the bottom of the social hierarchy. He therefore describes himself initially as an outsider in two senses: he is an outsider in the world of the aristocracy, which does not recognize him (since after all he is only a servant); yet he does not belong to the footmen's world (because his "talent" and his heart raise him above the condition to which he has been subjected). This double impossibility will ultimately be converted into a twofold power. Therein lies the source of the freedom that he will later claim to usurp noble language (without dissimulating his bourgeois origins) while deliberately making use of base language (claiming that the nobility of his sentiments makes him immune to its degrading effects).

For the moment, however, in Turin, Jean-Jacques is doubly deprived of speech: he *cannot* talk to either his peers or his masters; he is condemned to silence. He has the right to speak only when ordered to do so. He is then discharging a *duty*, analogous to the other duties of his office. Twice in this passage he speaks after being requested to do so. Each time—in responding to the brother and explaining the motto—is a triumph. The supremely *free* autobiographical narration here takes as its theme Jean-Jacques's time of apprenticeship, of clumsiness, and of *transition* from imposed silence to triumphant expression: the inception of the *power to reply and to interpret* that will bring glory to the name of Jean-Jacques Rousseau. The author of the *Confessions* writes at a time when he considers himself important enough to preserve the smallest details of his life from oblivion. He is pleased to describe a time when he was still a person of no significance, but in this case he is describing the scene of his first success, a momentary foreshadowing of what the celebrated author's life will be like. The dinner at Turin as described by Rousseau can therefore be seen as a symbolic anticipation of the writer's relation to his audience (a relation of seduction and prestige). It is in a sense the prototype of all the musical and literary successes by which Rousseau will subsequently *distinguish* himself. How could it be otherwise, since Rousseau is here recreating an episode in his youth through all the glory, power, and experience gained as a result of his mastery of the literary language? It is the whole *future* of the writer that casts its light on the dinner at Turin. The mode of expression used in the passage reveals a sovereign mastery of language. In theme (or content) it is the story of an inaugural passage, in which the denial of the right to speak is overcome by a twofold verbal prowess. It might be argued that the narrative power that enthralls us in the *Confessions* is here used (and the example is not unique) to create a simplified, dramatized paradigm of its own origins. A free man, who has freed himself through writing, tells us—in the ironic tones appropriate to the assertion of freedom—how he passed from servitude to the initial stages of emancipation. He comfortably communicates a situation in which communication was impossible, and he reconstitutes the scene in which he broke the curse of compulsory silence. The text—a perfect verbal fabric—has as its "pretext" the shifting back and forth between preverbal desire and the barely emergent verbal ability to communicate.

The narrator who so tenderly reconstructs this brief and abortive romance is the acclaimed author of *La Nouvelle Héloïse*. The success of the novel has given him the power to recount the failure experienced in life, and to do so in a minor masterpiece of irony. Light is thus shed on the life prior to the literary vocation. We are invited to notice how what was incomplete and unfinished in real life laid the groundwork for glorious achievement in fiction. "Things past" are remembered in their proper perspective. Now there is no reason why the story of Jean-Jacques's youth and loves cannot be reconstituted by way of the discourse that proved so successful in his masterworks.

To be sure, by the time he came to write the *Confessions* the writer had moved beyond his major doctrinal and fictional works. All his energy goes to deprecating the fate that his literary daring and success had brought him: that of being a stranger, an outsider (foreignness of a second kind). He renounces not his ideas or his principles but the glory that has made him a target of widespread persecution. To recover the memory of his years of obscurity and enforced silence is to regain a luminous paradise. Therein lies the paradox of nostalgia. Once discovered, literature's ambivalent powers are not easily dismissed. Through his wish, expressed in his late works, to turn his back on literature, Rousseau discovered literature's great modern dimension, and especially the inner torment that comes of wanting to proclaim one's innocence through a medium—the language of eloquence—that bears the mark of evil. In the depths of a joyless glory, Rousseau employs the sovereign art to which he imputes his misfortune in order to reconstruct the enchanting image of an obscure but happy youth, before sentiment had found its outlet in the form of literature. The magic of narrative is impure to the extent that it is *too* successful: Rousseau recaptures the imperfect experience of his adolescence in a perfect narrative, a narrative perhaps unduly preoccupied with perfection. The disturbing effect of the *Confessions*, so often ascribed to the murky sentiments that Rousseau dares to avow, has more to do with this unstable compound of free reflexivity and asserted innocence. The narrator's perceptive and astute mastery is used to conjure up an existence whose happiness consisted in oafishly savoring the plenitude of feeling without being able (at that time) to externalize it.

*   *   *

Turning once more to the details of the writing, we see evidence of Rousseau's mastery in the many sentences whose syntax creates a close bond between Mademoiselle de Breil and Rousseau, *she* and *I*. Even when the writer recounts a situation of separation, of sexual and social taboo, he takes pleasure in joining himself with the once-distant figure of the young woman. Now he can indulge himself by expressing *separation* through the language of relation, comparison, and complementarity. "Mademoiselle de Breil was a young lady of more or less my own age." The text *entwines* the words that refer to the two adolescent heroes, treating each in turn as subject or direct object of the transitive verbs that establish a relation between them. Hence it matters little whether or not these verbs are affected by negation. Syntactic position creates the relationship. Of course all literature is predicated upon *loss of the object* and its replacement (I do not say representation) by words. In the passage that concerns us here, nostalgia is focused on a double loss: a closed chapter of the past and a love that never was, that was only dimly divined. Thus there is even more work to be done by verbal manipulation, which must express the loss and at the same time create a close relationship between the verbal substitutes for the two young people who failed to connect. Obviously the "compensation" lies in the free play with the *verbal sign* that takes the place of the lost prey. In the narrative, for example, Rousseau takes a judgmental stance toward Mademoiselle de Breil, and in a tone of approving condescension adopts an attitude toward her worthy of the pedagogue-demiurge in *Emile*: "I loved to see Mademoiselle de Breil, to hear her say a few words that displayed her wit, her good sense, her modesty."

Initially the absence of reciprocity is total. Rousseau is sensitive to Mademoiselle de Breil's charms but, zealous though he may be, he remains unnoticed. The verb *to notice* (*apercevoir*) is repeated, seemingly only to allow the introduction of the negative to mark a radical opposition:

> But still I did *notice*.
> She did not even *notice* that I was there.

The same opposition between a gaze and a "nongaze" is found in:

I loved to *see* Mademoiselle de Breil.
What would I not have done for her to give me . . . a single *glance*.

In fact, between the initial situation (in which Jean- Jacques is both unspeaking and unseen) and his access to speech and recognition, we must first pass through a stage of preverbal communication. The reader will of course recognize the several stages in the development of language as described in the second *Discourse* and the *Essay on the Origin of Languages*. Do we not witness the development of a language of gesture, and do we not recognize the "language of action" transposed from its primitive setting to the denatured world of culture? In five propositions of nearly constant length (ten to thirteen syllables each) a rapid pantomime is sketched:

If her footman left her chair for a moment
I took up my place there
At other times I stood facing her
following her eyes to see what she might want
watching for the moment when I could change her plate.

Yet for all Rousseau's attentiveness and glances, he elicits no response. The enthusiasm of "what would I not have done" gives way to the curt and elliptical "But no," which drops like a portcullis. The object of desire refuses herself, whereupon utensils like the chair and the plate enter the scene as substitutes. Desire, whose fortunes this passage recounts, seems temporarily obliged to assume a masochistic and fetishistic posture: zeal in service, joy in silent contact with objects graced by the touch of the beloved. Access to Mademoiselle de Breil's *consciousness* is not even hoped for. "Following her eyes" seems to describe a moment of indiscreet intimacy, but the following "to see what she might want" immediately forces us back into the world of objects.

The next two propositions culminate the enunciation of nonreciprocity, but their syntactic arrangement yields one of the most marvelous interlacings of *I* (Rousseau) and *she* (the young woman). For Rousseau, to express separation is to weave a knot. The personal pronouns actually form a chiasmus:

To my mortification *I* meant nothing to *her*;
she did not even notice that *I* was there.

An identical construction occurs in the scene of the antechamber at the moment when separation is reestablished:

> *She* came in and went out without looking at *me*,
> and *I* scarcely dared to glance at *her*.

The episode involving the response to the brother is the beginning of a more complex relationship, in which Jean-Jacques's first speech elicits Mademoiselle de Breil's first glance. Provoked by the brother, Jean-Jacques is implicitly granted the right to speak; he takes advantage of the opportunity to make a brilliant riposte. (His answer is described as *fine, bien tournée*, eminently the qualities of an art cultivated by "polite" society in the eighteenth century; but these adjectives could be applied not only to a witty riposte but also to a leg or a waistline—well-shaped and nicely turned.) Without speaking to Mademoiselle de Breil, Rousseau has gained the upper hand before her very eyes, and this earns him a glance. The relationship remains asymmetrical, without real reciprocity. To a speech that was not directly addressed to her (though intended for her nonetheless), Mademoiselle de Breil cannot and will not reply. The analysis could be rephrased as follows: the hero, having received a verbal insult, offers a triumphant riposte, which, when reflected back to the first speaker, immediately takes on the value of an indirect query to the leading witness, whose response does not go beyond the preverbal stage. This is a moment of great importance, for Mademoiselle de Breil suddenly shifts from unseeingness to sight, from the absence of all signs to a movement of the eyes that *can* be interpreted as a sign. This initial sign, lacking the univocal quality of actual speech, is therefore both deeply moving and inadequate; being inarticulate and indeterminate, it can mean anything.

As Rousseau describes his first speech, it seems deliberately to be intended for two recipients. Explicitly addressed to one interlocutor, his response seeks and finds an emotional reception in the consciousness of a second listener. This split reception gives Rousseau's repartee a double significance, erotic as well as social. Responding to the brother, the witty servant wreaks vengeance on an insolent master; drawing the attention of the sister, he accepts her glance as a gift of love. His "smart" answer therefore has two values, two effects, and Rousseau collects twice on his gamble. Distinct as the social drama and the libidinal drama may be, they come together in the recourse to language. At the conclusion of these exchanges, a final echo reaches Rousseau in the form of a nonverbal sign, which he receives with "transports of delight." The cycle is complete.

The episode of the formal dinner, which follows immediately, begins with a description of aristocratic etiquette and the symbolism of dress. Rousseau, who is encountering all this for the first time, speaks from the standpoint of the servant: "I saw the steward for the first time waiting with his hat on his head and his sword at his side." If the servant Rousseau fails to comprehend the significance of the steward's ceremonial livery, an inverse incomprehension is evident among the noble guests when it comes to the ancient motto. "The conversation chanced to turn upon the motto." The language of the motto is misunderstood, in part because it is archaic, in part because it is foreign. "Someone discovered a spelling mistake in this motto." This indeterminate personage (someone) here takes the place previously assigned to Mademoiselle de Breil's brother. He throws down a challenge to Jean-Jacques (this time indirectly), only to be vanquished by the young servant. Once again, a representative of the master class, precipitously availing himself of his right to speak, makes himself vulnerable to correction by an inferior. In this case the correction takes the form of an accurate interpretation of the motto. (Hence the response, like the challenge, is also indirect.) Despite the fact that the ignorant guest enjoys undisputed precedence over the servant when it comes to expressing his views, it does him no good because he has lost contact with the language of old, with the archaic message of the motto, to which the wise servant has free access. By giving his interpretation the servant shows that he is not a servant "by nature," that he does not deserve his humble station. Not only is he capable of deciphering a *forgotten* language, but even more to the point he is able to reestablish the original significance of a statement in which the authority of the masters is concentrated in a fetishized verbal symbol. Knowledge thus gives him a grip on the figurative essence of the family of masters as embodied in the coat of arms; intelligence brings the servant into contact with the very source of nobility. Since he can decipher the primary language, why should he not enjoy *priority*? If an echo can be heard in this passage of the medieval conflict between cleric and noble, it is even more legitimately seen as an exercise of historical intelligence by a "man of the people," who is thus able to trace the existing social order back to its roots. The steward's sword, the coats of arms on the wall, and the verb *fiert* in the motto are all reminders of a civilization based on the force of arms and the prestige of the warrior. In Turin in 1729, however, if feudal ritual had not entirely disappeared, it was already more than half sunk into oblivion. Vehement denunciation would soon follow. In the second *Discourse* Rousseau wrote in a contemptuous tone of criticism: "There must have come a time when the eyes of the people were so fascinated that its leaders had only to say to the humblest of men, Be great, thou and all thy race, and immediately he appeared great to all the world, and his descendants rose higher and higher as they became more and more remote from their ancestor."[19] As a man of the Enlightenment, Rousseau substituted for the abusive language of armed violence that of verbal violence, of critical speech: the skill of interpretation through etymology and the quest for origins, first principles, and deduction from those principles. Thus a new force appeared on the scene, ready to transform itself into political power. The *knowledge* of the common man stood ready to inaugurate a "new age of the spirit" (Hegel). In the dinner at Turin we already witness a minor revolution, one that does not go beyond an overfilled glass. Note, moreover, that as the age of feudalism draws to a close, feudal society is vulnerable to the prestige of criticism; it allows itself to be fascinated by the brilliant words of the reasoners who will soon challenge its very foundations.

At this point it is well to emphasize the complexity of the "linguistic relationship" in this passage. Earlier I called attention to the wealth and ineffectiveness of nonverbal or preverbal expression (preverbal because it was a question of gestures that precede the use of language). But now the *intransitive* language of the motto and coats of arms establishes a priority of another kind. Here we have not something that is *not yet* articulated language, but something that was language in the past but is *no longer* fully understood. It is what people talk about, but as if it were a riddle: the meaning is to be recaptured. Interpretation must compel what is no longer understood to speak. Knowledge of past language then becomes the touchstone of a present destiny.

Old Count de Gouvon, an "ancestral" figure, is perfectly aware of the meaning of the family motto. It is his place to instruct the ignorant guest. But he chooses to reply indirectly. He has seen the *smile* of his gifted servant and interpreted it as a sign of knowledge and superiority. Jean-Jacques therefore began by indiscreetly listening to the conversation of the guests he was serving, an obvious infraction of the rule according to which a servant has neither eyes to see nor ears to hear anything that is not a direct order. But the old count, far from scolding him for his indiscretion, invites him to speak. To respond through Jean-Jacques will yield a double triumph: first restoring the truth, and second demonstrating the talents of a young man whose services the count has been shrewd enough to obtain. The glory will redound to the house of Solar. But what is an ostentatious display of *possession* for the master becomes for Jean-Jacques a pretext for an ostentatious display of *existence*: he demonstrates his mettle for himself. Of course this is still an inferior form of self-assertion, since the servant still serves the master's pride. (Later, self-assertion will be linked to opposition to the privileged and their principles.)

"They all looked at me (*me regardait*) and at one another (*se regardait*) without saying anything." The exhibitionist pleasure in this astonishing sentence is plain to see, and the repetition of the verb places the singular Jean-Jacques on a footing of equality with the collective "they." In the world of separation, a universal gaze circulates and ultimately converges upon the hitherto unnoticed figure of insignificance. In the series of *echoes* aroused by the interpretation of the motto, this unanimous movement marks a still silent initial phase dominated by a social act: recognition of hitherto unrecognized talent. The narrator's tendency from the beginning of this passage to attach values of intimacy to the silent communion of the gaze betrays a predilection for eroticizing social situations. (The whole episode, dominated by the figure of Mademoiselle de Breil, can also be interpreted as a socialization of an erotic situation.) The first, still silent wave of admiration is succeeded by a second, which culminates in a noisy concert of praise. The important thing about this more intense admiration is that it originates in the gaze of Mademoiselle de Breil. The flow of the language suggests the progressive enlistment of more and more *voices*:

> But what flattered me more was to see a look of pleasure on Mademoiselle de Breil's face. That haughty young lady condescended to throw me a second glance, every bit as precious as the first. Then, turning toward her grandfather, she seemed to wait almost impatiently for him to give me the praise which was my due. Indeed he did compliment me so generously and whole-heartedly, and with such an air of pleasure, that the whole table hastened to join in the chorus.

The hitherto impossible communication is for a brief moment achieved. Jean-Jacques had previously worked to *see* without receiving any compensation. Now he is gratified with a second glance. Like the first, this glance is not the result of a direct dialogue but a reward for an exploit on the "battlefield" of impersonal language. In the terminology of Saussure, the objective explanation of a *fact of language (langue)* takes on, in the narration of the exploit, the value of a *deed of speech (parole)*, that is, an act in which the speaker expresses his singularity. The deed of speech, insinuated in clandestine fashion, results obliquely in a libidinal advantage.

"That haughty young lady condescended to throw me a second glance . . . Then . . ." These two sentences form one long sentence, whose two parts distinguish the two successive initiatives of Mademoiselle de Breil, both of which culminate in her use of her only resource, the glance. The first glance, whose significance is more emotional, is directed to Rousseau alone. The second, more "social," solicits from the grandfather his explicit praise, which is then amplified in the joyful *tutti* of the guests. The conjunction of glory and love (in which Freud saw the typical daydream of the adolescent and writer) is here fully realized. For an instant the fantasy of the wandering adolescent, intoxicated by the novels he has read, comes true in "reality." Young Don Quixote has met a real princess, and talent, its rightful place restored, compensates for the deficiencies of birth. Equality won (or regained) by merit glimmers fleetingly in the exchange of glances. The desired object is no longer taboo; social distance is deceptively annihilated. The moment is "brief but delightful." Rousseau always insists on the brevity of pleasure. Paradise is regained only to be lost immediately thereafter, for desire thrives on the preservation of distance. Here the chorus of praise is presented as the work of Mademoiselle de Breil. It is her mediated response to Jean-Jacques. These young people have invented a circuitous means of communication: the motto explained, the concert of praise. The space between their two bodies remains inviolate.

The emotional crescendo culminates in a third wave. We come to the final event, in which Mademoiselle de Breil and Jean-Jacques are linked via intermediate objects:

> Some minutes later Mademoiselle de Breil lifted her eyes to me again and asked me in a shy but friendly voice to give her something to drink. Of course I did not keep her waiting. But when I came to her

I was seized with such a trembling that I overfilled her glass, spilling some water on her plate, and over her. Her brother stupidly asked me why I was trembling. This question did not help to put me at my ease, and Mademoiselle de Breil flushed to the whites of her eyes.

This is the first and only time in the story that Mademoiselle de Breil speaks to the footman she had until this day ignored. What progress—first a glance, then a speech! To be sure, the speech is an order that recalls Jean-Jacques to his servile station. But his desire, as we know, is apt to seek pleasure in desperate submission. To receive an order from an "imperious mistress" is not something that displeases him. In such a situation Rousseau submits happily to humiliation. Here the initiative, the invitation, comes—and can only come—from the young lady. Rousseau obeys as a lover: after the success he has just won, nothing offends him. Indeed all the conscious aims of desire are combined in a kind of synthesis: the masochistic passion to serve, the narcissistic need to be recognized. The social act (a servant fills his mistress' glass) is disturbed, distorted, sabotaged by emotion. Instead of a precise action from the universe of *labor*, we witness an uncontrolled movement raised to the function of a sign in the "fictional" universe of passion. The failure of the functional gesture becomes the appropriate language of love. The trembling, the spilled water, the blush, all point to the realm of the body and are tumid with erotic significance. Whereas at the beginning of the tale we witness an unrequited declaration of love, now we see, written in the language of love, a perfect correspondence between Jean-Jacques's trembling and Mademoiselle de Breil's blush. The emotions are nearly synchronous though felt at a distance. For the narrator of the *Confessions* this is the most exquisite of communions. The scene as relived here is characterized by that quality of magical participation which several times in the *Confessions* Rousseau declares to be preferable to possession itself. The two young people are almost simultaneously unsettled by emotion, at once obvious and unacknowledged. The social and physical distance between them remains. In this final echo of the successful interpretation, it is not difficult to see a substitute for a more real possession, which, if the author of the *Confessions* is to be believed, was something that never occurred to the adolescent servant. Few readers today would be unwilling to admit that the spilled water might well be an apt symbol for a more organic fluid. Even the most traditional textual scholarship reinforces this view: in the first version of the text, the scene of the spilled water takes place on the day *after* the formal dinner. The final version, with keener appreciation of the emotional significance of the scene, places the events closer together and joins them in a progressive sequence that culminates in the equivalent of an orgasm. Readers with more background knowledge will probably be unable to refrain from noting the passive and urinary coloration of the event: Rousseau *allows* water *to flow* onto Mademoiselle de Breil. This is the same lad who one day "made water in one of our neighbor's cooking pots while she was at church; her name was Mme. Clot."[20] He is also the boy who first dug a ditch and then built an aqueduct to divert toward his own seedlings the water intended by Pastor Lambercier for the walnut tree in his garden. This is the same man who could not walk with "impunity" from the Hermitage to the garden at Eaubonne because of the mere image of Madame d'Houdetot. And he is also the man who would inflict upon himself the daily torture of the urethral probe, to be freed from it only after paranoid delusions had become a permanent affliction.

Yet if the scene of the spilled water is subject to interpretation in these ways, it is because we find in it a language that is at once eloquent and obscure. Something *is being said* by way of gesture and "physiological reaction." We are in the realm of nonverbal expression. But can we call it preverbal, when in this case the expression follows speech? What we see now is no longer an *attempt* but a *repercussion*. The two young people signal to each other, not with words but by way of events that affect their bodies. Use of such silent signs is due not to a *want* of communication but to an *excess*. Emotion inadequately conveyed through words overflows its vessel. The nostalgic narration, with its abundance of verbal resources, successfully captures in writing an exalting situation in which language is eclipsed by somaticized emotion, and in which the feelings converse through physical symptoms. Thus the writer gives himself both the pleasure of telling (albeit after a lapse of time) and the pleasure of reliving a moment that, to judge from what he says, was experienced ineffably.

At the beginning of our passage Rousseau wrote: "My desires remained under control." Such was the situation at the outset, but the ensuing events produce a radical change. The entire passage can in fact be read as the history of an *emancipation*, at once social and erotic. But the decisive emancipation, the power to speak, is ultimately realized only in the act by which it becomes possible to give voice to the muteness prevailing at the outset, that is, in the writing of this page of the *Confessions*.

The scene in the antechamber marks a return to the prior situation, with the social distance greater than ever. Now the gestures of desire are limited to the footman's stubborn loitering about the antechamber. The glove that *falls* from the hand of Mademoiselle de Breil might have been an almost symmetrical response to the spilling of the water. But the expressive act (retrieving the glove and smothering it with kisses) does not take place. It is mentioned only as an unfulfilled wish: "I had not the courage to move." Jean-Jacques is trapped in a position of subordination (and says so in the language of liberty that he subsequently conquers). A centrifugal movement begins. Madame de Breil *banishes* Jean-Jacques from her antechamber. And the narrator, as if accepting part of the responsibility for his banishment, alludes to his own *distractions*.

At first sight there might seem to be a tremendous difference between the wordless emotion that grips the young people in the episode of the glass and Jean-Jacques's futile zealousness, when he is reduced to hoping for brief contact with mere objects (a plate, a chair, a glove) that serve both as obstacles and mediators. But these substitute objects are precious because they preserve the distance between the lovers and thus make it possible for them to feel emotion at a distance. It is as if direct contact were too dangerous given both prevailing social norms and Rousseau's libidinal structure. Here the objects serve not as fetishes but as transitional objects (in the modern psychoanalytic sense). The question arises whether there is not, at some symbolic level, an equivalence between the various transitional objects (the chair, the plate, the glove, the glass of water) and the triumphal interpretation. The motto stands between Jean-Jacques and Mademoiselle de Breil. It stands for the social distance that makes the young woman inaccessible. By giving the correct interpretation of the family motto, Jean-Jacques does not succeed in overturning the obstacle that stands in his way; he strengthens it. Thus the gap between the self and the beloved is preserved. The ability to speak *about* the motto is a way for Jean-Jacques to protect himself against the emotion he would have felt had he spoken to the girl directly. He accepts a substitute in every sense of the word. Yet at the same time he bridges the gap; his response to Count de Gouvon is coupled with an *implicit*, oblique, indirect appeal for the girl's attention. The desired relationship is therefore obtained in the seemingly innocent circumstance of an absence of relations. The common denominator between the verbal exploit and the spilled water is that both are *interposed*; both arouse intense attention, thanks to the gap but also in spite of it, and that attention takes the place of physical contact. The energy of desire, having chosen its proxy, is free to flow back over Rousseau's own body. The cherries thrown from the top of the tree into the corsages of Mademoiselle Galley and Mademoiselle de Graffenried are another example of this (*Confessions*, book 4). This is also the function of the letter in *La Nouvelle Héloïse*. Independent of the message it contains, the letter is a transmitted object, an instrument permitting generally clandestine contact and communion. Touched by the hand and quill of the writer, bathed in tears, the letter becomes the physical receptacle of its passion. It solicits its recipient's emotion. The lovers suffer from the distance that forces them to write rather than see each other. Yet that very distance, which the letter bridges, becomes the indispensable prerequisite of a separate pleasure, a pleasure of which each sentence— written and then read—deploys, modulates, controls, and contains the rhythm and melody.

The passage we have been studying reveals an aptitude for eroticizing a series of objects in contact with the "beloved." Ultimately Rousseau's prime substitute object will become imaginary representation and its narrative transcription. In the dinner at Turin and its linguistic exploit, we witness the awakening of the very power that will enable the narrator of the *Confessions* to limn the remembered image of Mademoiselle de Breil and elicit the disconcerting blush. Even when the literary powers whose first glimmerings are depicted here have fully matured, language does not cease to serve, as we have seen it do in this scene, as an indirect means of seduction. In the strategy for winning Madame d'Houdetot's love, the gift of the manuscript of *La Nouvelle Héloïse* serves the same purpose as the explanation of the motto in the presence of Mademoiselle de Breil. Finally, however, *La Nouvelle Héloïse* makes the actual conquest of Madame d'Houdetot superfluous. For if initially Rousseau believed that he had found in Sophie d'Houdetot the real embodiment of the imaginary Julie, he could equally well love in Julie the articulated image of Madame d'Houdetot's perfections. The explanation of the motto was a way of gaining access to the heart of Mademoiselle de Breil, but it was no substitute; by contrast, the prose of *La Nouvelle Héloïse* and the female characters in the *Confessions* are substitutes for love. In the emotional narration, the moment of explaining the motto and that of spilling the water have become one.

As so often in Rousseau, the advent of speech takes on the value of an initiatory event. The narrative conforms to the rule of *inchoateness* that Rousseau so often applies in telling of his life. Here it is as if love caused Rousseau to speak for the first time. Hence we may consider this passage an illustration of the origin of language in the passions, a theory that Rousseau sets forth in his *Essay on the Origin of Languages*: "The *first* causes that made man speak were the passions."

Once again we can profit by closely examining the syntax in those parts of the text where the narration traces the transition to speech. Far from losing our way in a forest of pedantic detail, we actually discover a structural model valid not only for the syntax of the sentence but for the very syntax of Rousseau's thought.

Let us turn once more to a sentence that we examined previously in another context:

> Her brother, however, did sometimes speak to me at table, and on
> one occasion, when he said something to me that was pretty uncivil,
> I gave him so neat and smart an answer that she noticed it and threw
> me a glance.

Leaving aside the explanatory clause ("did sometimes speak to me at table"), this statement can be divided into three parts. The first establishes the circumstances: "and on one occasion, when he said something to me that was pretty uncivil." The second contains the principal assertion: "I gave him so neat and smart an answer." And the third reveals the consequences: "that she noticed it and threw me a glance." Each part of the sentence has a different subject: "the brother," "I," and "she." It is immediately apparent that the act performed by "I" (the smart answer) comes between a prior provocation and a later consequence, and in both cases, before and after the answer, the role of "I" is that of object rather than subject. Thus the system of three propositions divides time into three parts: a provocation, a response, and a consequence.

This "figure" of three propositions, three times, and three actors relates an *event*. Previously Rousseau had to face Mademoiselle de Breil alone, and the language of gestures he used while waiting on her at table remained without effect. Nothing happened. The event occurs only when the situation shifts from the illusory duo to a trio. The brother's speech provokes Rousseau's reply, which in turn elicits the girl's interested glance.

The episode of the explanation of the motto seems to me to conform to a similar three-part pattern, but on a considerably larger scale. The schema is no longer so obvious at the level of syntactic structure, but it can be perceived clearly in the sequence of the action. In the first phase, the stage is set: first the guest makes a mistake, then the Count de Gouvon gives his order. In the second phase, we have the act itself: the etymological explanation of the verb *fiert*. In the third phase we have the description of the effect of the revelation of Jean-Jacques's knowledge: first admiring silence, followed by a crescendo of praise ending in a *tutti* in unison.

The three phases are heralded in summary fashion in the introductory sentence: "The next day I had the opportunity (1) of earning another (3), and availed myself of it (2)." The event is then set forth in three clearly distinct sentences:

1. Provocation: "he ordered me to speak"
2. Response: "Whereupon I said"
3. Consequence: "They all looked at me and at one another"

The subjects of the first phase are the ignorant guest and, later, the Count of Gouvon. In the second phase, Rousseau is the sole subject. And in the third the subjects are, successively, everyone, Mademoiselle de Breil, her grandfather, and the whole table. With still closer scrutiny it is not difficult to make out a subordinate tripartition within the first phase, which follows the same pattern. The guest's error and the discussion that ensues *provoke* Jean-Jacques's smile, and the *consequence* of this smile is the order to speak issued by the count. Here the syntactic structures do not conform strictly to our primary model, but the *rhythm* of events is precisely the same. The subject occupies a central position between an outside provocation and an unforeseen consequence:

1. Provocation: "*someone* discovered a spelling mistake"
2. Response: "*I* was smiling, though I dared not say anything"
3. Consequence: "*he* ordered me to speak"

The central phase, occupied by Rousseau's exploit, cannot be subdivided. But the subsequent phase, that of the consequence,

unfolds as a series of linked repercussions, syntactically concluded by
a mark of consequence, "so . . . that," which precedes the peak of the
chorus of praise: "she seemed to wait . . . for him to give me the praise
which was my due, and indeed he did compliment me *so* generously
and whole-heartedly, and with such an air of pleasure, *that* the whole
table hastened to join in the chorus." This last moment is compressed
into one long, hypotactic sentence where all the active agents are
external to the self, which, in a position of receptivity, is grammati-
cally present only as an indirect object.

Finally, we find tripartition once more in the scene of the overfilled
glass. Initially it comes in a scene involving just two figures:

1. Provocation: "Mademoiselle de Breil . . . asked *me* . . . to give
   her something to drink"
2. Response: "Of course *I* did not keep her waiting"
3. Consequence: "But when I came to her I was seized with *such* a
   trembling *that* I overfilled her glass"

In the last sentence the indication of consequence is indeed present.
But in contrast to the other cases examined so far, the subject-actor of
the consequence is still "I." But the anomaly is more apparent than
real. In reality the consequence is not under Rousseau's control, and
the subject is implicated in a passive construction, "I was seized,"
which clearly indicates a consequence not under his *control*. His
passivity is such that in the next triad, where Mademoiselle de Breil's
brother once again intervenes in phase one, Jean-Jacques loses the
initiative in phase two; emotion deprives him of his opportunity to
"respond." The narrative includes a "failed response," whose comic
effect is increased by the contrast with the preceding instances of
successful response. The narrator consoles himself in the concluding
sentence with two linked, symmetrical statements, in which the young
servant's emotion is coupled with that of Mademoiselle de Breil:

1. Provocation: "*Her brother* stupidly asked me why I was trembling"
2. Failed response: "This question did not help to put me at my
   ease"
3. Consequence: "and Mademoiselle de Breil blushed to the whites
   of her eyes"

In this instance it is as if the second phase were contaminated by the
passivity regularly found in phase three. We witness the triumph of

the *consequence passively endured*, a triumph that corresponds not only to the failure of the hero's voluntary powers but also to the peak of his emotion.

Thus a characteristic sequence first detected in a syntactic pattern has been found to recur in a narrative schema, or series of events. The order that governed the organization of the sentence has also been found in the organization of a series of episodes, which develop fairly regularly according to the same rhythm. Such a homology is not fortuitous. It can be argued, in the first place, that it is characteristic of art: the use of the same principle of organization at different levels—both in the detail and in the broader elements of the work—achieves effects of harmony and economy. But what is at issue here is even more important. It is a question of the place that Rousseau assigns himself as the subject of his actions. On his account, he does not act in response to a primary impulse or drive that contains its own justification. Rather he reacts, replying to some stimulus, responding to some external circumstance. In fact when he refers, in the *Confessions* and the second letter to Malesherbes, to the moment of illumination he experienced at Vincennes—the central event in his life—we see yet another striking illustration of the ternary schema discovered in the dinner at Turin. The question posed by the Dijon Academy—a "happy chance"—plays the role of external stimulus. The sudden illumination is Rousseau's response, a response that is at once active and passive (being a kind of "movement" that takes place within him). The immediate result is an extraordinary welling up of uncontrollable tears, which moisten Rousseau's clothes, much as Mademoiselle de Breil's plate and even her person were moistened during the dinner at Turin. Once again Rousseau uses a particular syntactic construct to express uncontrolled consequence. Consider these two sentences:

> I was seized with *such* a trembling *that* I overfilled her glass, *spilling* some *water* on her plate and over her.

> I spent a half hour in *such* agitation *that* upon getting up I noticed that the whole front of my vest had been *moistened* by my tears without my having been aware that I was *crying*.[21]

But the ternary schema's reappearance is most striking when Rousseau, in the *Confessions*, alludes to the encouragement he received from Diderot. This time the uncontrolled consequence is Rousseau's entire life after the moment of illumination at Vincennes. Compared with the original syntactic model, we do not find the same characteristic order of propositions (circumstance, principal action, consequence), but we do find the same succession of subjects (he, I, the rest) and above all the same pattern, beginning with a provocation from outside and ending with an uncontrolled consequence:

1. Provocation: "He encouraged me to give my ideas wings and compete for the prize"
2. Response: "I did so . . ." (Compare, in the Turin dinner scene, "Whereupon I said.")
3. Consequence: ". . . and from that moment I was lost. All the rest of my life and of my misfortunes followed inevitably as a result of that moment's madness"[22]

Here it is clear that the ternary scheme serves the purpose of *exoneration*. Personal responsibility for the action ("I did so") is assumed only momentarily. Before and after the act, on either side of it in time, Rousseau declines all responsibility. The prior impulse came from the *other*, and the ultimate, "inevitable" effect rendered the subject a stranger unto himself, estranged from his true nature against his will.

In this we recognize the schema that governs Rousseau's historical thought. Upon encountering certain "obstacles" the man of nature is obliged to respond, by going to work and inventing language. At that moment history begins, and the only process that leads from virtual perfectibility to the perfection of the present is set in motion. Yet the consequences of this process are uncontrolled, and through it man falls prey to evil according to an inexorable logic whose workings cannot be foreseen when man first sets to work and begins to reflect. In the second part of the *Discourse on Inequality* we clearly discern the three phases that have caught our attention:

1. Provocation: "Sterile years, long, harsh winters, and scorching summers . . . *demanded* new industry *of them*"
2. Response: "Along the seacoast . . . *they invented* the fishing line and the and the hook. In the forests *they made themselves* bows and arrows"
3. Consequence: "This repeated application of diverse individuals

to themselves and to one another naturally *engendered* in the mind of man the perception of certain relations"[23]

A fuller commentary on Rousseau's philosophy of history would not be out of place. But I shall content myself with pointing out that the external provocation here interrupts a *stationary state* whose duration is indeterminate, namely, the state of nature. In the state of nature every need is immediately gratified; hence desire never has an opportunity to appear. As it happens, the story of the dinner at Turin includes a similar state, however great the distance may be between the young servant and the "man of nature." This preliminary state is marked by ignorance and the absence of desire:

> *Confessions*, book 3 (dinner at Turin): "I did not forget myself, I stayed in my place, and even my desires remained under control." (In the first draft we read: "perhaps because I was not sure what they ought to settle on.")

> *Discourse on Inequality*: "His desires did not outstrip his physical needs ... His imagination painted him no pictures; his heart demanded nothing of him."[24]

This preliminary state—a time of repose fraught with the potential for catastrophe—has often been compared with the Garden of Eden. Carrying the theological analogy somewhat further, one might compare the provocation (first phase) to the speech of the Tempter, the response (second phase) to the original sin, and the uncontrolled consequence (third phase) to the unfolding of historical time.

If there is a time prior to the provocation, there is also a time following the uncontrolled aftermath, a time of *emotional repercussions* or, perhaps better, of *emotional interpretation* of the consequences of the action taken in response to the provocation.

Rousseau responds to external provocation by way of an active reaction: he does something, he speaks. But to the uncontrolled consequences of his action, he responds with an emotive reaction, the final quintessence of the whole event. When Jean-Jacques makes his smart reply and Mademoiselle de Breil finally lifts her eyes to him, her action finds a strong echo in Jean-Jacques's heart. He savors the pure affective quality of what has just happened to him. "That glance was short enough, but it threw me into transports of delight." The same thing happens after the chorus of praise from the masters: "That moment was short, but it was in every respect delightful." Thus there is a secondary reaction to the event; in this case it takes the form of pleasure, but more often, when the uncontrolled consequences are hostile or unfavorable, it will be expressed in tones of anguish or suffering.

The ternary schema is therefore sufficiently ubiquitous to be singled out as one of the primary "structures" in terms of which Rousseau interprets himself, the world, and his situation in the world. It is, as we have just seen, a characteristic feature of his *writing*, and therefore of his thought (to the extent that his writing traces an image of the world) and his sensibility (to the extent that his writing is intimately associated with a personal way of being in the world). At the time the *Confessions* were written, Rousseau had a penchant for interpreting himself in accordance with the ternary scheme, which enabled him to exonerate himself by incriminating others and to dissociate himself from the undeserved albeit inevitable consequences of actions he was compelled to take.

The complexity of this passage excerpted from the great work in which Rousseau interprets his destiny and present situation derives from the fact that its subject is an *act of interpretation*. Perhaps we can draw from this scene of interpretation something of value for a *theory* of interpretation. This, incidentally, need not be a theorization of all that is explicitly or implicitly contained in the passage.

Focusing on the explanation of the motto, the act of interpretation at first sight appears to offer nothing of unusual interest. Jean-Jacques, the occasional scholar, follows the same procedure as any philologist: he restores the meaning of an archaic word by tracing its etymology back to the linguistic source. In this way he explains the presence of a letter that is not pronounced and dispels the illusion created by the apparent homophony. But this little exercise in historical linguistics only restores the literal meaning of the word. Rousseau in this passage says nothing about the meaning (or semantic value) of the statement itself, even though it too requires interpretation. What is the meaning of "some strike and do not kill"? Oddly enough, an oral tradition, preserved by the count's family, suggests that Rousseau did not refrain from offering a commentary on the motto as well. He is supposed to have said that "what wounds without killing is love," thus applying the motto to his own situation, using it as an emblem of his desire.[25] (This bold lover's sally is omitted from the *Confessions*, and in a moment we shall see why.)

Where did Rousseau acquire the ability to reason in terms of etymology? Just as he looks to the original word *ferit*, we may look to the origins of his capacity to invoke Latin models. Where did he gather this knowledge? It is not difficult to trace the "Roman theme" in Rousseau's background. As an apprentice he idled away hours inventing medals "to be used as orders of chivalry," and he studied about the Romans with Pastor Lambercier. Going still farther back, we find books taken from his father's study, such as Plutarch's *Lives*, which taught him about the world of the Roman republic, and a whole series of sadomasochistic fantasies: "Continuously preoccupied with Rome and Athens, living, as one might say with their great men, myself born the citizen of a republic and the son of a father whose patriotism was his strongest passion, I took fire by his example and pictured myself as a Greek or Roman. I became indeed the character whose life I was reading . . . One day when I was reading the story of Scaevola over table, I frightened them all by putting out my hand and grasping a chafing dish in imitation of that hero."[26] The motto as *interpretandum*, an object to be interpreted, is both the starting and the ending point of an operation where both the workman (*interpreter*) and his conceptual tool (*interpretans*) embody a *prior discourse*—a discourse that constitutes the person of the interpreter (or at least an important part thereof) and gives him a grip on the object of interpretation.

But what is going on when Rousseau declares that "what wounds without killing is love"? This appears to be a deeper interpretation of the meaning of the motto. In fact, however, it is an *emblematic embodiment* dictated by the need to dramatize the circumstances and to create a chance for something to happen. The emblematic exegesis becomes a way of explicitly characterizing the moment of experience and at the same time a way of modifying it. The motto itself, when used to further the interests of the young lover, is no longer the starting and the ending point of the interpretive act. It is, as I just indicated, a *means*, an instrument, a mediator. For Rousseau, then, the object of interpretation (*interpretandum*) is not the motto itself but, thanks to his witty explanation, his own role, his own figure as a potential lover. Thus the emblematized motto becomes an interpretive instrument (*interpretans*) in an operation of self-interpretation. Once again the prior situation is important. In order to use the motto in this way, its literal meaning first has to be worked out. A preliminary "objective" interpretation is required. The situation, moreover, must be cast as a "romantic" one. This is the purpose of the second preliminary interpretation, which is "subjective" in nature and associated with the subject's presence vis-à-vis others, inseparable from his current feelings. Coming as a tertiary interpretation, the emblematic commentary is overreaching, overinterpreting.

Again we must look to the interpreter's history to account for his powers of interpretation. To sense the romantic possibilities in a scene, to take advantage of opportunity by availing oneself of a duly "solicited" pretext, to describe for oneself and others the adventurous significance of the situation—these are things that can be done only by one who is utterly at home in the world of fiction. He must be familiar with the traditional *discourse* and legendary mythology of passion in order to establish a relation between these and the events of his own life. In the case of Rousseau, we know that the heroic and amorous world of the novel was associated with the image of the mother he never knew. His nocturnal reading of works of fiction was a substitute, a "compensation," for the mother he lost at birth, the symbolic object who both marks and spans the gap. If the erotically emblematized motto can be seen as an instrument for interpreting the situation with Mademoiselle de Breil, it is because that situation was from the outset decoded in terms of texts stored in the deepest past of Rousseau's consciousness, that is, in terms of the rhetoric of the novel, "the first interpretive instrument." The discourse contained in books that *took the place of* Jean-Jacques's lost mother give meaning to the encounter with Mademoiselle de Breil and make it possible to sustain and extend the "objective" interpretation of the motto by way of its "subjective" embodiment. Now we can understand why in writing the *Confessions* Rousseau no longer needed to add the comment that "what wounds without killing is love." His entire narrative is conceived as a romance. The romantic and amorous interpretation of the scene is present in its composition and tone from the very first portrait of Mademoiselle de Breil. The amorous purpose to which the philological exploit is put is too obvious to require redundant emphasis in the form of additional comment by the hero. The circle of objective (philological) interpretation, which occupies a distinct moment in the tale, is itself included and subsumed in the wider circle of emotive self-interpretation. In this passage Rousseau is composing a "romance" patterned after those that enchanted him as a child, whose rhetoric was powerful enough to give form and meaning to both the actual and the remembered experience of the events of Turin. In this interpretation of self (and of the lived situation) through the discourse of "books" we recognize the delusion of Don Quixote.[27]

Assume that the subjective interpretation takes precedence, that the external object loses its autonomous reality and is subordinated to the requirements of a prior fiction, and that the object ceases to be anything more than a means of self-interpretation in which the meaning of the situation is emotionally prejudged: the possibility of delusion then exists. Ignoring the resistance of the object, interpretive discourse bends the world to its own law, resulting in a radical misinterpretation of the exteriority of the other. Objective interpretation no longer has its proper place; it is preceded by a *projective* interpretation, which begins and ends with the subject. The meaning of the object is no longer governed by the manner in which the object stands before the subject. The object does not even figure in the interpretation. It is caught up, rather, in the subject's concern and becomes the material pretext that the subject needs to crystallize its awareness of its situation.

As long as the circle of objective interpretation counterbalances and compensates for the movement of subjective interpretation, the danger of delusion is avoided. A risk arises when there is a relative weakening of objective interpretation. One cause of this weakening may have to do with the substitution of an image (a memory or fantasy) for the object itself. If, under the impact of emotion, representation takes precedence over perception, the image becomes malleable and can be incorporated into a cycle of subjective-projective interpretation. This is true of all the figures that an autobiographer includes in his narrative. Whatever their initial status, their final status in the writing is that of image, which lends itself to the imaginative exegesis of anxiety. But anxiety is unwilling to recognize that it is master of its interpretations. It feigns submission to the object, respect for its individuality. Hence it will mimic the procedures of objective interpretation. It will pretend to search for incontestable *etymologies*. Read the Turin dinner scene once again. It is full of interpretations of expression, in which Rousseau claims to recognize in a certain *look* or *tone* positive proof of a *feeling* or *attitude*. He goes back to the source, to the cause, just as he traces the etymology of *fiert* to *ferit*. Consider only the most obvious instances of this:

"a look of pleasure on Mademoiselle de Breil's face"
"he did compliment me . . . with such an air of pleasure"
"asked me in a shy but friendly voice"
"Her brother stupidly asked me"
"she asked me very coldly"

Appearances are always characterized in such a way as to pinpoint the intention that lies behind them. Admittedly Rousseau varies his method. Sometimes he reveals the physical sign, or *seme*, without explicitly elaborating its significance; sometimes he first discloses the significance (*astonishment*, for example) without mentioning the physical signs; and frequently he slips in an interpretation in the form of an adverb (*stupidly*). Yet the diversity of method reveals a constant need to define verbally the nature (essence) of sentiments of which he is the object. In the Turin passage the interpretation is generally favorable (with the exception of the mother's words and *tone*). But in the passages most typical of Rousseau's paranoid delusions, it is striking to note a style of writing and mise en scène strangely similar to that of the Turin episode. Rousseau is the object of some external provocation, he must speak, a collective gaze is focused upon him, and a murmur spreads through the assembled company. But now what happens is just the opposite of what took place in Turin: his tongue is tied, the gaze that focuses on him is perceived to be full of hate, the chorus is one of slanderous rumor and hostile whispers. One brief example, in all respects a mirror image of the Turin dinner, will suffice:

> Some time ago Monsieur Foulquier persuaded me against my custom to go for a kind of alfresco dinner with him and his friend Benoît at Madame Vacassin's restaurant; our hostess and her two daughters also dined with us. During the meal the older daughter, who had recently been married and was expecting a child, suddenly looked hard at me and asked if I had had any children. Blushing deeply, I replied that I had not had that happiness. She smiled maliciously at the company; none of this was particularly obscure, even to me.[28]

Here, as in Turin, Rousseau is at the center, exposed to the attention of "all," of the "whole table," the "company." And just as in Turin the language of the body ("blushing deeply") is presented as the organic repercussion of the spoken word. The three phases—

provocation, response, consequence—are plainly evident. The narcissistic element is of course present in both scenes. But with guilty anxiety Rousseau interprets the question, the smile, and the look as expressions of hostility. He reads the situation as yet another proof of his persecution. Rousseau's plight is the primary object of interpretation (*interpretandum*), and the young woman's hostility, which is perceived as the etymology behind her question, her smile, and her look, is interpreted only to be used at once as a new interpretive instrument (*interpretans*) in an enigmatic situation.

I I I

The Interpreter and His Circle

We have just read a narrative text whose central event is an act of interpretation. Why—if our purpose is to develop a theory of interpretation—this lateral text, this oblique reference? What does it tell us about interpretation? Can its lesson be carried over, like some quasi-mythical model, to the work of the modern interpretive disciplines, including even psychoanalysis?

The idea is tempting. We have here an archetypal scenario ingenuous enough to contain, in a dramatized form, various revealing clues that lay bare social and emotional factors generally—and wrongly—overlooked in theoretical discussions limited exclusively to the epistemological aspects of interpretation. The fact that the interpreter in this text is an inferior, the outsider, should certainly not be ascribed to mere chance or to the realm of the anecdotal. There is a more substantial lesson to be drawn, a lesson that bears on the interpreter's position in the world. This should be read in conjunction with another lesson to be derived from the picaresque tone of the passage. Traditionally the picaresque expresses the illusionless world view of the outsider. It has rightly been argued that, in its original form (*Lazarillo de Tormes*), the picaresque adopted the lucid and ironic point of view of the "new Christians" (Jews ostensibly converted to Christianity) by way of the moral fictions claimed by the hidalgo class. In this we recognize the traditional demystifying role of the outsider. But whereas the picaresque hero is content to achieve respectability by devious means in a society of which he knows the ins and outs and whose hypocrisy he turns to his own advantage, Rousseau (the foreigner, the Genevan) refuses to limit himself to an ironic description of success achieved through industry. In his theoretical works he will interpret the *origins* of the social relations that he feels have excluded him from his rightful place. Interpretation, the philosophical complement of persiflage, deepens ironic criticism to the point where it takes on revolutionary proportions. The line from the picaro to Rousseau continues on to Freud. Freud is also an outsider, but one who compensates for the disadvantages of his situation by using interpretation to capture the secrets of the *insiders*, by restoring the meaning of a forgotten tongue, and by relating every element of the message to its overall meaning. He is thus, in turn, promoting a revolution through interpretation. This revolution or circle, which is expressed in part in the notion of the "return of the repressed," can be extended in a sociological sense: Freud, the descendant of a people whose theological discourse lies at the source of "gentile" society and yet who were expelled from that society (or confined in its ghetto), conquered through interpretation the right to a place in the inner sanctum of a scornful and thankless world.

Another lesson has to do with the emotional value of the interpretive act. It is clear that a successful interpretation yields a libidinal gain with an important narcissistic component. To understand is to "eliminate the gap," and to make others understand (to teach) is to move from a peripheral position (perhaps a perilous pulpit) to a central one; it is to seek to become the focus of general interest, and since every audience includes a Mademoiselle de Breil, it is to seek the comfort of loving approbation. Since the energy of desire is transferred to the successful act of interpretation, to the hermeneutic feat, it is conceivable that the image exhibited by the interpreter is that of a victor—an emphemeral image subject to eventual defeat and persecution. Someone may object that I am going rather far afield in search of those traits common to the actor and the intellectual, who both present their thoughts for others to see (or hear): *interpreter* is, significantly, a word applied to the actor or soloist as well as to the grave hermeneuticist. Recent psychoanalytic literature on the specific content of the psychoanalyst's work has not failed to consider this problem. A look at some very old books would do just as well, however: Socrates was already quite familiar with the facts we have so laboriously extracted from the passage in Rousseau. To interpret the ambiguous language of appearances is to go back to a forgotten source, but it is also to seduce and to derive pleasure from the exhibition of truth. It is, moreover, to risk being accused of corrupting youth. In recalling the name of Socrates I myself am performing the same feat of anamnesis as Rousseau in tracing *fiert* back to *ferit*, or as the psychoanalyst in tracing a symptom back to language buried in the unconscious.

Let us carry this one step further. I surprise myself dreaming that Freud in his own way interpreted the same maxim as Rousseau, and that in this interpretation the verb *fiert* (from *ferit*, he strikes) became the act of Oedipus. Everything in the original account can be taken as an adumbration of the Freudian interpretation, even the comment preserved in the memory of one of those present: "What strikes and does not kill is love." Chance (if it is chance) contrived to arrange things fairly well. But it is unnecessary to invoke coincidence. Freud himself confronted the question of the most effective relationship compatible with the preservation of distance. Observing the rigor required of the scientist, he chose to remain even more aloof from "Mademoiselle de Breil" so as to heighten the impact of the moment of interpretation. It is well known, moreover, that it was because Breuer found himself unable to maintain this necessary distance that he turned his patient over to his young colleague.

Is it legitimate, though, to ascribe such emblematic dignity to Rousseau's passage? Don't we diminish Rousseau's singularity and uniqueness, upon which he particularly prided himself, when we read him in such general terms as an apologist for interpretation? Aren't we transforming what is symptomatic of Rousseau's individual psychosexual makeup into an exemplary myth? Aren't we also neglecting what is absolutely original in the interpretive work of the modern critic, what cannot be traced back to earlier models?

The time has come to ask about the way in which I have chosen to comment on this passage from Rousseau. I sought to identify the complex web of social and emotional relations that it depicts, using an essentially stylistic analysis of a text that describes a scene. After first identifying the key vectors, I then tried to describe them in the currently available vocabulary. I do not claim to have done anything other than make empirical use of terms and concepts from psychology and social philosophy. My use of these terms and concepts is more literary than scientific. Had it been otherwise, would I have used certain vague terms, fetish words such as "revolution" and "transgression," in the way I did? I measured my object against the abcissa and ordinate of a language fairly widely used in discussions of social and emotional problems, nothing more. I gave a translation, or reencoding, or, better still, a free transcription of elements from the text itself. In this connection it is well to bear in mind the "entropy" of terminology in the human sciences, quite apart from any process of vulgarization. Although this language is, at a certain stage of development, sometimes (but I think not always) endowed with a degree of technical precision, it quite rapidly degenerates into a somewhat vague mode of sensibility, a means of immediate perception. We are no doubt wiser as a result, but at the expense of systematic rigor. Similarly, in medicine, the clinical method degenerates into what is called clinical flair, frequently not without practical benefits but at the sacrifice of genuine "scientificity." True, for a work of language an initial *understanding* invariably precedes any methodical explanation, and inevitably our spontaneous apprehension of the work includes echoes of old methods that have become habits.

I make no causal hypothesis. For me, description of evidence drawn from the text itself is enough. Behind the social event we have glimpsed the confrontation between the artisan class, the hereditary nobility, and nascent industry. And behind the emotional event, or through it, we have investigated earlier life experiences and conjectured about possible fantasies. With respect to the history of ideas and attitudes, I might have called attention to the autobiographical emphasis (or self-indulgence) of the text, which marks the decisive moment when the idea of the self and of individual existence as an absolute value first took hold in Western consciousness (in tones at once defiant and seductive). I have been satisfied to make just a few comparisons, abandoning the text only briefly, and to elucidate significant analogies. Does this somehow reflect a "structuralist" bias, hostile to all genetic explanations? Not at all. But the very economy of the interpretation, I think, made it imperative to emphasize description. Does anyone doubt that the social conditions of an era and the experiences of childhood necessarily have an influence on the work produced by the adult writer? That is no reason to crown with usurped privilege a causal theory that is as difficult to challenge as its claims are unspecific. The less attention one pays to the individual character of literary works, the easier it is to persuade oneself that all questions can be answered merely by enumerating the conditions under which those works were necessarily produced. The critic who respects the particular configuration of texts or events will be less readily satisfied with explanations too broad and too supple to be truly pertinent.

Thus, rather than ascribe constraining antecedents to Rousseau's text, I chose instead to show how this passage might be applied to our own enterprise, to raise it to the status of a model or emblem. Just as Rousseau used his motto for his amorous designs, I have used the entire scene as a paradigm for interpretation in general.

One possible objection must be addressed, however. This passage, which I have taken to be typical of interpretation in general, has proved to be so eloquent only because I interpreted it with the aid of theories and concepts of which I see it as a precursor. It was able to instruct me only because I already spoke the language I was so amazed to discover in it. Nothing is simpler than to shape the past so as to make it fit into our own project or discourse. The scene of interpretation, as interpreted by me, has become the model of what I have to say about it. Haven't I contrived to produce a true echo of my own voice? Haven't I arranged to have my own discourse faithfully reflected back to me? In this way, it will be objected, I have constructed a tautological circle, on which a single discourse travels, reverberating back upon itself and always certain of confirmation by its object.

A circle? Why not acknowledge the fact? It is a circle in which our theories are turned back upon themselves, in which everything begins and ends with what we say but only after passing through our object, which functions much as a crystal does when it diffracts a beam of particles or rays focused upon it. Isn't it legitimate for an interpretive discourse first to explore its own style, structure, and possibilities before demonstrating its powers and characteristic qualities on an object of study? In this way, the language of our knowledge and consciousness stands revealed in its historical particularity and universal ambition. Surely explanatory language is not the same at the end of its circuit as at the beginning. In between it encounters an obstacle, a challenge, a provocation, and even if it were concerned only to reduce a foreign presence to its own terms, even if its only ambition were to prove its ability to triumph over whatever stands in its way, it will have had to perform a task, to expend energy on assimilation of its object. And yet the *alien* object, thus reduced to the terms of an unvarying discourse, always identical to itself, does not disappear. Once explained, the object is subsumed; it ceases to be simply an illustration and application of a preexisting method and becomes an integral part of learned discourse. It provides an opportunity for the transformation of methodological principles through practice, so that in the end the interpreted object becomes yet another element of the interpreting discourse. It is no longer an enigma to be deciphered and becomes in its turn an instrument of deciphering. This is true (with certain provisos) of formal systems of explanation, which are enriched and toughened through practice. It is especially true of methods that rely upon emblematic models, for which the interpreted object becomes a new explanatory emblem, a new operational model. Recall that *Oedipus Rex* was first a text read by Freud (in high school) and that it later became not an object but an instrument for deciphering. The same is true of *Hamlet*, initially a puzzle to be solved but later a typical specimen of neurosis. When a psychoanalyst speaks of a patient's "oedipus" (small *o*), I presume he has forgotten about Sophocles' character. The explanatory discourse inherited from Freud has become the repository in which the mythical figure resides. That figure has been subsumed at a new level, assigned a secondary signifying function. Yet the name of the hero, now a common noun, has not disappeared; it has acquired a new meaning and a place in the "metalanguage" of science.

Let us imagine a generalization of this absorption of the interpreted object into the language of interpretation. In such a process the asymptotic limit, as it were, is a kind of dream: an all-embracing discourse that would abolish the separation between language and its theme, between the interpreting subject and the interpreted object. The object would be spoken and would speak for itself, would speak and be named within the context of a unique discourse that is the discourse of both reality and knowledge. There would be a homogeneous text, a universal algorithm in which, bound by a single set of models and metaphors, the reality to be explored is indistinguishable from the language in which its laws are enunciated. Today, as research into infrastuctures progresses hand in hand with the elaboration of ever more sophisticated metalanguages, the mixture (or synthesis) sometimes takes surprising forms. When it is possible to say that the unconscious is "structured like a language," it is perhaps not outrageous to point out that interpretive discourse tends to conform to the logic of dreams: the syntactic rules of metalanguage are confounded with those of infrastructure, and each points to the other as its mirror image.

Let me neglect here the philosophical implications of this new version of Absolute Knowledge (or the *mathesis universalis*). The desire for coherence and continuity is obvious, as is the ambition to pursue implications step by step. Ambition, to be sure, is not to be confused with achievement. What can be achieved remains to be seen. But the striking thing about the new discourse, the new "interpretive circle," sometimes presented in a utopian perspective, is the curious way in which it combines a scientific ideal with a theology that no longer dares to speak its name. The reductionism of natural science, eager to establish the unambiguous trace of physical causality, leads to a monism that is subject to misinterpretation and lends encouragement to the residual pantheistic tendencies of natural theology. It should not be forgotten that the art of interpretation was first developed for purposes of religious exegesis. It was essential to prove that all myths and all historical events revealed a single Providence—its mysterious advent and progress toward meaning and salvation. Interpretation became indispensable at the moment when a unique and exclusive faith wished to see in the world, in history, and in texts nothing but proof of its own validity, its own prefigurations, tribulations, and triumphs. Ultimately, theological interpretation relates all things through their common dependence on a single "principle." Its proofs are based either on analogy or on the concatenation and filiation of events. A glance at the past is enough to reveal the circularity of such a mode of argument. In the return unto itself of a language that has produced and in the process subsumed all reality, we recognize *apocatastasis*, the restoration of all things to the bosom of God (the One, Logos), which Johannes Scotus Erigena and certain cabalists saw as the axis of history. Another example of circularity can be found in an entirely different quarter of the religious spectrum: Pascal maintained that man's misery is explained only by Scripture. Hence man's present condition, incomprehensible in any other way, is primary proof of the truth of the Revelation, which in turn illuminates man's supernatural fate. The human condition, explained by the Bible, becomes an integral part of the explanatory discourse.

A circular language that always comes back to its point of departure, that establishes the reign of identity, and that subsumes all it touches in its coherent universality: this is not an adequate definition of interpretation. Here Rousseau encounters the risk of delusion, and we encounter the dangers of dogmatism and hypothetical deductive reasoning, the delusion of intelligence. To leave it at that would no doubt be to furnish those who suspect interpretation with arguments to strengthen their case. It must be recognized that interpretation also proceeds by way of a second circle, contemporaneous with the first but stemming from a different source. This second circle starts and ends with the object. It begins with a particular, distinctive, significant occurrence and ends with the same occurrence, only now legitimized in its particularity and significance. In the interim the circle proceeds by way of explanatory language, which along with the work of reason enriches the object. This is the thought process that, from Schleiermacher to Dilthey, Spitzer, and Gadamer, has been known as the "hermeneutic circle." In this view of the matter, it is not my discourse that assimilates and absorbs the object, but the object that elicits and absorbs my discourse. This is no mere play on words, even if the inversion of terms seems to be a matter of simple permutation.

Instead of an "assumption" of the object in a universalizing discourse, there is a "descent" of the universalizing discourse into the particular object, into otherness. (Is it by chance that the language of theology gleams once again on the surface of my text? The hermeneutic circle also derives from theology.) What preserves us from tautology is no doubt the fact that there are two circles, not just one. We may say that interpretation seeks both to abolish difference (through an inclusive and totalizing discourse) and to preserve distance (by understanding the other as other). More generally, interpretation aims to achieve both maximal coherence and maximal individual specificity.

The circle that begins and ends with the object is important for other reasons as well, which derive from primary truths that should not be forgotten. In the interpretive disciplines, everything begins with the choice of an object, and that choice is never accidental. The object commands our attention as one "in need of interpretation" or "deserving study." No one would bother to study something considered unimportant or insignificant. We interpret only that which spurs our interest, which seems promising, which stands out as *already* important but *not yet* sufficiently explained. The object of interpretation stands out because it has meaning for us; it stands out as historically important for us as historical individuals. It is history, behind me and within me, history in the name of culture or in the guise of current urgency, which gives me a reason to be interested in Rousseau, in his rebellion and his writing. It is my present choice, in my present situation, under current conditions—my choice, I say, which, by electing new objects or confirming the significant value of objects commended by the judgment of generations, commits me to my study and brings under scrutiny events, persons, and works of past eras that I do not wish to see consigned to oblivion. Their wealth of possible meanings has yet to be explored, and dialogue with them seems likely to yield a profit. By expanding and renewing my understanding, I hope to derive an advantage in the present.

The interpreter and his *interpretanda* therefore confront one another in historical time. Historicity must be restored not only to methodology, not only to the object of our interest, but to our interest itself. I am not displeased that the current climate requires that we pay attention to such questions by obliging us to justify our choices, to reexamine their foundation, their relevance, and, with full knowledge of what we are about, to restore confidence not only in our working methods and objects of study but in the very purpose of our work.

Our choice of starting point is already pregnant with meaning and not without consequence for our choice of method. The choice of an object for interpretation—whether it be Michelangelo's *Moses*, the coup d'état of December 2, or the *Confessions*—determines a concrete, global phenomenon whose meaning already exists in a powerful form prior to any explanations that I may subsequently have to offer. Hence I start with a defined figure, a clearly delineated form, a text whose significance is powerful enough at *first glance* to attract my attention and to provide the *pretext* for further investigation, for a project of research or construction whose purpose is to transform prior significance (*présignification*) into developed significance (*signification dévelopée*).

The starting point is of course also the point to which the study must return. The object invested with prior significance expects us to come back to it, to ascribe a motivation, an origin, a function in some larger complex, or something of the sort. All genetic constructions know in advance where they will end, in what global presence or complete organism. They know where they will end because they start with it at their backs. Sometimes they create the impression that they discovered their end point by some miraculous means, whereas in fact they only rediscovered what they had pretended to ignore. (Think, for example, of Descartes constructing a hypothetical mechanical model of man and the world; he cannot avoid rediscovering these images, because it is with them that he begins.) To be sure, the object of an explicit explanation appears quite different from what it seemed before the explanation was available, when it possessed only a promise of meaning and a power to elicit explanation. The initial object is restored to us in the guise of the result. Henceforth it will be seen as a product of labor; it has absorbed all the stages of its elaboration. Interpretation has added innumerable qualities. The object has been enhanced by the revelation of its structure, the retracing of its origins, the unearthing of its historical foundations, the restoration of its context. It has been revised and "revisited." But in contrast to scientific explanation, which is always subject to experimental verification, interpretation of the significant object (the "meaningful" object adduced in every "humanist" study) is subject to no standard other than coherence, internal consistency, completeness, and in some cases formal rigor.[29] It is highly unlikely that the interpreter will seem to fall short of his goal, since his goal is nothing other than the point of departure at last regained, and the gaps and contradictions in the interpretation are not evident at first glance. The exegete who knows how to present his product can often win an easy victory. (I do not except myself.)

Since circularity and return to the point of departure are to be taken for granted, there is no explanatory method or technique that, if skillfully applied, cannot claim to make some contribution, whether it be one of pure description, causal filiation, or homology. There is no method that does not tell us at least something about the object of interpretation, as long as the text is not misconstrued. Hence no method can be rejected on principle. The question, rather, is whether any particular method is adequate, specific, and complete enough for the task at hand, whether it encompasses the whole of the object or simply one of its components, one of its forms of existence or levels of meaning.

But here, where the hermeneutic circle is closed, it is once again the historical subject, the "investigator," who must decide whether he is satisfied or whether further research is needed. If, when the experiment is over, no new meaning has been added to the world or to the life of the interpreter, then what was the point of the effort? The dinner at Turin, to which I come back in order to complete the circle, contains in its stark dramatic outlines a lesson as simple as it is fundamental: an interpretation that strikes home and commands attention is a wonderful way to turn the wheel of fortune, provided that desire also takes a hand.

Notes

Translator's note. Reference is made to the following English translations of Rousseau (page numbers of the English edition are indicated in parentheses after the citation to the Gallimard *Oeuvres complètes* in French):

A Discourse on Inequality, trans. Maurice Cranston (New York: Penguin, 1984).
Reveries of the Solitary Walker, trans. Peter France (New York: Penguin, 1979).
The Social Contract, trans. Maurice Cranston (New York: Penguin, 1968).
The Confessions, trans. J. M. Cohen (New York: Penguin, 1953).

2. Jean-Jacques Rousseau and the Peril of Reflection

1. *Confessions*, book 1, p. 37(45). The first page number given refers to the *Oeuvres complètes*, ed. Bernard Gagnebin and Marcel Raymond, 4 vols. (Paris, 1959–1960); this edition will henceforth be abbreviated O.C. The second page number (in parentheses) refers to one of the English translations of Rousseau's works mentioned above.
2. Ibid.
3. Paul Valéry: "Human relations are based on *ciphers*. To decipher is to become confused. The cipher has the advantage of saying without saying, of holding reciprocal opinion in suspense, in a reversible state. It protects us against bringing decisive and definitive judgments, which are never true but for a moment." *Choses tues* (Paris, 1932), pp. 103–104.
4. *Confessions*, book 1, O.C. 1, p. 5(5).
5. *Ebauches des Confessions*, O.C. 1, p. 1149.
6. On the ambition to tell all, see my *Jean-Jacques Rousseau: La Transparence et l'obstacle* (Paris, 1957); in English, *Jean-Jacques Rousseau: Transparency and Obstruction*, trans. Arthur Goldhammer (Chicago, 1988).
7. Sören Kierkegaard, *Journal*, trans. Knud Ferlov and J.-J. Gateau (Paris, 1957), vol. 4, p. 252.

8. Eugène Ritter, *La Famille et l'enfance de J.-J. Rousseau* (Paris, 1896), pp. 89–103.

9. *Confessions*, book 1, O.C. 1, p. 24. When Rousseau discusses his childhood thefts or his "illumination" on the road to Vincennes, it is difficult to believe he did not have Augustine in mind.

10. Ibid., p. 31.

11. Ibid., p. 33.

12. Ibid., p. 34.

13. Ibid., p. 27.

14. All of Rousseau's escapes put him back in the same state of mind he was in when, at the age of sixteen, he escaped from his native city into the wider world, only to find that other cities and societies (Turin, Venice, Paris) would also hold him hostage. In the period of the *Reveries* escape coexists with the sedentary life: every stroll outside the gates of Paris is like a small escape.

15. Compare the way in which Rousseau describes in *Emile* the urban youth's entry into society. Persecution by the gaze is not absent from his account: "What does he see upon opening his eyes? Multitudes of alleged goods of which he knew nothing, and most of which, being within reach for only a moment, seemed to show themselves only to make him regret his not possessing them. If he goes walking in a palace, you can see by his anxious curiosity that he is wondering why his father's house is not like this . . . Soon everything comes together in concert. The disturbing glances of a man of grave mien, the mocking words of a sarcastic onlooker, are not long in reaching his ears. And were he disdained by but a single man, that one man's contempt would instantly poison the applause of the others." *Emile*, book 4, O.C. 4, pp. 512–513.

16. *Confessions*, book 1, O.C. 1, pp. 36–38.

17. *Confessions*, book 3, O.C. 1, p. 89.

18. *Confessions*, book 2, O.C. 1, p. 75(78). This episode is preceded by several mute scenes: "I trembled with embarrassment, I dared not look at her or breathe in her presence, yet I feared leaving her more than I feared death. I feasted my eyes greedily on everything I could see without being observed—on the flowers of her dress, the tip of her pretty toes, the glimpse of her firm white arm between her glove and her sleeve, and her bosom, which was sometimes visible between her kerchief and her bodice. Every detail added to the general impression. When I looked at all I could see, and somewhat beyond, my eyes swam, my chest grew tight, and my breathing became more difficult every moment" (p. 74[77–78]).

19. *Confessions*, book 2, O.C. 1, p. 75(78).

20. *Confessions*, book 1, O.C. 1, p. 34(42).

21. *Confessions*, book 2, O.C. 1, p. 75(78).
22. *Correspondance générale de J.-J. Rousseau*, ed. T. Dufour (Paris, 1924–1934), vol. 1. p. 41.
23. Ibid. Another passage from the same letter gives a precise description of the magical effects of eye contact: "In the instant in which your eyes encountered mine, my trembling knees and dimmed vision nearly prevented me from continuing on my way."
24. *La Nouvelle Héloïse*, part 1, letter 26, O.C. 2, pp. 89–93.
25. Ibid.
26. Ibid.
27. *Confessions*, book 4, O.C. 1, p. 174.
28. *Confessions*, book 3, O.C. 1, p. 108.
29. Ibid.
30. *La Nouvelle Héloïse*, part 1, letter 54, O.C. 2, p. 147.
31. *Confessions*, book 9, O.C. 1, p. 436(406).
32. *Confessions*, book 3, O.C. 1, p. 107(107).
33. Ibid.
34. *Confessions*, book 1, O.C. 1, p. 8.
35. In particular in *Reveries*, V, O.C. 1, p. 1047.
36. On the prophetic aspect of certain of Rousseau's reveries, see Marcel Raymond, "Deux aspects de la vie intérieure de J.-J. Rousseau," *Annales J.-J. Rousseau*, vol. 29, p. 44.
37. See the chapter on Rousseau in Georges Poulet, *Etudes sur le temps humain* (Paris, 1950), pp. 158–193.
38. See Robert Osmont, "La Genèse de la Nouvelle Héloïse," *Annales J.-J. Rousseau*, vol. 33, pp. 93–148.
39. *Confessions*, book 1, O.C. 1, p. 41(48).
40. Ibid.
41. *Dialogues*, II, O.C. 1, p. 814. No one has shown better than Rousseau the truth of Hegel's idea that the end of desire is unity of the self. For Rousseau the final stage of desire lies not in the world of images but at the point where all determinate objects disappear, where all images give way to pure transparency. If traces of the material world remain at this stage, they thin out, liquefy, and become fluid limpidity, or else take the form of gentle, rocking motion, escape into open space, or meditation in a withdrawn and very private place.
42. "Third Letter to Malesherbes," O.C. 1, p. 1141.
43. *Confessions*, book 13, O.C. 1, p. 644.
44. In his introduction to the *Reveries* Marcel Raymond shrewdly observes that "Rousseau, the man of desire, had to reach a point where he no longer desired or imagined anything." O.C. 1, p. xciii.
45. "Second Letter to Malesherbes," O.C. 1, p. 1134.
46. *Emile*, book 5, O.C. 4, p. 762. Cf. Martin Rang, *Rousseaus Lehre vom*

Menschen (Göttingen, 1959), pp. 316–317. See also the valuable remarks on imagination in P. Burgelin, *La Philosophie de l'existence de J.-J. Rousseau* (Paris, 1951).

47. "Third Letter to Malesherbes," O.C. 1, p. 1140.

48. Ibid.

49. *Reveries*, VII, O.C. 1, p. 1066(112).

50. *Discours sur l'origine de l'inégalité*, O.C. 3, p. 144(90).

51. *Emile*, book 4, O.C. 4, p. 657.

52. "I would have to be the clumsiest of men not to inflame him with passion before knowing the object of that passion. It makes no difference if the object I paint for him is imaginary. It is enough that it should discourage his interest in all that might tempt him. It is enough that he find everywhere comparisons that will make him prefer his fancy to the real objects that will strike his senses. And what is true love if not fancy, falsehood, and illusion? One much prefers the image that one makes to the object to which it is applied." Ibid., p. 282.

53. Ibid., p. 647.

54. Ibid., p. 648. As Rousseau himself says: "All my ideas are in images." *Confessions*, book 4, O.C. 1, p. 174.

55. *Discours sur l'origine de l'inégalité*, O.C. 3, p. 132.

56. *Confessions*, book 8, O.C. 1, p. 388.

57. See Jean-Paul Sartre, *L'Imaginaire* (Paris, 1940), p. 189. And Valéry, *Choses tues*: "What is real cannot be desired, because it is real."

58. Alain, *Système des Beaux-Arts* (Paris, 1953), p. 18.

59. "Final response to M. Bordes," O.C. 3, pp. 90–91.

60. *Dialogues*, II O.C. 1, p. 819.

61. "First Letter to Malesherbes," O.C. 1, p. 1131.

62. *Confessions*, book 1, O.C. 1, p. 9.

63. Ibid., p. 25.

64. Similarly, Baudelaire: "Being a child, I sometimes wanted to be pope . . . sometimes an actor."

65. *Confessions*, book 1, O.C. 1, p. 20(30).

66. *Ebauches des Confessions*, O.C. 1, p. 1140.

67. La *"Profession de foi de vicaire savoyard,"* ed. P. M. Masson, p. 283.

68. Ibid., p. 141.

69. Immanuel Kant, *Beantwortung der Frage: Was ist Aufklärung*, in *Werke*, ed. Cassirer, vol. 4.

70. *Confessions*, book 1, O.C. 1, p. 7(5).

71. *Confessions*, book 7, O.C. 1, p. 314.

72. *Confessions*, book 12, O.C. 1, p. 641.

73. Marcel Raymond, "Lecture du premier livre des Confessions," *Lettres d'Occident* (Neuchâtel: La Baconnière, 1958), p. 184.

74. *"Profession de foi,"* p. 227.

75. *Discours sur l'origine de l'inégalité*, O.C. 3, p. 144(90).
76. *Dialogues*, II, O.C. 1, p. 818. "Reflection and foresight, sources of all worries and woes, scarcely trouble a soul intoxicated by the charms of contemplation." Ibid., p. 822.
77. "Third Letter to Malesherbes," O.C. 1, p. 1141.
78. *Reveries*, I, O.C. 1, p. 999. Hölderlin, who attended deeply to Rousseau, compares the breathing of the gods to the sleep of a child: "Schicksallos, wie der schlafende / Säugling, atmen die Himmlischen." "Hyperions Schicksalslied," Werke (Berlin, 1958), p. 181
79. Thomas Aquinas, *De veritate*, q. 18, a. 1.
80. Marsilio Ficino: "To indicate divine objects the Egyptian priests used not letters but whole images of plants, trees, and animals, for God surely has knowledge of things that is not a complete, discursive thought but somehow their simple, direct form." *Opera*, vol. 2, p. 1768.
81. Henri de Lubac, *Surnaturel* (Paris, 1946), p. 446.
82. John Locke, *An Essay Concerning Human Understanding* (New York, 1959), vol. 2, pp. 304–305.
83. *L'Homme machine*, ed. Solovine (Paris, 1921), p. 81.
84. *Essay on Man*, III, lines 145–152.
85. *Reveries*, V, O.C. 1, p. 1046(87–88).
86. *Dialogues*, II, O.C. 1, p. 862.
87. *Reveries*, VII, O.C. 1, p. 1051(95).
88. *Discours sur l'origine de l'inégalité*, O.C. 3, p. 142(88).
89. Ibid., pp. 191–192(135).
90. "*Profession de foi*," p. 229.
91. *Confessions*, book 12, O.C. 1, p. 642(593).
92. Fénelon, *Explication des maximes des saints*, ed. A. Chérel (Paris, 1911), art. 13, pp. 210–211. We know that Jean-Jacques, when he was with Mme de Warens, becomes "devout almost in the manner of Fénelon." *Reveries*, III, O.C. 1, p. 1013.
93. Ibid.
94. *Dialogues*, I, O.C. 1, pp. 668–669.
95. Malebranche, *Recherche de la vérité*, book 1, chaps. 1, 2.
96. Condillac, *Traité des systèmes*, I, 6, art. 1.
97. *Discours sur l'origine de l'inégalité*, O.C. 3, p. 138(85).
98. The word and the idea can be found in Cicero, *De finibus*, 1.30, in the general sense of deviated, turned aside. In the eighteenth century this initial meaning had not vanished, but the word had taken on a highly pejorative coloration.
99. "You see nothing in my account but natural religion. It is quite strange that another is necessary!" "*Profession de foi*," p. 305. On this point see Burgelin, *La Philosophe*, and Henri Gouhier, "Nature et histoire

dans la pensée de J.-J. Rousseau," *Annales Jean-Jacques Rousseau*, vol. 33.

100. *"Profession de foi,"* p. 81.
101. *Discours sur l'origine de l'inégalité*, O.C. 3, p. 193(136).
102. Henri Guillemin has made this point quite well in *Cette affaire infernale* (Paris, 1942).
103. *Fragments politiques*, O.C. 3, p. 479.
104. *Ebauches des Confessions*, O.C. 1, p. 1154.
105. Ibid.
106. Ibid.
107. *Reveries*, I, O.C. 1, pp. 1000–1001.
108. Descartes, *Dioptrique*, ed. Adam and Tannery, vol. 6, pp. 106ff, and *Traité de l'homme*, vol. 11, pp. 174, 176.
109. Locke, *Essay Concerning Human Understanding*, IV, 2, 6.
110. *Dialogues*, O.C. 1, p. 665.
111. Jean-Paul Sartre, *L'Etre et le néant* (Paris, 1943), p. 329: "I cannot be an object for myself because I am what I am. Reduced to its own resources, the reflective attempt to achieve splitting ends in failure; I am always recaptured by myself."
112. *Correspondance*, ed. Dufour, vol. 3, p. 354.
113. *Confessions*, book 1, O.C. 1, p. 5.
114. *Confessions*, book 3, O.C. 1, p. 116(116).
115. *Dialogues: Histoire du précédent écrit*, O.C. 1, p. 985.
116. *Confessions*, book 4, O.C. 1, p. 152.
117. *Confessions*, book 12, O.C. 1, p. 642.
118. *Narcisse*, scene 3, O.C. 2, p. 983.
119. *Emile*, book 4, O.C. 4, p. 492.
120. *Pygmalion*, O.C. 2, p. 1226.
121. Ibid., p. 1228.
122. *Dialogues*, II, O.C. 1, p. 839. See the important study by Maurice Blanchot in *Le Livre à venir* (Paris, 1959), pp. 53–62.
123. *Confessions*, book 8, O.C. 1, p. 351.
124. Ibid., p. 352.
125. *Confessions*, book 9, O.C. 1, p. 431(401).
126. *Corrrespondance*, vol. 6, p. 209.
127. *Confessions*, book 4, O.C. 1, pp. 174–175(169).
128. For further information see the studies by Ernst Cassirer and Robert Derathé.
129. *"Profession de foi,"* p. 91.
130. *Reveries*, III, O.C. 1, pp. 1016, 1017, 1018(53, 54, 55).
131. Ibid., p. 1022(60).
132. Rousseau frequently associates pain with reflection. By way of example consider the following passage from the "Profession of Faith," p. 97:

"Pain has little hold on anyone who, having reflected but little, has neither memory nor foresight."

133. Heinrich von Kleist, *Über das Marionettentheater*, in *Sämtliche Werke*, ed. Siegen (Leipzig, n.d.), vol. 3, pp. 122–213.
134. *Dialogues*, II, O.C. 1, p. 812.
135. Ibid., p. 850.
136. *Reveries*, III, O.C. 1, p. 1020(57–58).
137. Ibid., p. 58.

3. Pseudonymous Stendhal

Translator's note. A portion of this essay was previously translated by B. A. B. Archer as "Truth in Masquerade" and published in Victor Brombert, ed., *Stendhal: A Collection of Critical Essays* (Englewood Cliffs, N.J.: Prentice Hall, 1962), pp. 114–126. I found it useful to consult Archer's translation before making my own.

1. *Souvenirs d'égotisme*, in *Oeuvres intimes* (Paris, 1955), pp. 1449–1450.
2. *Journal*, in *Oeuvres intimes*, p. 1041.
3. *Privilèges*, in *Oeuvres intimes*, pp. 1559ff.
4. *Journal*, in *Oeuvres intimes*, p. 611.
5. Maine de Biran, *Premier Journal*, ed. P. Tisserand (Paris, 1920), p. 52.
6. *De l'amour*, ed. Divan (Paris, 1957), p. 240.
7. *Journal*, in *Oeuvres intimes*, pp. 655–656.
8. Ibid., p. 678.
9. *Vie de Henry Brulard*, in *Oeuvres intimes*, p. 407.
10. *Correspondance*, ed. Divan, vol. 5, p. 241.
11. *Journal*, in *Oeuvres intimes*, p. 549.
12. Ibid., p. 677.
13. *De l'amour*, p. 92.
14. Of course only a good opera buffa, superbly acted, will produce such an exalting effect. When the performance is mediocre, Stendhal is well aware of the defects in the work and the actors: pure sensation is not free to develop.
15. *Journal*, in *Oeuvres intimes*, pp. 1104–1105.
16. Ibid., p. 626.
17. *Correspondance*, vol. 6, p. 24.
18. Lautréamont, *Oeuvres complètes*, (Paris, 1940), pp. 52–53.

Readers will also wish to consult the now indispensable work of Georges Blin, *Stendhal et les problèmes de la personnalité* (Paris, 1958), and Jean-Pierre Richard's essay on Stendhal in *Littérature et sensation* (Paris, 1954).

5. Psychoanalysis and Literary Understanding

1. Sigmund Freud, *Gesammelte Werke*, ed. Anna Freud (London, 1940–1952), vol. 14, p. 34.

2. Ludwig Binswanger, "Mein Weg zu Freud," in *Der Mensch in der Psychiatrie* (Pfullingen, 1957).

3. Thomas Hobbes, *De cive*, ed. Sterling P. Lamprecht (New York, 1949), "Praefatio ad Lectores," pp. 12–13.

4. Cited by Lionel Trilling in his excellent essay, "Freud and Literature," *The Liberal Imagination* (London, 1951), p. 34.

5. "It looks now as though Freud's view of the Oedipus complex were a psychological conception that throws some light on literary criticism. Perhaps we shall eventually decide that we have got it the wrong way round: that what happened was that the myth of Oedipus informed and gave structure to some psychological investigations at this point. Freud would in that case be exceptional only in having been well read enough to spot the source of the myth. It looks now as though the psychological discover of an oracular mind 'underneath' the conscious one forms an appropriate allegorical explanation of a poetic archetype that has run through literature from the cave of Trophonius to our own day. Perhaps it was the archetype that informed the discovery: it is after all considerably older, and to explain it in this way would involve us in less anachronism. The informing of metaphysical and theological constructs by poetic myths, or by associations and diagrams analogous to poetic myths, is even more obvious." Northrop Frye, *The Anatomy of Criticism* (New York, 1969), p. 353.

6. Victor Hugo, *Les Contemplations*, preface.

7. André Breton, "Le Message automatique," in *Le Point du jour* (Paris, 1934), p. 241.

8. Emile Benveniste, *Problèmes de linguistique générale* (Paris, 1966), pp. 86–87.

9. Freud, *Gesammelte Werke*, vol. 14, p. 399.

10. Freud, *Gesammelte Werke*, vol. 16, p. 276.

11. Sigmund Freud, *Beyond the Pleasure Principle*, trans. James Strachey (New York, 1959), chap. 6, pp. 104–105 (sightly modified).

12. Concerning possible pitfalls in Freudian exegesis, see Marthe Robert, *Sur le papier* (Paris, 1967), pp. 221–250.

13. Maurice Merleau-Ponty, preface to A. Hesnard, *L'Oeuvre de Freud* (Paris, 1960).

14. Ludwig Binswanger, "Erfahren, Verstehen, Deuten in der Psychoanalyse," in *Ausgewählte Vorträge und Aufsätze* (Berne, 1956), vol. 2, pp. 67–80.

15. On the myth of Actaeon see Pierre Klossowski, *Le Bain de Diane* (Paris, 1956).

This essay is the text of a paper presented in June 1964 to the Psychiatric Hospital of Cery (Lausanne), in March 1965 to the C.U.M. (Nice), and published by the review *Preuves* in March 1966.

6. Hamlet and Oedipus

1. Sigmund Freud, *The Origins of Psycho-Analysis: Letters to Wilhelm Fliess, Drafts and Notes, 1887–1902*, ed. Marie Bonaparte et al., trans. Eric Mosbacher and James Strachey (New York and London, 1954), pp. 216–217.
2. Ibid., p. 219.
3. In fact, Hamlet has no idea that the tip of his foil has been unbuttoned and poisoned: he kills Laertes unintentionally. For what reasons, in writing to Fliess, did Freud ascribe to Hamlet the intention of deliberately committing a kind of fratricide? Or has he, in a striking slip, substituted the name of Laertes for that of Polonius?
4. Freud, *Origins*, p. 223.
5. Ibid., p. 224.
6. Ibid., p. 229.
7. On this point see Paul Ricoeur, *De l'interprétation* (Paris, 1965), p. 188.
8. Sigmund Freud, *Standard Edition of the Complete Psychological Works of Sigmund Freud*, trans. James Strachey (London, 1953–1974), vol. 4, p. 264; hereafter abbreviated *SE*.
9. Freud returned to idea of a "secular progression of repression" in *Totem and Taboo*, among other places, and Otto Rank made it the central theme of his *Das Inzest-Motiv in Dichtung und Sage* (Vienna, 1912), a long book filled with documents and interpretations and in which a chapter is devoted to Shakespeare's "paternal complex" (see pp. 204–233). In chapter 2, which deals with "types of incest dramas," Rank examines *Oedipus Rex, Hamlet*, and Schiller's *Don Carlos*. In his view, Sophocles' tragedy and Schiller's play represent "two extremes in the process of repression of psychic life" (p. 45). *Hamlet* stands midway between these two extremes: herein lies the decisive turning point in the evolution of repression.
10. Sigmund Freud, *Correspondance* (Paris, 1966), p. 469.
11. Ibid., p. 483.
12. Freud, *Gesammelte Werke* (London, 1940–1952), vol. 11, pp. 347–348 (hereafter abbreviated *GW*); *SE*, vol. 16, pp. 347–348.
13. *GW*, vol 5, pp. 127–128.
14. On this problem, mentioned here only in passing, see Jean Laplanche and J.-B. Pontalis, "Fantasme originaire, fantasme des origines, origines du fantasme," *Les Temps modernes*, 215 (April 1964), pp. 1833–1868.
15. *GW*, vol. 6, p. 37.

16. *Hamlet*, IV.5. 7–10
17. Charles Mauron, *Des métaphores obsédantes au mythe personnel* (Paris, 1963), is the most important French theoretical work to date on psychoanalysis in literary criticism. An interesting comparison of *Le Cid* and *Hamlet* may be found on p. 260.
18. *GW*, vol. 14, pp. 89–90; *SE*, vol. 20, p. 63.
19. *GW*, vol. 17, p. 118; *SE*, vol. 23, p. 191.
20. *GW*, vol. 7, p. 457; *SE*, vol. 10, p. 241.
21. *GW*, vol. 5, pp. 18–19.
22. *GW*, vol. 14, p. 214.
23. *GW*, vol. 6, pp. 43 and 10.
24. Sigmund Freud, *Correspondance avec le pasteur Pfister* (Paris, 1966), pp. 185–186.
25. Ludwig Binswanger, *Erinnerungen an Sigmund Freud* (Berne, 1956), p. 14.
26. Freud, *Correspondance*, p. 431.
27. *GW*, vol. 14, p. 96.
28. *GW*, vol. 17, p. 119. On this subject see Ernest Jones, *The Life of Sigmund Freud* (New York, 1953), vol. 3, chap.16.

The variorum edition of *Hamlet* edited by H. H. Furness (1877) contains an ample bibliography and selection of commentaries. A. A. Raven, *A Hamlet Bibliography and Reference Guide, 1877–1935*, covers an additional period. More recent works are mentioned in Gordon Ross Smith, *A Classified Shakespeare Bibliography* (University Park, Penn., 1963). A "Reader's Guide to *Hamlet*" may be found in volume 5 of *Stratford upon Avon Studies* (London, 1963). Also worth consulting is Morris Weitz, *Hamlet and the Philosophy of Literary Criticism* (Chicago, 1964). An anthology of modern German writings on Hamlet may be found in Joachim Kaiser, ed., *Hamlet, heute* (Frankfurt, 1965).

7. *The Interpreter's Progress*

1. See G.-G. Granger, *Essai d'une philosophie du style* (Paris, 1968), pp. 7–8.
2. Obviously I have in mind the concept of stylistics characteristic of the early work of Leo Spitzer. See his *Linguistics and Literary History* (New York, 1962), pp. 11–14.
3. Emile Benveniste, *Problèmes de linguistique générale* (Paris, 1966), p. 242. See also Harald Weinrich, *Tempus. Besprochene und erzählte Welt* (Stuttgart, 1964), and Gérard Genette, *Figures II* (Paris, 1969), pp. 61–69.
4. "In narrative, since the narrator does not intervene, the third person is

not opposed to any other; it is actually an absence of person." Benveniste, *Problèmes*, p. 242.

5. On the role of autobiography in the history of culture, see Georg Misch, *Geschichte der Autobiographie* (Berne-Frankfurt, 1949–1969).

6. An excellent discussion of this problem may be found in Weinrich, *Tempus*, pp. 247–253.

7. Pierre Fontanier, *Les Figures du discours* (Paris, 1968), pp. 143ff.

8. O.C. 1, p. 3.

9. Ibid., p. 7(17).

10. Cf. Jacques Voisine, "Le Dialogue avec le lecteur dans *Les Confessions*," in *Jean-Jacques Rousseau et son oeuvre. Commémoration et colloque de Paris* (Paris, 1964), pp. 23–32.

11. O.C. 1, pp. 1153–1154.

12. Ibid., p. 226(216).

13. *La Vie de Lazarille de Tormes* (Paris, 1958), "Prologo," p. 88.

14. I am referring primarily to the *Discours sur l'origine de l'inégalité*; see preface and critical commentary in O.C. 3.

15. O.C. 1, pp. 94–96(95–97). [The English translation is that of J. M. Cohen, with minor modifications.]

16. I am indebted to Roland Barthes for this observation.

17. See Erich Auerbach, *Mimesis* (Princeton, 1953).

18. If we are to believe the remarks reported by Hérault de Séchelles in his *Voyage à Montbard*. See Hérault de Séchelles, *Oeuvres littéraires* (Paris, 1907), p. 41: "Rousseau has all the vices of a bad education."

19. O.C. 3, p. 188.

20. O.C. 1, p. 10(21).

21. "Second Letter to Malesherbes," O.C. 1, p. 1135.

22. O.C. 1, p. 351(328).

23. O.C. 3, p. 165.

24. O.C. 3, pp. 143–144.

25. Emile Gaillard, "J.-J. Rousseau à Turin," *Annales J.-J. Rousseau*, vol. 23, pp. 55–120.

26. O.C. 1, p. 9(21).

27. See Marthe Robert, *L'Ancien et le nouveau* (Paris, 1963).

28. *Reveries*, IV, O.C. 1, p. 1034(75).

29. See Eric Weil, "On Language in Humanistic Studies," *Daedalus* (Fall 1969), p. 1005.

Index

Harvard Studies in Comparative Literature